ATOMIC SALVATION

**HOW THE A-BOMB
ATTACKS SAVED THE LIVES
OF 32 MILLION PEOPLE**

Published in the United States of America in 2020 by
CASEMATE PUBLISHERS
1950 Lawrence Road, Havertown, PA 19083, USA

Hardcover Edition: ISBN 978-1-61200-944-5
Digital Edition: ISBN 978-1-61200-945-2

Printed and bound in the United States of America by Sheridan

Licensed from Big Sky Publishing Pty Ltd
PO Box 303, Newport, NSW 2106, Australia
Phone: 1300 364 611
Fax: (61 2) 9918 2396
Email: info@bigskypublishing.com.au
Web: www.bigskypublishing.com.au

Cover design and typesetting: Think Productions

ATOMIC SALVATION

HOW THE A-BOMB ATTACKS SAVED THE LIVES OF 32 MILLION PEOPLE

Tom Lewis

CASEMATE

Philadelphia & Oxford

To Peter and Linda

CONTENTS

ACKNOWLEDGMENTS

My thanks to Dr Peter Williams, military historian, for his as-always perceptive insights. Simon Loveday in Japan, provided clear advice from a Western perspective but also from someone who took up residence in Tokyo several decades ago. I appreciated Jared Archibald's armour advice and Bob Alford's comments on aircraft. Ric Fallu's fearless eye was most welcome indeed. Much appreciation to Dr Lloyd Browne. Clinton Bock's honest views were most appreciated. As always, Kaylene's comments have been gratefully received.

Notes:

The term "Japs" and "the Jap" and so on were in widespread use in World War II. They are considered offensive by many in today's world, but their presence in verbatim quotations was sometimes unavoidable.

Sections of this work, discussing modern battlefield behavior, have appeared in the same author's book *Lethality in Combat*. Thanks to Big Sky Publishing for their assent in reproducing them.

PREFACE

A nation that loses the vast majority of its population in a war, from teenagers to middle-aged adults, will never again arise from the ashes.

If the World War II Japanese male population, from 12 years upwards, had fought and died as intended in the defence of the Home Islands, this is precisely what would have happened.

If the Japanese females from 14 years upwards had died wielding single shot rifles and pikes in their country's final defence, there would have been no one left to bring new lives into Japan.

Japan's houses, temples, fortresses and gardens would have succumbed to ferocious artillery bombardments designed to ensure no protection was left for what remained of the country's military forces, infantry and militias.

Japan would have been a smoking ruin, blasted to pieces by artillery and air strikes, and ground to rubble beneath the tracks of armoured vehicles as they rumbled through the ruins.

The atomic bombings prevented all that, and ended the war.

Within days Japanese soldiers were obeying the will of their Emperor and co-operating in harvesting the meagre economic resources left to ensure survival for all.

So didn't the atomic weapons bring about a great peace?

Since the initial grateful acknowledgement of the success of the A-bomb attacks in ending World War II, there has been a steady reversal of opinion and sentiment: from at first a hearty appreciation to a condemnation by many of the United States for its actions.

Atomic Salvation investigates the full situation of the times to a previously unplumbed depth. It examines documents from both Japanese and Allied sources, but it uses logical in-depth analysis to extend beyond the mere recounting of statistics. It charts the full extent of the possible casualties on both sides if a conventional assault akin to D-Day had gone ahead.

The content discussed is concerned solely with the military necessity to use the bombs, but it also investigates why that necessity has been increasingly challenged over the successive decades.

Controversially, the book shows that the Japanese nation would have lost many millions of their people – likely around 28 million – if the nation had been attacked in the manner by which Germany was defeated: by amphibious assault, artillery and air attacks preceding infantry insertion, and finally by subduing the last of the defenders of the enemy capital.

The work looks at the depth of the resolve of the Japanese Empire and the extent of their capabilities, including massive attacks by kamikaze forces. *Atomic Salvation* outlines and investigates the attempted coup that took place even after both atomic weapons had been used, which was still mounted by fanatical elements of the Japanese military committed to extending the war. It examines the attempts by Japan, said by some to be remarkably successful, to achieve their own atomic weapons.

From the other side, the book investigates the enormous political pressure placed on America as a result of their military situation. The book shows that the United States' Truman Administration had little choice but to use the new weapon, given that the Allied forces would have undoubtedly suffered more than a million deaths through conventional assault.

Through investigation of reactions then and since, *Atomic Salvation* charts reactions to the bombings. It looks briefly at a range of reactions through the decades, and shows that there has been relentless pressure on the world to condemn what at the time was seen as the best, and the only, military solution to end the war.

The book shows the Japanese death toll in the A-bomb attacks, although horrific, was less by many millions than those that would have been incurred through conventional assault. Although it can hardly be suggested that the Japanese nation of the 1950s should have thanked the Allies for thus avoiding the deaths of its people, given the extent of actual and psychological shock involved, it would be remiss of the world today, including modern Japan, to mutely acquiesce to the criticism of the United States without taking this into account.

The crux of *Atomic Salvation* is that the deaths of 200,000 Japanese in the A-bomb attacks prevented the deaths of more than a million Allied troops, around 3.5 million dead in territories the Empire held, and around 28 million Japanese. Millions more on both sides would have been wounded.

Yet somehow over time, the A-bombings have become seen as militarily unnecessary, or military overkill.

This book proves these assumptions wrong.

INTRODUCTION

How many lives did the A-bombs save?

In mid-1945, Japan was being pressed back to its Home Islands as the Allied war effort intensified.

To calculate the cost of World War II in the Pacific as it reached its height, we might conclude that the simple mathematics of this are too difficult to contemplate.

But why?

War comes at a cost, and if we are arguing for its non-conclusion when such an option is open to us, then that accounting must be made.

General Sweeney, pilot of the second atomic B-29 aircraft *Bocks Car*, suggested that '900 Americans were killed or wounded each day' at that period of the war, and therefore delay in forcing the Japanese surrender was a critical factor.

J Samuel Walker cites a figure in the US Army alone of 3233 deaths for the month of July 1945, and he notes that if that had continued without the use of the bombs and the invasion plans had been running to plan, then another approximate 9700 deaths would have occurred by November.

That is 104 deaths a day for delaying the end of the war, in the US Army with its air forces alone. The US Navy lost 1/5th of the personnel of the Army. Therefore, it might be accurate enough to say 125 fatalities a day were being incurred by the US military every day as the war continued. The other Allied forces, although not present in such great numbers, saw their share of the fatalities too. It would seem, given their comparative strengths, safe to add another 25 to the tally.

The numbers of fatalities elsewhere are grim to contemplate. Although Germany was defeated, Japan's forces still ranged throughout their shattered Empire of South-East Asia. Civilian personnel, huge numbers of them Chinese, died as military operations impacted literally on their existence.

Robert Newman argues that 250,000 were dying every month from starvation, disease, executions, and battle deaths, in all of the areas held by the Japanese across their conquered territories. If we were to add up the amount of people dying every day due to the war, that would add 8064 to our total.

What of the Japanese fatalities?

General Slim noted that in the last stages of the war: 'We were killing Japanese at a rate of over a hundred to one.' So, if 150 Allied military personnel were dying every day as the war continued, then so are 1500 Japanese.

In other words, in the terrible accounting of war operations, as World War II continued through 1945, 9714 people were dying as a result every day. That is without any accounting of the POW operations.

Can we bring that figure to 10,000 a day?

For the first time ever, this book gives the calculated figure of how many Allied deaths *would have been* caused by a conventional invasion of Japan at the end of World War II. A figure of 767,600 combat deaths would have been incurred.

But this grim picture does not stop there. Three hundred thousand prisoners would have been executed. And in an invasion lasting until the end of 1946, 3.5 million people who were scattered throughout Japanese territory would have perished.

By saving 4,567,600 people, the two atomic strikes were justified in taking around 200,000 Japanese lives.

And given around four people are wounded for every war death, 3,070,400 people did not have their lives impacted by injuries and pain.

But there is more.

The Japanese people – military and co-opted civilians – would have died in their further millions for their Emperor.

Atomic Salvation shows calculations of 27,879,717 deaths for the defenders of the Home Islands – far higher than previously suggested. The analysis shows that a total of 32,447,317 Allied and Japanese people would have died in a conventional invasion – with caveats on these numbers, this may have been as high as 35 million or as low as 30 million. (We might admittedly round up the figures above to show there can be no precise calculation.)

Atomic Salvation's military factors analysis also examines:

- The troop strengths both sides would have brought to an invasion.

- What resolution did the Japanese people have to continue the war – and what rebellion did those who refused to surrender engage in?

- Would the 10,000 kamikaze aircraft have been a significant factor?

- How capable would the 9200 suicide speedboats, submarines and divers being readied have been?

- Did Japan explode its own nuclear test device in its quest for the ultimate weapon?

- Were the forces of the USSR a possible decisive factor?

- Why blockade, starvation, and intensive aerial bombing were not able to bring the war to a conclusion.

- Why has argument risen since the war, saying that the United States was not right in its action?

Never has such an exhaustive analysis been made of the necessity to bring World War II to a halt.

Timeline of Events

Date	Event	Detail
7 April 1945	The Koiso government is replaced.	It had failed to halt the invasion of Okinawa. On the same day, the giant battleship *Yamato* was sunk. This resulted in the loss of 2488 men[1] with a total of over 3000 from the battle group.
5 April	The Soviet Union declares it will not renew Neutrality Pact.	
30 April	Hitler commits suicide.	Japan's main Axis partner falls.
8 May	Truman's Victory in Europe Day address is given.	
26 May	500 B-29s strike the government and palace districts of Tokyo.[2]	
17 June	Truman writes in his diary:	'I have to decide Japanese strategy – shall we invade Japan proper or shall we bomb and blockade? That is my hardest decision to date. But I'll make it when I have all the facts.'[3]
18 June	Japan's Supreme War Council meets.	It determines 'to propose peace through neutral powers, especially the Soviet Union'.[4]
Mid-1945	Baron Kantaro Suzuki takes office in mid-1945, but 'was forced by the army to promise that his government would continue the war "to the bitter end"'.[5]	
9 July	Lord Keeper of the Privy Seal of Japan, Kōichi Kido meets with the Emperor.[6]	Commissioned to consult the Prime Minister and the heads of the Army and Navy and Foreign Affairs, and to set about trying to bring a peace plan forward immediately

Date	Event	Detail
21 July	Potsdam conference – the leaders of the United States, Britain, and the USSR meet in defeated Berlin.	They set out a strategy for dealing with Japan.
4 August	720, 000 leaflets dropped across Japan.	Warning, as the Potsdam conference had outlined: 'of the inevitable and complete destruction of the Japanese armed forces and just as inevitably the utter devastation of the Japanese homeland'.[7][8][9]

Monday 6 August – *Tokyo time; 13 hours difference to Washington*

2.45 pm	Seven B-29s take off to form the first atomic attack group. *Note: narratives generally cite six aircraft as one diverts as backup.*	Three as 'weather ships'; No. 82, just repainted with her new name *Enola Gay*; one to be diverted to Iowa Jima as a backup A-Bomb carrier, and two camera and blast measurement-carrying aircraft.[10]
Pre-8.00 am	Weather B-29 detected; air-raid sirens sound.	B-29 dismissed as a reconnaissance flight only.
8.00 am	Hiroshima radar detects incoming B-29; city radio announces reconnaissance flight.	Due to lack of incoming aircraft numbers sighted, no major movement to bomb shelters.
8.15 am + 43 seconds	Bomb dropped.	Detonation approx. 43 seconds after drop at 1850 feet.[11]
12.00 pm (approx.)	Domei News Agency dispatch reaches Tokyo.	It advises basic details.
Unknown	Broadcast from Washington received in Tokyo.	Warning of 'rain of ruin from the air'.
Late afternoon	Tokyo receives advice from Second Army Headquarters through Kure Naval Yard.	Advice that only a few aircraft had inflicted tremendous damage with bomb of unknown type.

Date	Event	Detail
Tuesday 7 August		
Unknown	Army issues communiqué saying Hiroshima has been attacked.	… 'by a small number of B-29s', which caused 'considerable damage' from a 'new type of bomb'.[12]
Unknown	Further conventional bombings across Japan.[13]	
Unknown	Japan's Foreign Minister, Togo, informs Cabinet of Truman's announcement.	No action taken.
Wednesday 8 August		
Unknown	Togo advises Emperor of need to accept Potsdam Declaration.	Emperor tells Foreign Minister to advise Premier that war must be terminated with no delay.
Unknown	Premier Suzuki calls for emergency meeting of Supreme War Council.	Postponed, as one member unavoidably detailed by 'more pressing business elsewhere'.[14] Historian Stephen Harper describes it as 'the Supreme War Council which had so strangely failed to assemble'.[15]
Unknown	Further conventional bombings across Japan.[16]	
10.30 am	Moscow: Japanese Ambassador Sato meets with Molotov.	Advice given that from the next day the Soviet Union would be at war with Japan.
Thursday 9 August		
2.30 am	USSR enters the war.	9 August, 8.30 pm Moscow time; 2.30 am Tokyo; 1.30 pm Washington.[17]
8.00 am	Togo visits Premier Suzuki in Koishikawa, north-central Tokyo.	Demands meeting of the Supreme Council.
Unknown	Togo visits Admiral Yonai, Navy Minister.	Agrees that Japan must sue for peace.

Date	Event	Detail
10.30 am	Supreme War Council meets at Imperial Palace.	No consensus – 50/50 split of the Big Six: Prime Minister Suzuki, Foreign Minister Togo, Army Chief of Staff Yoshijiro Umezu, Navy Chief of Staff Soemu Toyoda, Army Minister Anami, and Navy Minster Yonai.
11.00 am	Nagasaki bomb dropped.	B-29 Fat Man mission harassed by fighters and AA fire.[18]
1.00 pm	Supreme War Council meeting continues.	(By now) word had reached them of the second bombing – of Nagasaki – and that Manchuria was now in Russian hands, but they could still not reach an agreement.[19]
1.00–3.00 pm	Director of the Information Bureau, Hiroshi Shimomura, meets with Emperor.	Unusual two-hour meeting (normally 30 mins), with Emperor agreeing to make broadcast telling the nation whether war would continue, or peace be made.
2.30 am	Cabinet meets at Premier's official residence.	No outcome.
5.30 – 6.30 pm		One-hour recess.
6.30 – 10.00 pm	Meeting continues.	No outcome.
10.00-10.30 pm (approx.)	Suzuki and Togo visit Emperor.	They request official meeting of Supreme War Council, which is granted.
10.37 pm	Emperor receives Kido.	Sixth meeting that day.
10.50 pm	Emperor meets with Supreme Councilors, as well as aides and two invited guests.	Chief Cabinet Secretary Sakomizu and President of the Privy Council Baron Hiranuma.
Friday 10 August		
2.00 am	Emperor speaks about deadlock before him, then leaves.	Advises decision to 'bear the unbearable' to 'accept the Allied Proclamation'.
Unknown	Premier's residence.	Meeting to decide the wording of the advice to Allies.

Date	Event	Detail
4.00–7.00 am		Advice dispatched to neutral countries Switzerland and Sweden.
9.30 am	War Minister Anami convenes meeting of all above the 'chief-of-section' rank.	Advises of outcome
9.30 am Washington	Conference at White House: President; Sec of State; Sec of Navy; Chief of Staff	Consideration of phrase 'said Declaration does not compromise any demand which prejudices the prerogatives of His Majesty as Sovereign Ruler' = need to consult with the other country signatories of the Potsdam Declaration.
Throughout morning	Tokyo and other cities bombed heavily.	Cited as 'the most impressive and nerve-wracking demonstration of the whole war'.[20]
Throughout day	372 carrier sorties flown off Allied carriers.	Met by strong AA fire.[21]
Throughout morning	Soviet declaration of war appears in morning newspapers.	Regarding news of the second A-bomb attack, the military ask the editors of the five leading Tokyo dailies to downplay the news of Hiroshima, and all five complied.[22]
Probably late morning	Meeting of the Jushin (Senior Statesmen), group of ex-premiers.	Had considerable influence at the senior levels of government.
Probably late morning	Meeting of the Cabinet.	General conclusion was a decision to say nothing about the Emperor's decision or the Japanese note; would issue radio statement saying something vague about forthcoming announcements.

Date	Event	Detail
Unknown	Supporters of War Minister Anami prepare statement saying Japan would fight on. Lieutenant Colonel Masao Inaba prepares initial draft and shows it to Vice Minister of War and Colonel Okitsugu Arao; redrafts with Lieutenant Colonel Masahiko Takeshita	'We have but one choice: we must fight on until we win the sacred war to preserve our national polity. We must fight on, even if we have to chew grass and eat earth and live in fields – for in our death there is a chance of our country's survival. The hero Kusunoki pledged to live and die seven times in order to save Japan from disaster. We can do no less ....'[23]
7.00 pm	Evening radio news broadcasts statements.	Evening radio news broadcast statements were contradicting each other: Cabinet statement says that they must rise to the challenge; Anami's statement given that 'we must fight on ....'
Overnight	Washington, London, and Moscow confer.	Agree on slight re-wording, saying that the Emperor must be 'subject to the Supreme Commander of the Allied Powers'.[24]
Saturday 11 August		
Throughout day	Marquis Kido moves into the Imperial Palace area.	Rationale to be closer to the Emperor and less vulnerable to assassins.
Morning	15 revolutionary officers meet in a bomb shelter in War Office.	War would continue, by means of revolution, if necessary. Suzuki, Togo, and Kido were to be assassinated.
Morning	Newspapers appear on streets.	Carrying both announcements.
8.00 am	Group of officers meet and decide that continued fighting is preferable.	Approach their force commanders in Tokyo and announce this.[25]
8.00 am	Foreign Minister decides Japan must accept the note.	

Date	Event	Detail
8.20 am	General Umezu and Admiral Toyoda visit Emperor.	Emperor unsure whether they are speaking for themselves or others; no action.
10.00 am	12 offices visit War Minister.	Urge him to continue fighting.
11.00 am	Foreign Minister meets with Emperor.	Emperor hears translation of note and orders his desire for a continuance towards surrender be relayed to Premier Suzuki.
11.00 am (approx.)	Premier is met by War Minister and President of the Privy Council.	Advise him of their opposition to surrender. Persuade Suzuki that the Allies have changed the status of the Emperor – he agrees to support.
Early afternoon	Cabinet meets and rises without a vote.	Debate as to whether to demand reinstatement of two conditions asked for which the Allies had discarded.
Late afternoon	Metropolitan Police throughout Tokyo.	Post guards at strategic points; mount watch over officers thought to be involved in a conspiracy.

Sunday 12 August

| Sunday night 9.30 pm | Suzuki meets Kido. | Peace is necessary to avoid death of millions; Throne must be defended. |

Monday 13 August

Throughout day	Army manufactures statement they will fight on.	
Throughout day	Many officers meet at War Office and Army General Staff office.	
4.00 am	Anami orders Major Hayashi.	
4.00 pm	Cabinet meets.	
Monday night	War Minister Anami visited by Lieutenant Colonel Ida and Major Hatanaka.	
8.00 pm	Ten officers call on Minister Anami.	
9.00–11.00 pm	Togo meets with his two chiefs of staff.	
11.00 pm	Navy's Admiral Onishi arrives.	

Date	Event
12.00 am	General Anami meets Colonel Arao.
Tuesday 14 August	
7.00 am	Kido was shown some of the leaflets dropped over Tokyo.
Unknown	Officer group visits Anami with demands.
8.40 am	Suzuki and Kido visit the Emperor.
10.30 am	Emperor meets formally with Cabinet, Supreme Council, and others. Field Marshall Hata attends.[26]
Following meeting	Anami, according to some sources, meets with Umezu, Hayashi, and Lieutenant-Colonel Takeshita, his brother-in-law.[27]
1.00 pm	Cabinet meets.
Afternoon	Radio broadcast prepared.
Afternoon	Anami makes officers sign loyalty oath.
Afternoon	A 2nd battalion of Imperial Guards enter Palace grounds.
11.00 pm –12.00 am	Officers of the 302nd Air Corps called to a meeting by rebel leader, Captain Kozono of the Atsugi Air Group.
11.00 pm– 12.00 am	Captain Sasaki, of the Yokohama Guards, makes his way to foment revolt within the Guards Headquarters Sojiji Temple, planning to issue arms to the men he found there.[28]
11.00 pm– 12.00 am	Recording made.
Wednesday 15 August	
1.00–2.00 am	General Mori and Lieutenant Colonel Shiraishi assassinated.
Unknown	Strategic order No. 584 sent to various units and regiments.
Throughout day	Imperial Palace controlled entirely by Imperial Guards.
Unknown	16 men imprisoned by Guards in Palace grounds; later this rises with more prisoners added.
Early morning	Rebels fire machine guns at the Premier's official residence and set it on fire.

Date	Event
4.30 am	Marquis Kido's residence attacked by Kempeitai.
4.30 am	NHK building surrounded by rebel soldiers.
Unknown	Machine guns set up outside the Emperor's residence of the Imperial Library.
Unknown	37 rebels attack the Premier's private residence and set it on fire.
Unknown	War Minister Anami commits seppuku.
Unknown	General Tanaka, commander of the Eastern Army, takes charge.
6.00 am	Emperor told of the revolution.
6.58 am	Rebels set fire to Privy Council President Baron Hiranuma's house.
7.21 am	NHK broadcast the news of the Emperor's noon broadcast.
8.00 am	Battalion of the Guard leaves the Palace.
Morning	Major Hatanaka and Lieutenant Colonel Shiizaki distribute leaflets outside the Imperial Palace.
Morning	Aircraft flown by crews from Atsugu Air Base.
11.20 am	Emperor meets with Privy Council.
11.30 am	Officer of the Kempeitai tries to stop broadcast.
12.00 pm (approx.)	Hatanaka and Shiizaki kill themselves.
12.00 pm (approx.)	Major Koga, of the Imperial Guards staff, kills himself.
Thursday 16 August	
Unknown	Captain Uehara kills himself.
12.00 pm	Emperor's Broadcast heard throughout nation.
After broadcast	At Kodama, pilots load torpedoes onto planes and attempt to take off.[29]
Evening	Captain Sasaki's rebels surrender.

Date	Event
Later events	
17 August	Mito Army Air Division attempts revolt.[30]
24 August	Attempt by military students to occupy the Kawaguchi broadcasting station.[31]
Up until MacArthur's landing (30 August)	At Atsugi, plans and attempts to attack enemy forces continue.[32]
2 September	Colonel Oyadomari kills himself and family.
11 September	Former military leader and prime minister Tojo shoots himself in an attempted suicide.[33]

CHAPTER ONE
THE A-BOMB MISSIONS

Overview: In this chapter, we assess the overall description of the war, as well as a simple chronology of the major events surrounding the atomic missions, and an account of the attacks from the bomber perspective.

The world had been at war for a long time by 1945. The Japanese had invaded Manchuria in 1931 and defeated Chinese forces there – the start of a long campaign of aggression in the Pacific. The attack on the United States' possession of Pearl Harbor, and other American outposts such as the Philippines in December 1941 had brought the United States into full-blooded combat across the world.

Prior to that, Germany's invasion of Poland in 1939 finally brought the major powers of France and Great Britain into a campaign to stop Adolf Hitler's assertive campaign to bring Europe under the Nazi jackboot. Britain's decision to go to war brought the Empire's possessions of Canada, Australia, India and more into the conflict.

Germany's defeat of Poland was followed by the blitzkrieg – literally 'lightning war' across the continent as she attacked Finland, Norway, and then turned on France, smashing her forces and almost driving the British Army into the sea at Dunkirk. Meanwhile, a systemic persecution of Jews and other elements of society the German command thought undesirable was gaining strength. The USSR's previous alliance, the so-called 'Pact of Steel', which saw Poland divided up between Germany and the USSR, came to an end when Hitler decided to attack the despised Slavic hordes.

In the Pacific, Japanese aggression was given further impetus with the success of a surprise attack on Pearl Harbor. The armies of their Empire swept south, with the Imperial Japanese Navy also gaining victory at sea. Italy entered the war as one of the Axis powers. The United States' initial reverses saw Japan checked at first at the Battle of the Coral Sea, and then its expansion halted at the Battle of Midway.

The plan for the war on this side of the globe was two-fold. Firstly, there was a sweep across the Pacific to use Australia – also under air attack in its north – as a base. And secondly, what occurred from that was a long war of 'island-hopping', with occasional success, paralleled with enormous cost as the Japanese forces fought in a way no other nation did: to almost total destruction rather than surrender.

The Battle of the Atlantic, meanwhile, was almost bringing Britain to its knees. Successful U-boat attacks were seeing a massive amount of tonnage sunk, and the island nation's supplies looked as if they would not last. But even in its darkest hour, planning was underway for an amphibious invasion of Europe, and this duly took place on D-Day in mid-1944. The armies of Britain, the United States, and the USSR began their march to Berlin, even as German possessions were taking more punishment from the air.

The strategic policy agreed on by these 'Big Three' was simple: 'Germany first'. In the Pacific, however, Japan had gained an empire and was determined to keep it. But they had not fully figured in the United States' massive industrial base. A nation already geared to turning out civilian aircraft, passenger ships, and road vehicles on production lines could be turned into a massive supply house capable of producing bombers, destroyers, and tanks by the hundreds of thousands.

The United States, in turn, had not figured out how to battle an enemy willing to accept massive casualties – far more than the normal 30 percent, which caused a normal army to break and run. This was to make the amphibious assault of island bases across the Pacific enormously costly. But while 1942 to 1943 was about the Allied forces – for the United States was joined by many other countries in the Pacific – learning how to defeat the Japanese, 1944 was to be about a more studied approach. The use of the aircraft carrier, in particular, changed the face of battle in the world's biggest ocean: airpower from the sea made enormous differences in when and where aircraft could strike.

Germany's defeat, slowly and steadily, and almost assured, despite breakout attempts such as the Battle of the Bulge, saw the European strategy through to success. But in the Pacific, an awareness was dawning that another D-Day-style attack on Japan would see the war continue through until the end of 1946. And it would be enormously costly: the steep hills and valleys of Japan would favour the defenders, and the entire country's population would become militia. The atomic bomb experiments – which began years before, and ironically in a response to German moves along the same lines – had come to fruition in the Trinity test blast in mid-1945. Although aerial bombing raids had inflicted massive destruction on Japan, the concept of 'one plane, one city' offered a new shattering possibility that the war could be terminated early.

The A-bomb assaults take place

Aug. 6, 1945 - This picture taken from Yoshiura on the other side of the mountain north of Hiroshima shows the smoke rising from the atom bomb explosion. Note the radiation spots almost ruining the film. (AP Photo)

The attack

Once the A-bomb attacks were decided on, targeting became a prime concern. Hiroshima was chosen for the initial attack, as it was both an important military production target and untouched by raids so far. Previously in the conflict, 'Hiroshima switched from producing everyday goods to making materials for the war.'[1] It had a military base on which worked 40,000 soldiers. Its civilian population had largely been conscripted in the effort to produce military supplies, even using the city's children as labour.[2]

The best description of the mission comes from the account of the command pilot, Paul Tibbets, who commanded the B-29, which carried the weapon itself.[3] Although the mission is often described as a 'one-plane attack' it actually saw a small fleet of bombers making their way to the target.

40,000 individual tiles, recalling those who died, make up the mosaic picture within the Hiroshima Peace Memorial underground section. (Author photo)

Special Mission 13, primary target: Hiroshima, 6 August 1945[4]

Aircraft	Pilot	Call sign	Mission role
Straight Flush	Major Claude R Eatherly	Dimples 85	Weather reconnaissance (Hiroshima)
Jabit III	Major John A Wilson	Dimples 71	Weather reconnaissance (Kokura)
Full House	Major Ralph R Taylor	Dimples 83	Weather reconnaissance (Nagasaki)
Enola Gay	Colonel Paul W Tibbets	Dimples 82	Weapon delivery
The Great Artiste	Major Charles W Sweeney	Dimples 89	Blast measurement instrumentation
Necessary Evil	Captain. George W Marquardt	Dimples 91	Strike observation and photography

Three weather planes flew ahead, taking off first and covering a target each so the weather could be assessed over the prospective raid site. Two other B-29 bombers accompanied *Enola Gay*, which had just been named after the pilot Colonel Tibbets' mother.[5] The two escort planes carried cameras and measuring devices.[6]

At 6.30 am, Hiroshima time, Captain Williams Parsons, who was in charge of the bomb, 'Replaced three green plugs in the bomb with three red ones. Little Boy was now live.'[7]

The Hiroshima weather plane, named *Straight Flush*, reached her target and made good observations, despite being harassed by light anti-aircraft fire. The city's fate was therefore sealed, if the bomb worked – for its design had not been tested previously: the test detonation back in the United States had been of a different type. *Enola Gay* climbed to her bombing height of 32,000 feet, reaching it by 7.25 am local time.

The instrument aircraft, *The Great Artiste*, throttled back until she was 1000 feet behind the bomber, and the camera plane, *Number 91*, began to circle for photographs. At 8.13 am and 30 seconds, the *Enola Gay* was handed over to Bombardier Ferebee for the target run. At

8.15 am and 17 seconds, the bomb bay doors opened and the weapon was released.[8]

It was to take 43 seconds to fall to its detonation height.[9]

According to Tibbets, the plane was 'instantly 9000 pounds lighter. As a result, the nose leapt up sharply and I had to act quickly to execute the most important part of the flight: to put as much distance as possible between our plane and the point at which the bomb would explode'.[10] At the moment the bomb was released, three parachute instrument packages were dropped from *The Great Artiste*, leading to some Japanese eyewitness claims that the bomb had been dropped by parachute.

A B-29 cockpit, with the bombardier's position in front and below. (USAAF)

The target was hit precisely at the Hiroshima time of 8.16 am on 6 August 1945. A picture of a fused clock, showing that exact time, was often circulated in later years.[11] It is 'often said that about 80,000 people died either of the immediate effects of the bomb or of exposure to gamma radiation, which killed victims in twenty to thirty days'.[12] The Japanese government summarised the damage six months later: 4.7 square miles of Hiroshima were destroyed; 40,653 dwellings were eliminated; 71,379 people were killed or missing; 68,023 were wounded.[13]

Nagasaki air raid shelter entrances (Author photo)

The second raid

The Nagasaki mission took place days later when no surrender was forthcoming. It was only just a success: all reports state the aircraft, named *Bockscar* and piloted by Major Charles W Sweeney, only just made it back to a secondary base after several delays caused by dubious decisions.

Special Mission 16, secondary target: Nagasaki, 9 August 1945[14]

Aircraft	Pilot	Call sign	Mission role
Enola Gay	Captain George W Marquardt	Dimples 82	Weather reconnaissance (Kokura)
Laggin' Dragon	Captain Charles F McKnight	Dimples 95	Weather reconnaissance (Nagasaki)
Bockscar	Major Charles W Sweeney	Dimples 77	Weapon delivery
The Great Artiste	Captain Frederick C Bock	Dimples 89	Blast measurement instrumentation
Big Stink	Major James I Hopkins, Jr.	Dimples 90	Strike observation and photography

Sweeney's account[15] seems to be the most truthful of several written after the second raid. He does not embark on histrionic accounting, or attempt to gloss over the many errors in the two attack raids: fairly standard problems in World War II flying, but nevertheless significant. (Tibbets' book paints a very dismal picture of the second raid, with the B-29 A-squadron commander criticising Sweeney personally.) For example, the photography plane, which was supposed to accompany the Nagasaki mission, failed to make the rendezvous point due to poor navigation, resulting in a significant failure in recording the effects of the second type of weapon; Nagasaki being an implosion type of A-bomb rather than the 'gun type' employed on the previous drop.

Casualty figures for Nagasaki vary, but one account cites 23,753 killed and 43,000 wounded.[16] The 'Japanese Council against A and H Bombs' cites Hiroshima deaths as being 130,000 by the end of 1945, and Nagasaki as 60,000.[17] The Hiroshima Peace Memorial carries 140,000 tiles in its underground circular display room, which it cites as being one for each person who died.[18]

However, the number of people who died in the A-bomb blasts is often given as much higher than that, and indeed is argued to extremes. For example, the 'Specialists Committee, Japan Council against Atom and Hydrogen Bombs' gives a figure for Hiroshima of 'approximately 200,000' people dying there, and 122,000 in Nagasaki.[19] Alternatively, historians Robert Lifton and Greg Mitchell suggest that 100,000 were killed in the Hiroshima attack. [20]

Nagasaki, taken 20 minutes after the bombing. (Public domain)

Nagasaki's hills can be seen beyond the modern streets. The containment of the A-bomb blast meant to a small degree there was some lessening of possible casualties. (Author photo)

The attacks killed various Allied Prisoners Of War scattered around the city. Many, such as Corporal John Long, from Pennsylvania, an air gunner from a downed B-24, are now commemorated at the Memorial in Hiroshima.[21] It was the ultimate irony that the weapon which was to save hundreds of thousands of POWs – as outlined later – would kill some in its detonation.

The B-29 *Enola Gay*, at the Steven F. Udvar-Hazy Center, a section of the Smithsonian National Air and Space Museum. (USAAF)

Similarly, POWs imprisoned at Nagasaki feature in the displays of the Nagasaki Atomic Bomb Museum. Accounts are featured from Australian soldiers Francis Fitzmaurice, Reginald McConnell, Murray Jobling, Eric Hooper, and Alan Chick.[22] Fitzmaurice says in one of the short films in the display: 'If the Americans had landed in Japan, our fates would have been terrible.' He goes on to say that: 'Many more people round here would have died if the A-bombs had not been used.'[23] It is with this often-controversial argument that this book is concerned.

Conclusion

If wars can be said to have a "satisfactory" conclusion, it was at this point the world could truly say World War II was coming to a halt. It was a faster capitulation than had been experienced in many conflicts, and therefore might well be said to be a better one, for the fatalities quickly petered out. Over time, however, many have disagreed with the means which achieved that end.

CHAPTER TWO

WAS JAPAN GOING TO FIGHT ON?

Resolution, refusal to surrender, and a second bomb

Overview: In this chapter, we discuss the quality of Japanese soldiers, their casualty rates, and casualty ratios as a measure of willingness to fight. We look at the US Strategic Bombing Survey, composed after the war, which argued that Japan would have surrendered, including a rebuttal by Maddox. The second bombing, at Nagasaki, is briefly analysed, and the leaflets dropped after the first are discussed. The construction of underground headquarters is outlined, as is Japanese love of country as a factor in continuing the war.

The situation and the resolve

The Empire lay in ruins, but Japan still fought on.

All across the Pacific, through the shattered islands and countries where the war had raged, the country's forces fought, stubbornly, proudly, fiercely and capably. Millions of men under arms still took lives every day – thousands from both the Allied forces and from the diminishing yet still formidable Japanese side still struggling against each other.

The Allies had made their determination clear at Potsdam. Japan was to surrender unconditionally. However, the surrender conditions had some leniency. But Potsdam made no difference, and so the atomic weapons were readied.

Potsdam Declaration

Proclamation Defining Terms for Japanese Surrender Issued, at Potsdam, 26 July 1945

1. We – the President of the United States, the President of the National Government of the Republic of China, and the Prime Minister of Great Britain, representing the hundreds of millions of our countrymen, have conferred and agree that Japan shall be given an opportunity to end this war.

2. The prodigious land, sea and air forces of the United States, the British Empire and of China, many times reinforced by their armies and air fleets from the west, are poised to strike the final blows upon Japan. This military power is sustained and inspired by the determination of all the Allied Nations to prosecute the war against Japan until she ceases to resist.

3. The result of the futile and senseless German resistance to the might of the aroused free peoples of the world stands forth in awful clarity as an example to the people of Japan. The might that now converges on Japan is immeasurably greater than that which, when applied to the resisting Nazis, necessarily laid waste to the lands, the industry and the method of life of the whole German people. The full application of our military power, backed by our resolve, will mean the inevitable and complete destruction of the Japanese armed forces and just as inevitably the utter devastation of the Japanese homeland.

4. The time has come for Japan to decide whether she will continue to be controlled by those self-willed militaristic advisers whose unintelligent calculations have brought the Empire of Japan to the threshold of annihilation, or whether she will follow the path of reason.

5. Following are our terms. We will not deviate from them. There are no alternatives. We shall brook no delay.

6. There must be eliminated for all time the authority and influence of those who have deceived and misled the people of Japan into

embarking on world conquest, for we insist that a new order of peace, security and justice will be impossible until irresponsible militarism is driven from the world.

7. Until such a new order is established and until there is convincing proof that Japan's war-making power is destroyed, points in Japanese territory to be designated by the Allies shall be occupied to secure the achievement of the basic objectives we are here setting forth.

8. The terms of the Cairo Declaration shall be carried out and Japanese sovereignty shall be limited to the islands of Honshu, Hokkaido, Kyushu, Shikoku and such minor islands as we determine.

9. The Japanese military forces, after being completely disarmed, shall be permitted to return to their homes with the opportunity to lead peaceful and productive lives.

10. We do not intend that the Japanese shall be enslaved as a race or destroyed as a nation, but stern justice shall be meted out to all war criminals, including those who have visited cruelties upon our prisoners. The Japanese Government shall remove all obstacles to the revival and strengthening of democratic tendencies among the Japanese people. Freedom of speech, of religion, and of thought, as well as respect for the fundamental human rights shall be established.

11. Japan shall be permitted to maintain such industries as will sustain her economy and permit the exaction of just reparations in kind, but not those which would enable her to re-arm for war. To this end, access to, as distinguished from control of, raw materials shall be permitted. Eventual Japanese participation in world trade relations shall be permitted.

12. The occupying forces of the Allies shall be withdrawn from Japan as soon as these objectives have been accomplished

and there has been established in accordance with the freely expressed will of the Japanese people a peacefully inclined and responsible government.

13. We call upon the government of Japan to proclaim now the unconditional surrender of all Japanese armed forces, and to provide proper and adequate assurances of their good faith in such action. The alternative for Japan is prompt and utter destruction.[1]

But how determined was the Japanese government to fight on? Was it the case the atomic weapons were unnecessary, for they did not have the resolve anyway?

As a measure of resolution, we turn first to the reaction of the Japanese government and people after the detonation of the atomic weapons. The measure of resolution here is shown as an example of how willing Japan was to fight, and therefore we can gain a measure of how resolute the country would have been in the face of a conventional assault.

This resistance to surrender is a measure of how many casualties the Allied forces would have taken as a result. That term – 'casualties' – will crop up again and again, and it is necessary to understand its use: generally a description of both dead and wounded. In most wars, and World War II was no exception, it is one killed for four wounded. It is a sobering and necessary thought to realise that this means 'seriously enough injured to necessitate withdrawal from battle' – so amputation, loss of a major part of the anatomy, inability to walk, and so on.

After the first bombing, the Supreme War Council of Japan met in Tokyo in an emergency session. Three out of six members wanted to accept the Potsdam Declaration: Premier Suzuki, Foreign Minister Togo, and Navy Minister Yonai. War Minister Anami and his two military heads, Chief of the Army General Staff Umezu and Navy Chief of Staff Toyoda, wanted to hold out and demand three extra terms.[2] Nothing was done.

The national Home Service radio sent out a broadcast at 6.00 am the next day, which these days would be labeled as ultimate 'spin'. It was breathtaking in its audacity:

The enemy, being faced with difficult conditions, is feeling rushed to turn the war into one of short duration. Hence he has begun to use this new type of bomb .... The enemy has been carrying out large-scale propaganda on the effectiveness of this new-type bomb since using these bombs, but as long as we formulate strong steel-like measures to cope with this new type of bomb, it will be possible to keep damage at a minimum.[3]

Matsushiro Underground Imperial Headquarters, Nagano (Author photo)

The physical resolve – the Nagano Command Cave System

That the Japanese were ready to keep up the conflict can be seen by their physical preparations. As a measure of their determination, the high command had planned a fallback headquarters. The site was at Nagano, north-west of Tokyo, some 300 kilometres away, in a mountainous area. Enormous tunnels were driven through solid rocky mountains, chosen deliberately for their impervious position and designed to be immune from the B-29 bomber threat.

Designated the Matsushiro Underground Imperial Headquarters, the tunnels would house the Imperial Family, supreme commanders, and a support staff. From here the Japanese would fight on. The Nagano complex is the biggest defence system, but it was by no means the only one. All over the country physical preparation was being made.

Visiting the Nagano tunnel complex today gives some idea of Japanese determination at the time. Although the entrances look like mineshaft openings, once inside, the tunnels go on for kilometres. An enormous complex was planned and although they were still being built when the war ended, enough had been completed so that final finishing and equipping could have been quickly carried out.

Some 6000 Korean workers laboured to produce the headquarters. The history of the complex is hazy: the tunnels were sealed off post-war, and only opened in 1985 by exploring high school students. Debate then ensued as to whether they should remain open, for the use of Korean labour aroused bitter arguments, as it still does today in Japan. It is said that many Koreans died in the work period, from poor treatment and from accidents.[4]

Nagasaki modern street. The trams were a feature of the city in WWII. Note one of the surrounding hills in the background, which helped contain the blast. (Author photo)

Hardened and hidden structures were the norm for the everyday command of the forces. Control of the Navy was already carried out through such tunnels in Yokahama, a city south-west of Tokyo.

The Navy tunnels were opened to journalists for the first time in 2015. Located in World War II – and still today – in the Hiyoshi campus of Keio University, the grounds that normally swarmed with students were empty of students in the final stages of the war: they had all been drafted into the forces. Like the Nagano complex, the Navy tunnels also used Korean forced labour for their construction. They were opened for use in mid-1944. The Yokahama centre is 30 metres underground and stretches for 2.6 kilometres in length.[5]

The cities featured strongly constructed air-raid shelters. Generally, these were located in the suburb next to each railway station.[6] Where possible, they used natural features for protection, such as overlying hills or mountains. With such civil protection measures, the high command reasoned that the population could be inured to a degree to the B-29s and any lesser measures the Allies could bring to bear.

The Nagasaki bomb was dropped in a similar fashion to the Hiroshima strike, from a B-29 on a city, left largely unattacked, that could be destroyed as a warning of how formidable the new weapons were. Despite a gathering of the storm over the country, no action had been taken to terminate the war. The conflict continued unabated. The Allied bombers kept on raiding and the targets were defended by Japanese assets. Lives continued to be lost. On 8 August, the city of Yawata was attacked by 245 B-29 bombers; four were shot down in the biggest loss of aircraft and crews by the Twentieth Air Force in two months.[7]

On Thursday 9 August, the USSR entered the conflict. On the same day, the Fat Man mission took off – this time with the second type of nuclear weapon on board. This was an implosion device rather that the 'gun' type of weapon; the Trinity test had ascertained that this type of bomb would indeed work, whereas the Little Boy gun bomb had not needed a test. This time the B-29s were not left alone, as had been the case with the Hiroshima attack; they were harassed by fighters and anti-aircraft fire to no effect.[8]

Even Nagasaki did not necessitate a sudden surrender:

According to both *Imperial Tragedy* and *Behind Japan's Surrender*, rather than make the admirals want to seek peace, the news from

Hiroshima and Nagasaki made them immediately want 'to isolate all Japanese physicists in the caves in Nagano Prefecture to have them produce atomic bombs'.[9]

On 10 July [former Ambassador to Japan] Joseph C Grew publicly stated:

> We have received no peace offer from the Japanese government through official or unofficial channels. Conversations relating to peace have been reported to this department from various parts of the world but in no case had an approach been made to this government, directly or indirectly, by a person who could speak for the Japanese government, and in no case has an offer of surrender been made.[10]

The War Minister's proclamation gives an insight into the determination to fight on: 'Even though we may have to eat grass, swallow dirt and lie in the fields, we shall fight on to the bitter end ... surge forward to destroy the arrogant enemy.'[11] Meanwhile there was no lessening of the pace of the war. There were 372 carrier sorties flown off Allied carriers during that day, and they were met with strong AA fire.[12]

The psychological war – Japanese love of Nihon as a factor

The natural Japanese love of their Home Islands was part of the unification of the country. Newspapers praised the resolve of the soldiers and civilians in locations such as Saipan. Headlines described the suicides with enthusiasm: 'Sacrifice Themselves for the National Exigency Together with the Brave Men,' and 'The Heroic Last Moments of our Fellow Countrymen on Saipan.'[13] Such attitudes exemplify the converse of the physical preparation: the psychological resolve.

Suzuki, as Premier of Japan, since 7 April 1945, was seen as a moderate by many, and the war was expected by some to take a different course, but that was not to be. In his first speech to the Japanese parliament, the Diet: 'He insisted that unconditional surrender could never be accepted. Japan's only course, he said, would be to "fight to the very end".'[14] Fear of the consequences of living on past surrender was also thrown into the psychological imperative to fight: the Japanese were 'told that with the occupation of Japan, [they] would be forced to live the life of slaves'.[15]

The population as a whole had by now been placed on a war footing. Children laboured to produce war materials as part of their normal day, with school as the compulsory alternative. One boy later wrote:

> I was 16 years old at the time … I was working at the time as a mobilised student, helping to make airplane parts in a temporary factory of the Mitsubishi Electrical Plant set up in the gymnasium at the Nagasaki University Faculty of Economics, a distance of about 2.8 kilometres from the atomic bomb hypocenter.[16]

For a long time, the Japanese soldier had been conditioned to think of his life as not his own; it was the country's, exemplified by the Emperor. There was a complete rejection of the concepts of not doing one's utmost, even to the end. The idea of surrender was not part of the system – let alone of being captured.

For example, the 1941 Field Service Code, issued by General Tojo, explained it bluntly and firmly: 'Do not live in shame as a prisoner. Die, and leave no ignominious crime behind you.'[17]

The Japanese pre-invasion patriotic song, 'One Hundred Million Souls for the Emperor,' says Sledge, 'meant just that'.[18] As one line went: 'The day is near when the 100,000,000 people as one man will be in active resistance to the enemy.'[19] Even post the two atomic blasts, the official line was propagated in the newspapers that the country would, and could, continue the war:

> The newspaper that same day had carried a story with the headline: 'No reason to fear new style bomb' and went on to review the new style countermeasures against the atomic bomb that had first been made public on 11 August.[20]

Hiroshima and Nagasaki were no obstacle to the steadfast orderliness of Japanese people to continue the processes of running the country. Soldier Toyofumi Ogura simply reported to his temporary job, while on leave in Hiroshima, as the supervisor of a student work group who were making hand grenades: they continued their task, even on the outskirts of a city that had seen massive destruction.[21]

Even two atomic bomb attacks were not enough to defeat the will of the Japanese people to the extent they clamored for surrender. Then again, they did not know of the full extent of the war casualties, and never had, not knowing for example of the close to 100,000 people who died in one night in the firestorm raids on Tokyo. One of the residents of Nagasaki later wrote:

> Even after all of this, we continued to believe that Japan was winning the war, and that, for the sake of the country, we must continue struggling. A few days later, enemy planes scattered leaflets over the city. Although I do not remember clearly, these said something like 'Japan is defeated, and the emperor has surrendered.' We scoffed at this information, calling it lies, but on 15 August (another day I shall never forget) we learnt that the war was over and Japan had been defeated. [22]

That such massive casualties could be inflicted and the population remain resolute is hard to understand today. But then there were no instant communications. The news was carried by newspaper, and they were vigorously controlled by the Japanese government. Telephones were not commonplace instruments in every home.

Conversations with families and friends who were far away were mostly by letter, and therefore communication back and forth could take weeks. And if it turned out that a home had been burnt down or bombed – well, the country was at war, and such things happened in wartime. That it would happen to hundreds of thousands of people within a city was incomprehensible: you were seeing one piece of a puzzle without comprehending that many other pieces told the same story of death and destruction.

In any event, the Chief Cabinet Secretary commented on Premier Suzuki's position that:

> The Army was determined to continue the war. Therefore if anyone had said 'end the war' he might have been arrested by the military police. Things were like that then.... If Premier

Suzuki had mentioned a cease fire at that time, the Army would not have co-operated with his Cabinet.[23]

Some of this was the 'Bushido' code, encapsulating that 'no retreat, no surrender, and an eagerness to die in defence of the homeland'.[24] Wilson Miscamble summed it up as: 'Indeed, members of the Japanese military appeared to relish the opportunity to punish American invaders who dared to intrude on their Home Islands.'[25] And indeed they had much reason to believe they could not be conquered.

The Japanese infantry in general in World War II were excellent fighters, determined and efficient, and extremely bloodthirsty. One study of them concluded that 'Japanese soldiers from the highest to the lowest are thoroughly imbued with the spirit of offence, in which they tend to see the solution of all problems.'[26] British General, William Slim, thought 'there can be no question of the supreme courage and hardihood of the Japanese soldiers .... I know of no army that could have equaled them'.[27]

A US Marine report assessed the Japanese as 'well trained and disciplined army troops of exceptionally high morale and splendid physical condition'.[28] Any illusions about their abilities and temerity were swept away after a few days of combat. On Okinawa, where the US Marines took extremely heavy casualties to take the island, one platoon leader told new green replacements in no uncertain manner about the calibre of the enemy they faced:

> Pointing his pistol at these bewildered lambs, he concluded, 'And if I hear any bullshit about the Japs being lousy fighters, I'll shoot you. If one of you motherfuckers says they can't shoot straight, I'll put a bullet between your fuckin' eyes before they do.'[29]

Bob Neiman, the Executive Officer of the 1st Tank Battalion of the US Marine Corps, thought of the Japanese as 'tenacious, among the finest fighters in the world, next to the Marine Corps ... well trained, well disciplined, with little regard for their own lives.'[30] Japanese determination was usually extremely strong, with the infantry holding their positions in the face of odds, which would have broken the hearts of many Westerners.

One account from a Japanese soldier describes advancing to the Allied positions at night in an effort not to take the ground – the Japanese unit was not strong enough for that – but to get the enemy to retreat enough so that the ammunition, food and equipment they left behind could be taken by the Japanese for their own use. Then they would go back to their own positions, to fight and die for another day. Those who could not contribute through wounds were apologetic:

> If he were heavily injured he would regret overtaxing his mates. Those men passed away saying, 'Excuse me. I regret dying.' They died apologising and weeping. The battlefield takes the life of such brave men, and there is no way of helping them. We were short of food, but most distressing was that we did not have bullets. Still, we did not give up .... [31]

Morale on the battlefield, even if it was not full of enthusiasm when things became hard, was always one of simply trying harder in the face of adversity. The life of a soldier was the property of the Emperor, and it was duty to die for him if necessary. And die they did. Frank notes the extreme rate of casualties:

Place	Fatality rate among troops[32]
Tarawa	99.7%
Makin	99.6%
Roi-Namur	98.5%
Kwajalein	98.4%
Saipan	97%

What became known as the 'Saipan ratio' emerged from a paper originating from the Joint Chiefs of Staff:

> In our Saipan operation it cost approximately one American killed and several wounded to exterminate one Japanese soldier. On this basis it might cost us half a million American lives lost and many times that number in wounded to exterminate the

Japanese ground forces that conceivably could be employed against us in the Home Islands.[33]

There was certainly a willingness in the senior command to continue to spend Japanese lives. War Minister Korechika Anami demanded that the Japanese must fight a last, glorious battle to defend their homeland. Almost at the same time the Fat Man bomb descended on Nagasaki, he was asking colleagues, 'Who can be 100 percent sure of defeat?' His colleagues were just as adamant. 'The generals of Japan – a nation that had never known defeat – vowed to fight on, and War Minister Anami blocked all suggestions of surrender.'[34]

This was despite a steadily growing shortage of crucial war material and food for the general population. Frank Richard in *Downfall* analyses Japan's industrial capacity succinctly. He charts their new ability to use oil supplies from their conquered territories of South-East Asia, but also their inability to transport raw crude oil back to refineries. Eventually, the capture of the Philippines by the Allies cut off the area from Japan, and 'No tanker reached Japan after March 1945.'

Further, aerial mining was crippling the ability of freighters and tankers to move, as was a highly aggressive and successful campaign by American submarines. Labour forces within the Home Islands themselves were being severely hampered simply by hunger, with food supplies becoming more and more depleted. However, in the end, Richard concludes:

> It might appear obvious in hindsight that Japan's leaders should have recognised the impossibility of continuing a modern war of attrition and that the clear course was to surrender. The reality, however, is that they chose a different path.[35]

The much criticised US Strategic Bombing Survey, written soon after the end of the war, concluded that 'certainly prior to 31 December 1945, in all probability prior to 1 November 1945, Japan would have surrendered even if the atomic bomb had not been dropped ....'[36]

Robert Maddox contends this was not true:

Some writers have argued that the cumulative effects of battlefield defeats, conventional bombing, and naval blockade already had defeated Japan. Even without extending assurances about the Emperor, all the United States had to do was wait. The most frequently cited basis for this contention is the United States Strategic Bombing Survey, published in 1946, which stated that Japan would have surrendered by 1 November 'even if the atomic bombs had not been dropped, even if Russia had not entered the war, and even if no invasion had been planned or contemplated'. [37]

He goes on to contend that 'Recent scholarship by the historian Robert P Newman and others has demonstrated that the survey was "cooked" by those who prepared it to arrive at such a conclusion.'[38]

A final word on resolve to fight can be noted by the non-acceptance of the Emperor's message by many in the armed services to lay down their arms. Fighter pilot Yasuo Kuwahara, who had already been notified that he would become a kamikaze pilot, later wrote:

I saw the stricken faces, expressions of growing relief on some, of anger on others. Then, suddenly, one of the Kichigai leaped to his feet with a strangled cry. 'Those rotten Americans! May God destroy them! Revenge! Revenge! Are we mere feeble women? Let us strike now, this very moment – before it's too late! We are expendable!'

'We are expendable!' rose the cry. A score of men arose and would have rushed to their planes had not the commander intervened.[39]

On 15 August, days after the two atomic detonations, a Judy bomber managed to make it into the heart of the Allied fleet and drop two bombs near the carrier *Indefatigable*, before being shot down. Two more attacks were defeated that afternoon.[40]

On the same day, a dogfight between American and Japanese fighters near Tokyo saw four of the former and ten of the latter shot down. Martin Gilbert points out that on the southern coast of Burma 'several hundred Japanese' died in fighting through September against the British.[41] Such fighting was continued, not out of disobedience but by acceptance of the explanation that the Emperor had been betrayed, and it was now the duty of all patriotic Japanese to fight on.

It is another measure of a most formidable enemy.

Little Boy lifesize replica bomb. Nagasaki Atomic Bomb Museum, 2015. (Author photo)

People were still fighting and dying. But cooler heads were prevailing. Marquis Koichi Kido, adviser to the Emperor in 1945, later wrote: 'The presence of the atomic bomb made it easier for us politicians to negotiate peace. Even then the military would not listen to reason.'[42]

A second meeting – of ten-hours duration – followed, and then a meeting with the Emperor where the same deadlock was presented. He listened to both sides, and then made a decision for unconditional surrender.

Conclusion

We have seen the Japanese determination to fight to the end. We have seen that they were capable of fighting and dying in enormous numbers. They did not have a countrywide realisation of what was happening to them. The concept of 'one bomb, one city' from an aircraft they were unable to stop was largely unknown to the population as a whole.

We have no evidence to show that the Japanese were on the cusp of a revolution. It took their Emperor – regarded as 'divine'– to stop them, and even that command was almost negated.

This early chapter is merely an introduction to such background, so we shall explore further.

WAS JAPAN GOING TO FIGHT ON?

Rebellion

Overview: In this chapter, we see that the decision to surrender was not easy to make. In fact, it was countered by a revolution within the senior commanders. This is of interest to our central argument as an indication of how fiercely the Japanese would have fought if a conventional invasion had been put into place. Even as the rebellion failed, and the Emperor broadcast the nation the instruction to surrender, there was widespread resistance to the idea that the country was giving in.

The rebellions that took place after the atomic bombs had devastated two of Japan's most important cities are testimony to the determination and ferocity with which the nation's military caste pursued their aim. It is indicative of the perseverance with which – despite the likely use of tactical nuclear weapons in any Allied invasion – the military and militia, and conscripted civilians would have defended the Home Islands.

Even before the first weapon had struck Hiroshima, the nation was being bombarded with Allied-psychological warfare. Millions of leaflets were dropped; and every 15 minutes, foreign radio broadcasted exhortations to surrender. However, from a modern perspective, communications were poor. There was no television or Internet in Japanese homes: the former was in its infancy in the West, and the latter was not even dreamt of in science fiction. Computers were confined to ballistic calculations for big artillery pieces, or the deciphering of cryptology. Newspapers were the main form of communication; however, in paper-starved Japan, the former broadsheets – which circulated widely – were reduced to a shadow of their former self.

A group of Home Defence officials pictured at a drill, with two gas mask wearing participants in the foreground. (USAAF).

But generally speaking no one in the population of 72 million was unaware that Japan was hard-pressed, and if not expanding, then was not capably defending itself against the Allied onslaught. Defeat had followed defeat since the Battle of Midway in 1942. Initial success had been followed by an attempt to consolidate the gains, but the far-flung borders of the Empire had been slowly pushed back.

Initially, Japan had taken all of South-East Asia and had even struck at Australia to keep it from being used as an American base and to nullify its efforts to take New Guinea, and confine the Americans to fighting from their own continent. That had failed, with a check in the Battle of the Coral Sea followed by defeat in the Battle of Midway.

Island fortresses were steadily taken by the Allies: Tarawa, Guam,

Peleliu, Iwo Jima, Saipan, and even Okinawa, only 640 kilometres from the Home Islands, had fallen at enormous cost in Japanese lives and resources. Okinawa was the closest island base available to the southern invaders constituting the Allied fleets. With the island in Allied hands its airfields were available to the bombers, which now had the capacity to steadily deliver raid after raid against shattered Japanese fighter protection and anti-aircraft guns.

A Japanese officer surrenders his sword to a British lieutenant in a ceremony in Saigon. (Public domain)

Across the nation there was knowledge that Japan was now fighting with its back against the wall. Baron Suzuki Kantaro had taken office as Prime Minister in mid-1945, replacing the ineffective Kuniaki Koiso, who had governed for less than a year; Koiso had replaced the militaristic Hideki Tōjō. Some saw the new leader as a more effective bringer of peace, but he 'was forced by the army to promise that his government would continue the war "to the bitter end"'.[1]

The nation's sword was still raised and there was energy left for strike after strike. Even as discussion circled the dangerous subject of surrender there was an animated argument against any form of surrender from many prominent people and organisations.

Even as the Potsdam Declaration was discussed and surrender was seen as a possibility, there was talk of resisting, even if it came as a 'divine' command.

The logic of this was curious. Given that the Emperor was considered 'divine', how could it be that his opinion was wrong?

Those who began to talk of further resistance took a devious path. Following the Hiroshima raid, at around eight o'clock on a Monday morning, the news of the attack slowly began to intensify in the national capital. It is, however, essential to understand that the mindset within the government was qualified by the fact that they had already seen such destruction at close hand months earlier. The March 1945 attack on Tokyo by Curtis le May's firebombing raid had in fact killed more and devastated as much geographically as did Hiroshima. Japanese Foreign Office member Toshikazu Kase noted that:

> One hundred and fifty B-29s subjected Tokyo to a mass raid by night, concentrating on the most densely populated districts. Within a few hours 300,000 houses went up in flames and a million persons were rendered homeless overnight. One hundred thousand charred and mutilated corpses were strewn amidst the smoking ruins.[2]

Kase also notes Osaka being similarly bombed, with '200,000' homes being lost; but in fact, Nagoya had also been attacked a day earlier on the 12th with a square mile of the city destroyed, and 2.5 square miles of Kobe.[3] On 26 May, Kase noted that 'some 500 superfortresses (sic) struck the government and palace districts of Tokyo'. During the raid the AA guns ran out of ammunition after firing 'some 10,000 rounds'.[4]

In fact, Kase's understanding that 150 B-29s had carried out the raid was wrong; it had been carried out by 200 aircraft. The loss rate was 14 aircraft, 7 percent of what set out, and that was an acceptable rate, but in the ten-day fire raid period only 22 aircraft were lost – a rate of 1.4 percent.[5] (The firestorm attacks are discussed fully in a later chapter.)

What hadn't been present, however, in the military and government consciousness in the March and May attacks, was the knowledge that such destruction could be caused by a single aircraft with a single bomb. This realisation, which must have filtered into the consciousness of the ruling caste over the week of the atomic attacks and beyond, is impossible to fully understand, as little reflective writings of significant actors have survived.

But it must have been a factor: now just one high-flying B-29, with little chance of being shot down, had to appear over a Japanese city for the target below to disappear in a blinding flash of light and heat. There was to be no reciprocal damage inflicted by the Japanese. There would obviously be a growing realisation among the Allied commanders that to destroy a Japanese centre now meant not enduring a high cost in return of men's lives and aircraft destroyed.

The next day, Foreign Minister Togo informed Cabinet of Truman's announcement. On Wednesday, Togo advised the Emperor of the need to accept the Potsdam Declaration. Premier Suzuki called for an emergency meeting of Supreme War Council – the cycle of accepting defeat, refusing, and then re-considering the option had begun. Even then, one member refused to meet, being unbelievably 'unavoidably' detained by 'more pressing business elsewhere', and the meeting was delayed until the Thursday.[6]

In the minds of many, even discussing surrender was an avenue down which they would not travel. War Minister Korechika Anami demanded that the Japanese must fight a last, glorious battle to defend their homeland. As one writer later put it somewhat melodramatically: 'Even as the Fat Man descended on Nagasaki, he was asking colleagues, "Who can be one hundred per cent sure of defeat?"'[7]

Meanwhile in Moscow, Japanese Ambassador Sato met with Molotov, only to receive the gloomy advice that from the next day the Soviet Union would be at war with Japan.[8]

Did the Japanese High Command dream of victory, even now? They were capable of some poor decisions: their submarines had routinely attacked warships, rather than freighters and oil tankers; they had failed to consolidate their Pearl Harbor and New Guinea strategic ideas; they had not exploited the Axis partnership. But they were practical soldiers, capable of good decision-making. Fighting on meant they could secure better surrender terms, and thus retain their own hold on power. But was it really the case that 'one bomb, one city' could become reality.

Emperor Hirohito and US President Ronald Reagan, with wife Nancy, in Tokyo, 9 November 1983. (US National Archives)

At 10.30 am on the Thursday, the Cabinet met, only to be split 50/50 along the question of whether surrender should be made. Coincidentally half an hour later, the city of Nagasaki was struck. News would not have been instantaneous, or even quickly transmitted and received by 21st century standards. But by 1.00 pm, the Cabinet meeting was still in session, and by now word reached them of the bombing of Nagasaki, and that Manchuria was now in Russian hands, but they could still not reach an agreement.[9]

Leaflets 'expressing the Allied desire to end the war without destroying Japan' were dropped over Tokyo. [10] [11] Yet still there was no agreement to surrender, even though:

The Ministers of Agriculture, Commerce, Transportation and Munitions ... pointed out that Okinawa was already being used as a bridgehead for the forthcoming invasion of Kyushu ... that the people of Japan were on the verge of exhaustion; that the present rice crop was the poorest since 1931, that air raids and bombings had been increasingly devastating in recent weeks, and likely to grow more so, that enemy ships were already bombarding the coastal cities of Japan – that Japan had neither the strength nor the means to wage war any longer. [12]

The future of the nation was now effectively deadlocked in a way alien to Western minds. The Emperor, it was in actuality agreed to, could not make a mistake, so therefore, to present him with a divided cabinet, which could force him to make a decision which might be wrong, would be a terrible breach of protocol. In such circumstances a cabinet would resign. The tradition was that the Emperor did not, would not, take sides, but approved what the government had laid before him. (This is not, however, accepted by all as the actual role of the Emperor.)[13] As one group of scholars later put it:

His August Mind was not to be disturbed by party strife and political ambition; the responsibility for decisions made and actions taken were never his. To present him with a divided cabinet was unthinkable; normally, if a cabinet could not reach unanimity, it resigned.[14]

Suzuki, however, had decided not to resign, but to do the unthinkable: to present the Emperor with the situation, and to urge him to decide. This set the scene for a tumultuous final week during which the government made virtually no decisions until it was faced with a final dichotomy: surrender via the Emperor commanding the nation to do so, or fight on by convincing the nation the Emperor had been misled.

The thinking of those who contemplated rebellion began along the lines that those around the Emperor had pressured him to accept the Potsdam ultimatum, but this would destroy the Japanese political system. The Emperor could not possibly have wanted that, therefore he had been cleverly manoeuvered into it. This meant that a true officer would seek to free the Emperor of this and therefore revolution was a good idea.[15]

Late on the Thursday night of the 9 August – the day of the Nagasaki attack – the Emperor met with the Supreme Councilors, their aides and two invited guests: Chief Cabinet Secretary Sakomizu and President of the Privy Council Baron Hiranuma. As the Friday began, he spoke about the deadlock before him, and then he advised them of his decision to 'bear the unbearable' and to 'accept the Allied Proclamation'.

At 4.00 am at the Premier's residence, a meeting began to decide on the exact wording of the advice to Allies, and three hours later it was concluded, with advice dispatched to the neutral countries of Switzerland and Sweden.

Once this was received in Washington there was a conference convened at the White House, with the President; Secretary of State; Secretary of the Navy, and the White House Chief of Staff in attendance. The main topic under discussion was a consideration of the phrase in the Japanese communication, which advised that 'said declaration does not compromise any demand which prejudices the prerogatives of His Majesty as Sovereign Ruler'. This, it was concluded, meant there was a need to consult with Britain and China, the Potsdam signatories, of what action should result from it.

Throughout Friday morning, Tokyo and other cities were heavily bombed by conventional means. One report cited the raids as 'the most impressive and nerve-wracking demonstration of the whole war'.[16] To add to the gloomy outlook, the news of the Soviet declaration of war was carried in the morning newspapers.

In the late morning, a meeting of the Cabinet came to a general conclusion to say nothing about the Emperor's decision or the Japanese note, but they would issue a radio statement saying something deliberately vague about forthcoming announcements. War Minister Anami violently disagreed. Afterwards, supporters of Anami prepared a statement saying that Japan would fight on. Lieutenant Colonel Masao Inaba prepared an initial draft and showed it to Vice Minister of War and Colonel Okitsugu Arao; it was soon redrafted with Lieutenant Colonel Masahiko Takeshita's help.

General Shizuichi Tanaka. (Public domain)

Hirohito's personal standard. (Public domain)   Kenji Hatanaka, leader of the coup. (Public domain)

Prime Minister Suzuki. (Public domain)

And so, it came to pass that two messages 'from the government' soon appeared on Saturday morning. The Cabinet's was as planned; however, Anami's was a complete contrast. It concluded:

> We have but one choice: we must fight on until we win the sacred war to preserve our national polity. We must fight on, even if we have to chew grass and eat earth and live in fields – for in our death there is a chance of our country's survival. The hero Kusunoki pledged to live and die seven times in order to save Japan from disaster. We can do no less ....[17]

Over that night, Washington and its major Allies concluded an agreement for a slight re-wording of their demands, saying the Emperor must be 'subject to the Supreme Commander of the Allied Powers'.[18]

Over the weekend in Tokyo, the proposed revolution festered and grew from a possibility to a certainty. Fifteen officers met in a bomb shelter in the War Office and agreed the war would continue, by means of revolution, if necessary. Suzuki, Togo, and Kido were to be assassinated. Aware of the rumours of rebellion, Marquis Kido moved into the Imperial Palace area to be closer to the Emperor and less vulnerable to assassins. A further group of officers met and decided continued fighting was preferable to surrender; they approached their force commanders in Tokyo and announced this.

Around 11.00 am, the Premier was met by the War Minister and the President of the Privy Council, who advised Suzuki of their opposition to surrender. Despite the rising opposition, the Emperor and his closest advisers now concluded that a radio address to the nation from the Emperor, something which had never been attempted before, would be necessary in order to bring enough power to any command to stop fighting. The recording session was planned with NHK, the national radio broadcaster.

Meanwhile, the rebels plotted and met, and eventually concluded the Emperor's person must be 'protected' in order to not let what they perceived as the national will being changed. Anami, visited by more officers urging resistance, although he had initially supported a revolution, now refused to move further, presumably thinking it had little chance of success. The recording was planned for Tuesday night, to be broadcast to the nation on the following day at noon. Throughout the afternoon, the Metropolitan Police presence around Tokyo grew visibly larger on the streets.

During Monday, more meetings took place, largely inconclusive. Anami was lobbied by two groups of rebellious officers, but largely remained unenthusiastic. Cabinet met, and towards the end of the day Navy's Admiral Onishi made an offer of spending '20 million lives in kamikaze attacks' to stop any invasion. (Whether this could have been backed up in actuality will never be known, although the kamikaze strength is analysed later.)

In secret, Army members prepared a communiqué and sent it to all of the Tokyo newspapers, saying they would fight on in an 'all-front and all-out war'. The message was only prevented from being printed by desperate efforts of government members.[19] Many officers met at the War Office and the Army General Staff Office, devising plans to carry on the war.[20]

On Tuesday 14 August, the Emperor met formally with the Cabinet, Supreme Council, and others, and the recording of the radio broadcast, onto vinyl records for replay over the national network, was fixed for later that night. In the afternoon a second battalion of Imperial Guards entered the Palace grounds, remaining in addition to the battalion already stationed there, which would normally have changed out.

Later that night, as the recording apparatus was being prepared, all of the officers of the 302nd Air Corp were called to a meeting by one of the leaders, Captain Kozono of the Atsugi Air Group, where he exhorted resistance to giving in. He received what seemed to be enthusiastic support, but Kozono's junior officers had received quiet orders from General Harada not to obey.[21]

At the same time, Captain Sasaki, of the Yokohama Guards, was on his way to foment revolt within the Guards Headquarters at Sojiji Temple. He planned to issue arms to the men he found there.[22] Neither knew of each other's plot, and such disparate planning, as well as a lack of a senior leader, was a substantial reason for the failure of the revolt.

The actual bloody part of the attempted coup took place during that night. The NHK engineers had nervously set up a recording facility near the Emperor's location, and planned to cut a vinyl record of his speech. The Emperor's staff brought him to the studio, and the recording was made. But the first recording had some imperfections, and the Emperor requested another try. This was carried out, and the two records were now ready for broadcasting back at the main facility of the NHK the following day.

The recordings made by the Emperor on the two discs were stored by the Emperor's now fearful chamberlains overnight in a small safe with papers piled in front of it: this kept them hidden. The concealment was a most fortuitous move. If they had been seized and destroyed, an official announcement to the nation – presumably an altered version of the speech read by an announcer – would have lacked much of the divine authority the voice of the Emperor would have imparted to his people, almost all of whom had never heard his voice before.[23]

It was now that the rebellion reached actuality.

Around 1.00 am, the rebels Captain Uehara and Major Hatanaka visited two of the officers perceived as obstacles: General Mori and Lieutenant Colonel Shiraishi. In what seems to have been a very short confrontation, the rebels assassinated them, utilising pistols and swords. Using the prize of Mori's official seal, 'Strategic Order No. 584' was sent to various units and regiments ordering their disposition. Shortly, the Imperial Palace was controlled entirely by Imperial Guards, and 16 key men were imprisoned within the Palace grounds. Later this rose in number as more captives were taken and added to the lockup.

Kido was advised of the revolt as soon as it commenced. He tore up relevant secret documents and flushed them down the toilet in his quarters. Then he and Imperial Household Minister Ishiwatari hid in a bomb shelter underneath the building. The rebels searched for him and also the recording of the Emperor advising of the intention to surrender. Presumably, once they had obtained it they would have destroyed it so it could not be broadcast then or in the future. Other rebels also searched Radio Tokyo.[24]

Various incidents of revolt began to take place around the city. Leaflets were distributed that argued for continued resistance. But the Premier was the main target. The rebels were intent on killing Suzuki.[25] In short order his official residence and then his private house were visited and set on fire; the former being doused just after the Premier and his staff left. Suzuki, despite his 77 years, was adept at keeping one step ahead – almost literally in some moments – of his pursuers. Thus the coup failed. Its main symbolic leader, General Anami, hearing of the failure of the combined effort, committed suicide around 4.30 am.

Around 7.00 am, with smoke from Privy Council President Baron Hiranuma's house – also set on fire – drifting across the city, an implied signal of the failure of any coup was broadcast across the radio network: the official broadcast would take place at noon. The recording discs had not been found, despite vigorous searches by some of the Guards. Major Hatanaka and Lieutenant Colonel Shiizaki were reduced to distributing leaflets outside the Imperial Palace, the former on a motorcycle and the latter on a horse. Nothing further eventuated. Almost as the opening address was being made, the two killed themselves in front of the Imperial Palace, using their personal weapons.

This was not the end of the matter, however. Popular reaction among civilians was not altogether one of positive acquiescence. It varied from meek acceptance, to angry rejection, to the allocation of blame. Professor Ienega cites examples of teachers blaming students for not trying hard enough for the country, and people saying that this was not a defeat but a postponement of revenge.[26]

Medical Doctor Michihiko Hachiya, who survived the bombing of Hiroshima, noted that confusion reigned, with all sorts of rumours abounding. These included stories that Allied cities in the United States were being destroyed by Japanese forces using the same type of bomb; Japan had turned the tide of the war, or that conversely the nation was about to be invaded. One rumour was true: the Emperor was addressing the nation, and Hachiya heard the broadcast. However, the reception and volume were both bad, and Hachiya only made out some essential words, being told afterwards at a medical staff assembly that the country was surrendering.[27] He also noted that many people – in fact with all of the responses he noted – cried out publicly and loudly for the war to be continued.[28]

The military attitude was similar. Given the nature of armed service, it was often in accordance with their tradition of lethal response. As Kodama pilots loaded torpedoes onto planes and attempted to take off, they were deterred by Major General Nonaka.[29] Another attempt at aerial attacks was foiled by General Masao Yoshizumi, the chief of the Military Affairs Bureau.[30] On 17 August, the Mito Army Air Division attempted a revolt.[31]

Toland records that an actual attack on Allied units did take place, probably on the afternoon of the 15 August, in the hours following the Emperor's broadcast. Eleven 'small bombers' took off from Oita Air Base on Kyushu, flying south to attack the Allied war effort at Okinawa. The attack was organised by Admiral Ugaki and personally led by him. The bombers were two-man machines (perhaps Val divebombers), and Toland records that when Ugaki took the rear seat of the lead plane, the displaced crewman became indignant and insisted on climbing in too. Four of the aircraft turned back with engine trouble, but the remaining planes reached Okinawa, and seven dived into their targets.[32] [33]

Located at Atsugi, Captain Kozono, who had not garnered earlier overall support, seems to have been in sufficient command to order aircraft into the air, probably prior to the Emperor's broadcast. According to Frank, he eventually was restrained on mental grounds, and the propellers were removed from the aircraft in his charge.[34] Toland reports that aircraft flown by crews from Atsugi Air Base dropped leaflets across Tokyo, accusing the Suzuki government of misleading the Emperor.[35]

On 24 August, there was an attempt by military students to occupy the Kawaguchi broadcasting station. It was stopped by General Shizuichi Tanaka, commander of the Eastern region of the army, who convinced the rebellious officers to leave. Tanaka committed suicide nine days later.[36] Up until MacArthur's landing on 30 August, at

Atsugi, plans and attempts to attack enemy forces continued.[37] Frank notes that fighting between Japanese and Soviet forces along the Manchurian border did not cease until the end of August.[38]

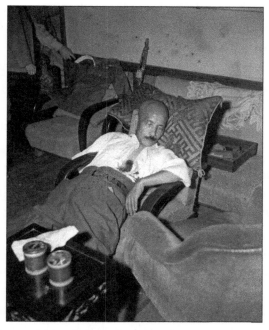

With a gaping bullet wound below the heart, General Tojo lies semi-conscious in a chair after he shot himself, 11 September 1945 in Tokyo. (AP Photo/Charles Gorry)

Senior diplomat Toshikazu Kase, who wrote the final communiqué to the Allies advising that Japan was willing to surrender, was *in situ* for the weeks following the decision. He observed much more than what has been listed so far in terms of rebellion:

> During the first few weeks following the surrender, the planes of our Navy Special Attack Corps several times flew over Tokyo and dropped leaflets which read, 'Don't surrender. Don't believe the imperial rescript. It is a false document.' Posters appeared and handbills were circulated in busy streets, which denounced the *jushin* for misguiding the Emperor and delivering the nation to the Allies. Lacking in organisation, however, such resistance to peace collapsed in a few days' time.[39]

Kase also noted a rebellion by 400 troops who seized 'Ueno Hill in the centre of the city'. Another group took possession of Atago Hill. Both were induced to disperse. Many of the leaders committed suicide, some with hand grenades.[40] Toland says there were ten 'young men' in the Atago Hill incident. They all blew themselves up with hand grenades after singing the national anthem.[41]

On 20 August, another planned coup to seize the Imperial Palace once more was prevented. On 26 August, a plan to use aircraft to attack Allied ships was stopped.[42]

Admiral Yonai, Navy Minister in various cabinets, and Navy Minister in the Suzuki Cabinet, said later in his interrogation:

> One thing that was a great source of worry to me at the end of the war was this: The Imperial Rescript was issued on 14 August and broadcast on the 15th; and being deeply concerned for what young officers in the Navy might do, I took every possible measure to forestall possible untoward incidents, and I believe that I was more or less successful, and the same may be said with regard to the Army. But after all, the thing that made it possible to avoid serious trouble of any kind was the power of the Emperor rather than anything that I or the Army were able to do. During my long career as Navy Minister, I probably never worried so much as I did during the period from the 14th to about the 23rd of that month, and I felt greatly relieved when we were able to go through this period without any serious trouble in the Navy.[43]

The war ended, but not for everyone. In 1944, Lieutenant Hiroo Onoda had been sent by the Japanese army to the remote Philippine island of Lubang. His mission was to conduct guerrilla warfare. Unfortunately, he was never officially told the war had ended; so for 29 years, Onoda continued to live in the jungle, ready for when his country would again need his services and information. Eating coconuts and bananas, and evading searching parties he believed were enemy scouts, Onoda hid in the jungle until he finally emerged from the dark recesses of the island on 19 March 1972.[44]

Other soldiers fought on unknowingly on small abandoned islands in the Pacific; one man in Indonesia, and two in Thailand – the latter not being found and induced to give in until 1991.[45]

Conclusion

It is hard not to be surprised at the level of resistance to surrendering. It is testimony to the different way Japanese people thought in those times: unity and harmony as a country was all-important, and the concept of an honourable death in the service of the nation seems to have been a genuine belief. There is perhaps too a suspicion that they knew too little of the extent to which their cities were being devastated. But in terms of a measure of the nation's resolve, it shows how determined the Japanese could be.

CHAPTER FOUR
HOW MUCH LONGER COULD JAPAN HAVE FOUGHT?

Overview: In this chapter, we discuss whether Japan could have been starved out? How effective was blockade? What comparison could be made of the casualties incurred in the invasion of Okinawa as a measure of how a conventional attack on the Japanese main islands would have looked?

That the war was reaching its height seemed obvious in mid-1945 as the Allied war machine got closer to the Home Islands. But there was little indication that it would end without a conventional invasion.

The US's Secretary for War Stimson thought:

> We estimated that if we should be forced to carry this plan [the invasion] to its conclusion, the major fighting would not end until the latter part of 1946, at the earliest. I was informed that such operations might be expected to cost over a million casualties to American forces alone. Additional large losses might be expected among our allies and, of course, if our campaign were successful and if we could judge by previous experience, enemy casualties would be much larger than our own.[1]

The Japanese economy relied almost utterly on imports of food and fuel. An American sea blockade had cut Japanese trade to almost nothing. The country faced starvation and the collapse of its transport system and its industries. Japan's cities were being battered and burned to ashes by mass air raids – Major-General Curtis LeMay reckoned that by September there would be no cities left worth bombing.[2] This and his earlier removal of some cities from the map of bombing targets due to having been destroyed are often cited as being evidence that

Japan was finished. But Japan's industry was much more scattered – as it is today – with commercial operations mixed in with housing.

1945 after a B-29 bombing attack on Tokyo. There is little left of the city and many, many families were without food and homes. (Public domain)

A Japanese naval attache, Fujimura, in Europe, emphasised that Japan could not supply itself with basically essential foodstuffs.[3] Koichi Kido, Lord Keeper of the Privy Seal, wrote:

Everything became scarce. The food situation was gradually becoming worse and worse. Under such conditions even the soldiers had not too much to eat .... With winter ahead, I said I cannot bear the responsibility for the lives of tens of millions of people dying a dog's death from hunger and exposure.[4]

The possibility of a siege

Japanese merchant shipping had been progressively destroyed from the commencement of the war. In what was named 'Operation Starvation', had the war continued it was estimated that seven million Japanese would have died of starvation by March 1946.[5] It is interesting to note therefore that this means the decision to deploy the two A-bombs was in keeping with this book's title: it was the 'salvation' of the Japanese rather than their slow destruction as a conventional assault got underway; the government of the nation put all its resources into the defence, and any food would therefore have been directed to the combatants. These would have included many millions of civilians, as we will see, but other civilians – the old, the sick, children under fighting age – would have been left to die.

Japan, like the United Kingdom, was a small nation surrounded by ocean, and depended on its far-flung resources to bring in what it could not produce on the Home Islands. But as the following table[6] shows, its shipping was being steadily devastated:

1942	1943	1944	1945
89 ships lost	157 ships lost	385 ships lost	550 ships lost

A confidential study carried out around May 1945, by Cabinet Secretary Sakomizu, under the instruction of Prime Minister Suzuki, found that 'within weeks' there would be no more production of steel ships.[7] These vessels were bringing in vital industrial essentials and foodstuffs. The loss of the food they would bring in was significant.

Rice production imports in 1943 were less than half of what it was the previous year. In 1944, it was two-thirds of the previous year, and in projected figures for 1945, it would be less than half of 1944. Grain production had fallen every year since 1942, and in 1945 – for a projected year – it would be around two-thirds of what it had been for 1944.[8]

In fact, the only success story in all of Japan's imports was soy, which was exceeding the 1944 figures. But this was of little consolation to hard-working troops and those engaged in physical labour, who needed calories imparted through protein-rich foods.[9]

Richard Frank analysed briefly the effects of starvation in his essay 'No Bomb, No End'. He concluded that the country's rice production had fallen from over 10 million tons in 1942, to 6.3 million tons in 1945. Bridging that gap with imports was impossible due to the destruction of Japan's merchant fleet and blockade.[10] He notes that even after the surrender and a new civil administration in place, the daily calorie intake for Tokyo residents was 1042 a day.[11] This was insufficient to maintain body weight.

Franks suggests the situation would have driven the residents into the countryside to seek alternative means of supplying food – and civilisation would have disintegrated as a result. Toland cites the people in cities already in mid-1945 venturing into the rural areas each weekend to sell jewelry, kimonos and furniture in exchange for food.[12]

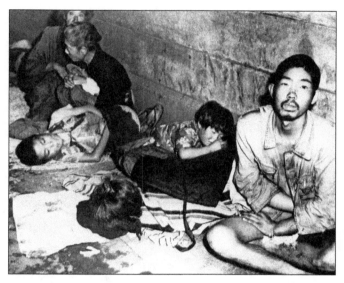

Hundreds of Japanese jam Ueno railway station, northeast Tokyo, 26 Oct 1945 seeking shelter. Homeless, the old and the young huddle together on matting and newspapers, trying to sleep. Police estimated two deaths nightly from starvation. (AP Photo)

One interesting aspect of any continued attempt to 'starve out' the defenders would have had exactly that effect – on the wrong people. The best, and in fact most of the food would have gone to the military forces within the Home Islands. With the convoluted logic that saw the Japanese forces use Banzai charges, place industrial capability in the middle of suburbs, and use super-battleships in suicide missions with no military achievements as outcomes, the High Command would likely have ordered babies to be depleted of food; old people to be allowed to die, and children under fighting age to starve. This would have been an unintended side effect of blockade.

Starving the Japanese into submission would also have resulted in them ceasing to feed their prisoners. Although the situation of

POWs is discussed in a later chapter, it is timely to remember that 'Allied POWs and internees in Japanese hands turned out to be nearly 300,000'. [13]

The situation for metals and minerals was grim. Although there had been a jump in imports in 1942–43, due to the acquisition of new territories, the situation had not been maintained and indeed rapidly worsened. [14] In projected figures for 1945, there would have been less than half the previous year of imports for iron ore, coal, bauxite, lead, and tin. Doing better than half, but still not reaching the 1944 totals, were zinc and rubber. [15] The metals and minerals situation meant that Japan's production of aircraft, ships, tanks, and ammunition was being steadily eroded.

Japan endured the loss of much of its shipping as the war progressed. A B-25 bomber of the US Army 5th Air Force strikes a Japanese ship in Rabaul Harbour, New Britain during an air raid on the Japanese-held air and naval base. 2 Nov 1943. (AP Photo)

By the end of the war, according to Willmott, 44 percent of 63 major Japanese cities had been laid waste; 42 percent of Japan's industrial capacity had been destroyed, and some 22 million people had been killed, injured, or rendered homeless. He estimates that 'she could not have sustained herself in terms of basic food requirements beyond November'.[16] Alperovitz's analysis agrees: 'There was a strong possibility that a considerable portion of Japan's various industrial areas will soon have to suspend operations for want of coal.'[17]

So was it the case that starvation would have worked? Not as a short-term measure. As was pointed out by the US's Secretary of the Navy Forrestal, even if Japan was besieged 'for a year and a half' it would still need to be invaded in the end.[18] Any discussion of a third way beyond neither bombing nor invasion though would have had to have taken into account the certainty that fighting in the rest of the Pacific theatre would have gone on while a blockade of the Home Islands continued.

As has been seen in previous chapters, any lessening of the ferocity of the assaults on the Empire would have had the converse and grimly ironical effect of convincing the High Command they were succeeding in their aim of gaining, through the fierceness of their resistance, better terms of a negotiated surrender for the country.

A figure cited in the authoritative study of the political dealings of the last days of the Empire, the Pacific War Research Society's *Japan's Longest Day*, often uses the debatable[19] figure of 'six million' men under arms by mid-1945, suggesting that three million of these were within the Home Islands group.

The other three million fighting men were overseas, either as prisoners – comparatively few, given the Japanese propensity for not surrendering – or still actively engaged. Those fighting commands in various operations areas would not have simply laid down their arms or retreated into impregnable fortresses while the operations around the Japanese mainland continued.

There had of course been immense victories in the Battles of the Philippines Sea, and Leyte Gulf, the largest naval battle of all time, where the final Japanese carrier ambitions had been crushed. There had been huge Allied achievements through several years in South-East Asia and in the islands taken throughout the Pacific, which had seen garrison after garrison fall. At sea, the Empire's naval fleets had been crushed. Her waters were now mined, and even sailing through them was a most dangerous act due to the prevalence of Allied carrier aviation and of submarines. Eight million tons of shipping was lost by Japan during the war, 60 percent of that due to the US Navy's submarine force.[20]

But Japanese forces had not given up, either partially or wholesale, and they were still a most formidable force that was not fighting with any less determination even in mid-1945. Bitter contests were still going on. In the Chinese mainland areas and in fighting throughout Asia where British forces were re-contesting India and Burma, the Japanese were beating fighting withdrawals and sometimes even counter-attacking.

Anyone disputing the ferocity and capacity of their existence can have their doubts dispelled by Field Marshal Slim's account of the taking back of Rangoon, which still left '60 to 70 thousand men' still facing him.[21] In isolated pockets around which the Allied offensive had surged, the Empire's soldiers still maintained a grip – for example, in Wewak, the Japanese were still holding ground; in New Britain; and in Bougainville.

In the northern Philippines, General Yamashita was still doing capable work with 50,000 troops of which 4/5^{ths} remained active at surrender.[22] On the day the Nagasaki weapon was dropped, George MacDonald Fraser observed one of his battalion's companies fighting against a Japanese unit and killing 21 of them: '*that* was the war, not what was happening hundreds of miles away'.[23]

The air units of both the Empire's Army and Navy had been pulverised, but there was still fighter opposition to the Allies over the Home Islands, such as has been mentioned at Nagasaki. The absolute air supremacy – not just superiority, which was the situation in actuality over Germany in the last days of Hitler's forces – was not the case through the Home Islands. That would still have to be won if a conventional assault went ahead. Added to the possibility of determined – if weak – fighter opposition was the potential of fatalities to be inflicted by anti-aircraft fire.

At sea, the naval forces – the mighty battleships *Yamato* and *Musashi*, the biggest ever built – were being lost to little account.[24] The carrier fleet, never recovering fully after the Battle of Midway, and decimated in further battles, lay in ruins. Any remaining battleships and cruisers and destroyers were an easy victim for the Allied aircraft carrier fleets, which now roamed the Pacific at will, while moving inexorably towards the mainland coasts. Of Japan's ocean-going submarines, three-quarters of the total of 174 were sunk. [25] None of this made any difference. The resolution of the men who remained was just as strong as it had ever been.

The radar on a B-29 is monitored by its crew member. Land outlines could be made out - an invaluable aid to navigation. The Allies steadily overtook Japan in the technology race through the war. (USAAF)

If a conventional assault had gone ahead, then the battle for Okinawa can't be ignored. The taking of this island was an example, not unusual when facing Japanese forces, of the inescapable mathematics of such an attack. The US forces lost over 12,000 in terms of Killed In Action, the majority from the Marines and Army, but around 5000 from the US Navy, which endured the loss of 34 ships, mostly due to kamikaze strikes. There were 36,000 wounded, and over 26,000 'non-battle casualties'.

It should be emphasised here that just undertaking war operations cost far more than the usual-imagined causes of death and wounding. The author's own war service is instructive. During that time in Iraq in 2006, at the height of the war there, deaths due to suicide were common – in the author's experience, four a week in the Coalition forces. There were frequent cases of deliberate wounding to escape the war theatre; although many forces had an aggressive stance towards their volunteer troops: once you have signed on for a period, then you had signed on, and you could not go home merely because life is horrible. (In the author's unit, a soldier who threatened to commit suicide had the firing pin of his rifle removed.) Psychiatric stress to the extent of making the recipient unusable is not uncommon, as is a simple refusal to stay. To any calculation of casualties from extending the war in a conventional assault must be added such losses.

The extent of Japanese losses on Okinawa were tremendous:

[There were] 107,539 soldiers killed and 23,764 sealed in caves or buried by the Japanese themselves; 10,755 captured or surrendered. The Japanese lost 7830 aircraft and 16 combat ships. Since many Okinawan residents fled to caves where they subsequently were entombed, the precise number of civilian casualties will probably never be known, but the lowest estimate is 42,000 killed.[26]

Okinawa is an island some 110 kilometres (70 miles) long, and 11 kilometres (seven miles) wide. The peninsula of Kyushu, where an initial Home Islands landing was being planned, has a similar topography. If the Japanese fought like this for an island 640 kilometres off the coast of the mainland, how would they have fought for their precious Home Islands? Their death total for Okinawa approaches that of Hiroshima and Nagasaki combined, but the High Command saw this sort of loss as acceptable. So too would have been the situation with mainland losses. To think the Japanese would have eventually stopped fighting due to morale being sapped by losses is to not understand their thinking.

As for the Allies, to think that their populations would have tolerated the thought that rather than invade, rather than employ the concept of 'one bomb, one city, no losses' is the stuff of fantasy. This will be examined further at length.

Conclusion

Japan was still well armed and capable by August 1945. They possessed the matériel, will and ability to keep fighting. All across the Pacific, the Allies were taking steady losses. Pressing onwards conventionally would have been tremendously costly, both in terms of Allies lives and wounding. Okinawa is a measure of how fierce the resistance would have been.

HOW WOULD THE WAR HAVE CONTINUED IF THE A-BOMBS HAD NOT BEEN USED?

The firestorm raids

Overview: In this chapter, we ascertain the effectiveness of the firestorm raids on Japan. It is quickly established that they caused a greater loss of life than the two atomic strikes combined, and if they had continued as an alternative to the A-bombings then even greater loss of life than what was undergone would have occurred.

Air raids indeed systematically destroyed Japan's ability to make war. The Home Islands' infrastructure was not sturdy enough to withstand repeated attack from the air: over 90 percent of Tokyo consisted of readily flammable buildings – factories, warehouses and dwellings.[1] Other target cities were similarly constructed.

In the commencement of using firebombing as a weapon, the Americans went to a great deal of trouble to build several blocks of 'test cities', complete with buildings duplicating those to be found in potential target cities in Germany and Japan. They were complete with structural barriers such as roofs, ceilings and walls, furnishings, carpets, including the tatami mats used everywhere in Japan, and even wallpaper. The test buildings retarded the bombs dropped on them so that penetration of the roofs was analysed, and how well they burnt could be ascertained. The buildings were constructed so that the typical narrow Japanese streets – only eight feet separating the houses – were duplicated. The bombs could therefore be designed accordingly, with their drop rates and penetration characteristics retarded or increased by manipulation of their fins, weight and drop characteristics.[2]

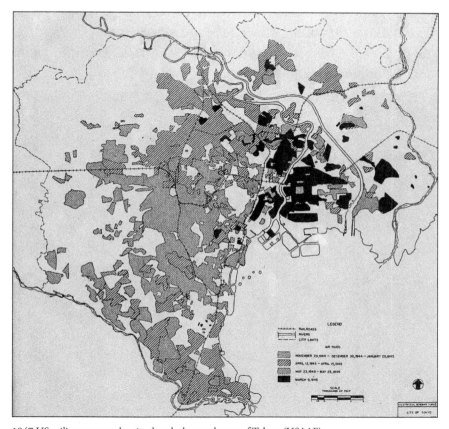

1947 US military survey showing bomb-damaged areas of Tokyo. (USAAF)

No single act of war, before or since, would exact as great a toll on life and property as was inflicted on Tokyo during the hours between midnight and dawn Saturday 10 March 1945.[3]

Three hundred and twenty-five bombers, all four-engined B-29s, carried out this raid.[4] Eighty-three thousand seven hundred and ninety-three people were killed, according to 'the police estimate made'.[5] However, there is dispute over this. Hoyt's *Japan's War* suggests 200,000, but he cites 'official US Army records' as saying this, and discredits Japanese accounts because of the disruption of society, giving another source that gives the higher figure.[6] Lifton and Mitchell state that 100,000 were killed in the 9–10 March 1945 firestorm raid on Tokyo.[7] Frank in *Downfall* cites the Tokyo raid death figures[8] of March 1945: Daniels, which he calls 'the best single study', uses a figure of over 90,000 in 'Great Tokyo Air Raid'; Edoin in *The Night Tokyo Burned* prefers 100,000, as does Kato in *The Lost War*, and as does Tillitse in 'When Bombs Rained Down on Tokyo'.

A B-29 bomb bay, showing some of the weapons in position. The A-bomb carrying B-29s needed special modifications to carry their special ordnance. The bombs shown are General Purpose demolition weapons. (USAAF)

The March firestorm attacks are the most commonly referred to in literature and films referring to such raids. In fact, as Kasi and

Kerr show, the assaults via flame-inducing bombs were carried out consistently and plentifully – though not to so massive an extent in terms of lives lost – in other months of 1945 beyond that.

Other firestorm raids included[9]

Target	Date	Aircraft / lost (all B-29)	Result	Lives lost
Tokyo	24 Nov 1944	111	Military target – but see footnote[10]	Unknown
Tokyo	29 Nov 1944	23/6[11]	1/10th of a sq. mile	Unknown
Tokyo	25 Feb 1945	172/maybe 229 (loss figures unknown)[12]	1 sq. mile	Unknown
Tokyo	9–10 March	325 (loss figures at least 2 but maybe several)[13]	25% of Tokyo; 15.8 sq. miles, 267,171 buildings; over 1 million people homeless	83,793, but see footnote[14] suggesting 200,000
Nagoya	10–12 March	285/0	2 sq. miles destroyed	Unknown
Osaka	13–14 March	301/0	8.1 sq. miles destroyed, with 130,000 houses	Nearly 4000
Kobe	16–17 March	300/0	2.9 sq. miles, with 65,000 houses	More than 2600
Nagoya	18 March	310 (loss figures unknown)	3 sq. miles destroyed	Unknown
Tokyo (arsenal area)	13 April	327/7	11.4 sq. miles destroyed	Unknown
Tokyo/ Kawasaki	15 April	303/12	6 + 3.6 sq. miles destroyed – Hoyt says 1.5 sq. miles of Yokohama were burnt out[15]	Unknown
Nagoya	14 May	500+/11	Over 3 sq. miles destroyed	Unknown

Target	Date	Aircraft / lost (all B-29)	Result	Lives lost
Nagoya	16 May	Less than 500/ unknown	Over 3 sq. miles destroyed	3000+
Tokyo	23 May	558 or 562[16]/13	5.3 sq. miles destroyed	Unknown but see entry below
Tokyo	25 May	464 or 502[17]/26	16.8 sq. miles destroyed (Tokyo now destroyed to an extent it was removed from the target list)	3000 to 'tens of thousands'[18]
Yokohama	29 May	500[19] 517[20]/ unknown	8.9 sq. miles destroyed; 85% of the metropolitan area 'in flames'[21]	4800
Osaka	1 June	458	3.15 sq. miles destroyed[22]	Unknown
Kobe	5 June	Unknown/9	'More than 100 sq. miles' destroyed,[23] Burnt out all assigned target area – Kobe removed as target	Unknown
Osaka	7 June	Unknown/nil	2.21 sq. miles destroyed	Unknown
Various	8–15 June	Unknown	Unknown	Unknown
Osaka	15 June	500+/nil	Burnt out all of assigned target area – Osaka removed as target	Unknown
Kagoshima, Omuta, Hamamats, Yokkaichi	17 June	Unknown/1	6.073 sq. miles destroyed	Unknown
Fukuoka	19 June	Unknown/nil	Unknown	Unknown

Target	Date	Aircraft / lost (all B-29)	Result	Lives lost
Kure	22 June	381/ unknown	Naval arsenal and 5 aircraft factories heavily hit	Unknown
Southern Honshu area	26 June	426/ unknown	3 arsenals, 4 aircraft factories, 2 metal factories	Unknown
Yokkaichi	26 June	Unknown/ unknown	Utsube Oil Factory	Unknown
Raids then continued at the rate of on average one a week against various targets, including leaflet drops.				
'Japanese cities'	31 July	1000[24]		
Toyama and 3 other cities	1 August	836/unknow; 6145 imperial tons of bombs dropped[25]	6 sq. miles destroyed, including 99.5% of Toyama's built up area – most devastating incendiary raid of the war	Unknown
'More cities'	2 August	800 or 820/1[26]	6600 tons of bombs	
Toyokawa	7 August	131/nil	Arsenal attacked	Unknown
Yawata	8 August	196[27] or 245/4	Military assets	Unknown
Tokyo	14 August	821[28]	Tokyo area	Unknown
3 targets	14 August	433/nil	Various damage	Unknown
2 small cities, oil refinery	14 August	366/nil	Various damage	Unknown

A total for those Japanese killed in all of the firestorm raids will probably never be known. A much-quoted figure of 168,000 can be found in many publications, for example:

It was estimated by the US Strategic Bombing Survey that 168,000 persons died, 200,000 were seriously injured, and nearly 8,000,000 persons were made homeless by the major incendiary attacks on Japanese cities. The great attack on Tokyo, March 9–10, 1945, alone accounted for half of the total deaths. This attack caused more deaths than either of the atomic bomb attacks, and more than the great Hamburg, Germany, attack. Probably more persons lost their lives by fire at Tokyo in a six-hour period than at any time in the history of man.[29]

B-29 bombers pass Mt Fuji on a mission. (USAAF)

After the March raid on Nagoya, the B-29s eventually ran out of the incendiary M-69 and M-47 bombs they were using. The bombers were then used for aerial mine dropping and conventional High Explosive strikes.[30]

Conclusion

If a conventional assault was undertaken, it is logical to assume that firestorm raids would have resumed. The loss of life to the Japanese would have been enormous. Given from the figures above, the B-29s killed more than those who died as a result of the Hiroshima and Nagasaki strikes, so it is fair to surmise that firestorm raids would have equaled that number soon enough: the target cities would have included Hiroshima and Nagasaki, as well as Kyoto and anywhere else left untouched so far. That such destruction is preferable to the two atomic strikes and the end of the war is unthinkable.

CHAPTER SIX

HOW WOULD THE WAR HAVE CONTINUED IF THE A-BOMBS HAD NOT BEEN USED?

A general appraisal, and anti-air defences

Overview: In this chapter, we appraise the air war and Tokyo anti-air defences, together with an interview post-war with Major Toga, formerly of the Japanese Army Air Forces. Conventional Japanese air assets – e.g. non-kamikaze – would likely have proved extremely limited in any conventional assault.

The overall thinking for the invasion of the Home Islands saw an invasion – Operation Downfall – mounted in two main thrusts: Operation Olympic, the invasion of the Kyushu peninsula, and Operation Coronet, following on with the invasion of the Tokyo area.

Olympic would commence on 1 November 1945, and Coronet, following the winter, on 1 March 1946. The reasoning behind the two assaults, rather than one, was that victory in the Olympic segment would not have been enough to subdue the Japanese wholly, nor induce an offer of surrender. That would be necessitated by Coronet, which would take place after the cold and debilitating winter weather of 1945–46.

The Japanese could see what was coming. Any strategic analysis would have concluded the same, for a direct assault on Tokyo would have left the left-hand flank of the attacking forces vulnerable to any defenders massing there. The defences built for Okinawa would have been duplicated. It is instructive to analyse how effectively these were constructed:

> Just above Okinawa's two largest cities, Naha and Shuri, the terrain was ideal for defence, and it was here that [Lieutenant General Mitsuru] Ushijima erected a defence line in depth, a series of concentric fortresses, facing north and extending across the island. Numerous caves, blockhouses and gun emplacements were carved into the ridges and hills connected by a complex system of tunnels. Even the Chinese lyre-shaped tombs, which dotted the countryside, were transformed into pillboxes.[1]

A captured Nakajima Ki-43 Oscar, date unknown. (USAAF)

Any conventional assault in 1945 assumed the following progression.

- Surveillance of defence lines and systems.

- Choice of landing sites.

- Attack phase one: naval gun and air assault against the defenders until they were either crushed or they abandoned their positions.

- Attack phase two: establishment of a beachhead; landing from assault boats against undefended positions. Opposition may have caused a withdrawal and a repeat of phase two.

- Attack phase three: consolidation of the landing with heavy equipment, including armour and artillery.

- Invasion phase one: breakout of the beachhead position, and advancing against any opposition.

- Invasion phase two: use of air and artillery assault against any perceived enemy position.

- Invasion phase three: taking and holding of any ground by infantry. Opposition would have caused withdrawal and a repeat of phase two.

- Invasion phase four: repetition of this up the main island of the mainland.

- Consolidation and holding: probably at a line no further than Kyoto.

- Beginning of the next main attack, this time against Tokyo, from the sea and from the established land forces combined.

The opposition to be subdued was formidable. A study of the air defence guns of Tokyo, *Headquarters AAF Intelligence Summary 45-10* (30 May 1945) began by advising that: 'About 500 heavy guns protect the area formed by the cities of Tokyo, Kawasaki, and Yokohama. This is as many guns as ever protected the German capital of Berlin.'[2]

The study concluded:

The Jap knows how to lay out his defences. We have seen him demonstrate that at Nagoya and here, at Tokyo. And upon occasion he has shown that he knows how to use them. We can't forget missions like the XX Bomber Command B-29 attack on the Singapore Naval Base on 2 March 1945 (see Hq.

AAF Intelligence Summary No. 45–8). In opposing this attack the Japanese defences were extremely well conducted, engaging formations attacking at altitudes between 19,000 and 25,000 feet with intense and accurate heavy AA fire. Throughout the engagement the flak defences exhibited a high standard of skill, accuracy, fire discipline and fire direction. It was no small-time flak defence that did this.

A Japanese plane is shot down during the Battle of Saipan in 1944. (USAAF)

The 25-page document examined fields of fire; the Japanese levels of ability of co-ordinating their AA fire with direction-finding equipment such as radar, and concluded further:

The main trouble that faces the Jap at the moment is his equipment. He has good directors, and he has some excellent AA guns. But at present he hasn't enough of them .... If right now the Jap cannot match the German in the quality of his flak, that doesn't necessarily mean that he cannot improve. Already he has made great strides.

In regards to aviation fixed-wing defence, the number of available aircraft around the time of the A-bomb raids is difficult to determine exactly due to document destruction, but one available source states that it was halved from its previous capability. The interrogation of Major Hiroshi Toga, Imperial Japanese Army, staff officer of the 10th Air Division from July 1944 until late 1945, yielded significant results. He stated that there were only 210 fighter planes (Army) available for the air defence of the Tokyo Area, but from 'about July, the number of available planes was 100'. The reasons for the decrease of availability was 'actual lack of modern combat type planes and lack of gasoline'.

Allied attacks resulted in rapid destruction of Japanese aircraft. Major Toga was interviewed shortly after the war. He co-operated fully about his role in the Japanese Army Air Force – the country, like the USA, did not have an air force; rather, sections of the army and navy had air components.

Q. Referring to American carrier attacks on the TOKYO Area on the 16 and 17 February, what combat losses were sustained by the 10th Flying Division?

A. I am not sure just what the combat losses during these two days were, but I think that it was about 30 planes.

Q. Were records kept of losses by the division?

A. Yes, but they have been destroyed.

And

Q. In the total loss of airplanes, what percentage were operational losses?

A. About two-thirds were lost in combat.[3]

It is most instructive to look through this interview. Toga was open about this situation, following the directive from the Emperor to co-operate with the Occupation forces.

Interrogated by: Captain T J Hedding, USN.

SUMMARY

Major TOGA was interrogated to obtain information on the Japanese Army air defence of the TOKYO Area, particularly against carrier-based air attacks. The 10th Flying Division of the Japanese Army Air Force was responsible for the air defence of the TOKYO Area. Its organisational strength was 210 fighters and 12 observation fighters, with a claimed operational strength of about 90 percent. Defence tactics called for a fixed defence in depth with two outer lines of defence with a final defence over TOKYO proper. During alerts, reinforcements were ordered to TOKYO by the Air Defence Commander of the EMPIRE Area, General Prince HIGASHI-KUNI. The number of reinforcing planes being determined by this command.

From February 1945 on, the number of aircraft available for defence decreased rapidly due to losses, conversion of aircraft types and shortages of aviation gas. Towards the last of the war, emphasis was placed on dispersal and conservation with consequent reduction in effectiveness.

Reports of losses are very unreliable due to reported destruction of records.

TRANSCRIPT

Q. What Japanese Army Air Force organisation was responsible for the air defence of the TOKYO Area?

A. The responsibility for the air defence of TOKYO was left up to the East District (TOBU). Direct Army command was under General TANAKA.

Q. Was the 10th Flying Division, which you joined in July 1944, part of this organisation?

A. They received their orders from TANAKA. In February of this year they became independent.

Q. Was the 10th Flying Division actually engaged in the defence of TOKYO Area?

A. The Division actually participated in the defence of the TOKYO Area. Up until April of this year, the Commanding Officer of the 10th Flying Division was Lt. General YOSHIDA, K. In April of this year the command changed to Lt. General KONDO, K.

Q. Are you familiar with the Operation Plans of the Japanese Army Air Force air defence organisation from the period of 15 February until end of hostilities?

A. I know only that with which my own command is concerned, that is the 10th Flying Division.

Q. What other flying divisions were included in the defence organisation of the TOKYO Area?

A. There was no other air division in the TOKYO Area. There was a naval organisation, however.

Q. What were the defence plans set up by the air force organisation for the defence of the TOKYO Area against carrier-based plane attacks?

A. Up until February of this year, when the command was under Lt. General YOSHIDA, the plan for the defence of the TOKYO Area against carrier-based aircraft was to meet the enemy in the air and shoot them down. However, in April when KONDO became the Commanding Officer, the plan was that they should not expend aircraft unnecessarily in defence against carrier-based raids, but should set up a defence by using the AA guns to the fullest extent as possible, and at the same time disperse their aircraft on the ground to minimise their losses.

Q. Where did they intend to seek air combat, over the TOKYO Area or attempt to intercept raids prior to the arrival of the attacking planes?

A. Expect to have air battle within the TOKYO Area. The first line of defence was built around CHOSHI, KATSUURA and SHIRAHANA, the second line of defence was at KISARAZU and CHIBA, and the third line of defence was the air coverage of TOKYO proper.

Q. Did the plan contemplate attacks on the American Carrier Force from which these air strikes were being launched?

A. My organisation had no plans for attacking American carriers, and I think that it was the responsibility of the First Air Army; also, the Navy had plans to attack the American carriers, but I don't know anything about that. Until July of this year, the First Air Army had no real plans for attacking the American carriers.

Q. What means were provided for co-ordination with the Navy Air Defence Force?

A. The co-operation and co-ordination with the Navy Air Defence was in actuality that the Navy defend beyond the first line of defence setup by the Army and that the Army would carry out the air defence over the land. The Navy, based at YOKOSUKA, KISARAZU and ATSUGI, was responsible for direct coverage of its own immediate area only. Liaison with the Army, between the Army Headquarters East District (TOBUGUN) and YOKOSUKA, existed in the eventuality of an attack. Until February of this year, both Army and Navy took to the air when attacks were made. However, in July these plans, as I have already stated, differed. It is believed, however, that the Navy carried out attacks in the air against the American Fleet.

Q. Was there a common Fighter Director Centre for the employment of both air forces?

A. They operated independently, but there was liaison.

Q. What were the actual aerial tactics employed in intercepting attacking aircraft?

A. The aerial tactics employed in intercepting attacking planes were that when planes approached one or between two Army bases in the first defence line, the planes at those two bases would attack in full force against the incoming planes. The planes in the secondary defence line were in the air, but would not attack unless planes got through the outer defence line. The same can be said of the direct air coverage of the TOKYO Area, that American planes that penetrated the secondary defence line were to be attacked by the planes performing air coverage over TOKYO.

Q. Was their primary target bomber planes or escort fighters?

A. Bomber planes were the primary target.

Q. What was the actual operational strength of the 10th Flying Division on 15 February 1945?

A. In the 10th Flying Division there were about 200 fighters and 12 observation planes.

Q. Was that authorised strength or operational strength?

A. The organisation strength called for about 210 planes, I don't know about the other.

Q. What was the normal availability, in percentage, of operational planes?

A. Generally 200 planes.

Q. You stated previously that the 10th Flying Division was the only defence air division in the TOKYO Area with an authorised strength of approximately 210 fighters. By this, do you mean that there were only 210 fighter planes (Army) available for the air defence of the TOKYO Area?

A. Yes.

Q. Were other air divisions ordered to reinforce the 10th Flying Division during air attacks; from where and in what strength?

A. Assistance in repelling incoming attacks was to be received from the Fighter Pilot School at MITO, TOKOROZAWA and TAMA. These did not include, necessarily, whole air divisions, but only certain flying units there. They came to help us in February.

Q. Who determined the strength of reinforcement ordered in this particular area?

A. The Air Defence Commander of JAPAN who was His Majesty Prince HIGASHI-KUNI.

Q. Was the 10th Flying Division able to maintain its operational strength throughout the remainder of the war?

A. No, they were not able to maintain 200 operating planes. In about July, the number of available planes was one hundred. The reasons for the decrease of availability was due to installation of armament in planes as well as some losses.

Q. Were you able to maintain the required number of pilots?

A. We were able to maintain sufficient number of pilots for the number of planes available, but we could not use all of the pilots because of the shortage of aviation gasoline.

Japanese anti-aircraft gun positions, Wewak, New Guinea 1944. The Home Islands would have been festooned with such positions for any invasion. (USAAF)

Q. The lack of operational planes then was due to two reasons, actual lack of modern combat type planes and lack of gasoline. Is that right?

A. Yes.

Q. Was the combat efficiency or calibre of the pilots maintained during this period? Were available spares and maintenance adequate?

A. The combat efficiency of the pilots decreased because of the lack of fuel for training purposes. The spares were inadequate, particularly as far as engines were concerned.

Q. How about maintenance facilities?

A. In comparison with the lack of engine parts for the planes, repair and maintenance facilities were considered sufficient. However, the repair and maintenance crews, which were sufficient in number, had been hurriedly trained and were not too skillful in their work.

Q. Referring to American carrier attacks on the TOKYO Area on the 16 and 17 February, what combat losses were sustained by the 10th Flying Division?

A. I am not sure just what the combat losses during these two days were, but I think that it was about 30 planes.

Q. Were records kept of losses by the division?

A. Yes, but they have been destroyed.

Q. Who ordered their destruction, and where are the copies of these records?

A. The order for their destruction came from Lt. General KAWABE, Shozo, who was the Commanding Officer of the Air Army. Duplicates of these records might be obtained at the Bureau of Investigation for Commendations and Awards (KOSEKI CHOSABU).

Q. During the carrier attacks, 16–17 February, how many planes were destroyed on the ground and what damage was done to the installations at the fields?

A. Approximately ten. Minor damage at the fields.

Q. What did the 10th Flying Division consider was the relative effectiveness of carrier-based fighter planes and American Army P-51 planes from IWO JIMA?

A. The P-51 were jeopardised by the distance they had to travel and return, therefore couldn't stay over the target very long; whereas the carrier planes could stay longer over the target.

Q. Which type of planes did the most damage to the Japanese Air Force and to their field installations?

A. Damage done by P-51 minor, both in the air and on the ground, whereas damage by carrier-based planes was greater.

Q. Which planes or type of planes did the Japanese fighter pilots consider the most effective combat fighters in air combat?

A. They considered the F-6-F carrier-based planes as most effective.

Q. That is in comparison with P-51 and F-4-U?

A. I think that is true.

Q. What type of planes did the 10th Flying Division have?

A. Type 3 fighters, Type 2 fighters (one with a one-engine and one with a two-engine). The two-engine fighters are night fighters, TORYU; single-engine fighters were SHOKI. The Type 3 above was called HIEN. The Type 1 was called HAYABUSA.

Q. Was any revision of defence tactics made as a result of the initiation of carrier attacks on the Home Islands?

A. The Air Defence Plan for the TOKYO Area was not changed from February on.

Q. Did they attempt any dispersal of planes to prevent damage on ground by air attacks?

A. Yes, in one particular case they moved them four or five kilometres away from the field.

Q. What effect did this dispersal have on the operating efficiency as a fighting force?

A. It prevented their planes from getting into the air. The principal object was to hide them and keep them from receiving any damage.

Q. Then late in the war you tried to avoid combat?

A. Because of previous damage, we were forced to hide our planes. It was not that we didn't want to go in to fight, but we had been ordered to hide our planes.

Q. Then losses were not acceptable?

A. That is correct.

Q. During the latter period of the war were your pilots trained for the Special Attack Corps?

A. Yes, but not all of them.

Q. Who decided which group of pilots would be trained for that type of operation?

A. They volunteered for it in the 10th Flying Division, and training was carried out for this Special Attack Corps.

Q. What did this training consist of?

A. They practised landings and take-offs with their bomb load and a bit of navigation in case they had to go out to sea. The only special equipment they had was to attach bombs to fighters.

Q. What was the normal number of night fighters attached to your organisation?

A. The organisation plan called for one SENTAI or 42 night fighters. However, they actually had only 25 or 26 night fighters.

Q. Did you consider them to be effective?

A. They operated satisfactorily against the B-29s. They shot them down.

Q. In the total loss of airplanes, what percentage were operational losses?

A. About two-thirds were lost in combat.[4]

Conclusion

Japanese air assets would have been much depleted at the beginning of any conventional assault, and likely lessened to almost extinction by the time of the second phase of the Home Islands assault. This, however, does not include kamikaze assets, which will be examined next. The effectiveness of the defenders' AA assets is more difficult to ascertain, but it would likely have been minimal to slight.

However, it must be pointed out that air losses in World War II came primarily not from enemy combat effectiveness, but the various forces' own limitations: more aircraft were lost to other factors than to enemy action. The Allies invasion effort would have seen thousands of aircraft in use, and a significant proportion of them would have been lost primarily due to the limitations of aircraft in the 1940s. This factor will be examined more fully in later chapters.

HOW WOULD THE WAR HAVE CONTINUED IF THE A-BOMBS HAD NOT BEEN USED?

Kamikaze forces – air

Overview: *In this chapter, we analyse the 10,000 kamikaze aircraft Japan would have used in its Home Island defence, and their efficiency, as well as examine the strike against the aircraft carrier USS* Bunker Hill *and other aircraft carriers.*

A suicide aircraft – background left – nearly strikes the USS *Missouri*. Note how many of the ship AA guns cannot now bear as the aircraft is too close. (US Navy Photo)

By 1944, the concepts of suicide were being embedded in the minds of the people. The Bulgarian Air Attaché to Japan was interviewed by a famous Japanese novelist for the government information agency. What, asked the novelist, impressed him about Japan. The spirit of sacrifice, unhesitatingly replied the attaché, embodied by the concepts of *tai-atari* (self-ramming); *jibaku* (self-destruction in the air), and *nikudan* (human bullet) concepts, the 'death or victory, victory or death ideal'.[1] And in a peculiarly Japanese way the concept worked: if one life equaled on ship, then proceed.

Glider corps units were intensified around Japan as the war continued. These gave teenage boys rudimentary lessons in flight. They were followed, although the progress was implied rather than advertised, by further unit training through an accelerated air cadet course, and then assignment to a suicide unit.[2]

Suicide diving was fostered as a concept in the naval air force, with a methodology that saw careful talks from flag rank officers that implied the idea had been forced upon them from the ranks below.[3] However, it was indeed routinely used in the war by pilots whose aircraft were so badly damaged they would not make it home. For example, the first air raid on Darwin, Australia, which saw four Japanese aircraft brought down, cites in the Japanese records that one was seen to 'voluntarily' dive into a building:

A unit of carrier-based bombers from *Kaga* (led by Lieutenant OGAWA Masakazu [or Shôichi]). The 1st Company (nine carrier-based bombers): Bombed the eastern airport, blasting two hangers which caught fire and bombed the western airport, blasting a hanger and barracks which caught fire, and strafing barracks and radio direction-finding facility; one bomber voluntarily crashed into the target [after being damaged], and another bomber received gunshot damage.[4]

The Japanese government, even in the hard-pressed days of 1945, was still producing a large number of aircraft. Foreign Ministry high official Tochikazu Kaze, who was in a position to know, noted in his autobiography that the nation was turning out in February

'1685 per month', although that included all types. It had built 28,180 in 1944.[5]

As 1945 moved on and the war came closer to the Home Islands, the prospect of using more and more suicide tactics became a reality. The Navy's Admiral Onishi offered to spend '20 million lives' in kamikaze attacks to stop any invasion.[6] One of the planners, Lieutenant General Noburu Tazoe, told his US interrogators:

> The [combined army and navy] air force plan was to attack the Allied Fleet by Kamikaze planes, and for that purpose the full air force, led by the Commanding general, was made ready to destroy the Allied ships near the shore. We expected annihilation of the entire air force, but we felt that it was our duty. The Army and Navy each had 4000 to 5000 planes for this purpose. Of that force, waves of 300 to 400 planes at the rate of one wave per hour for each of the Army and the Navy would have been used to oppose a landing on Kyoshu.[7]

The kamikaze technique was very effective in its accounting: one life sacrificed caused hundreds of enemy fatalities. The deaths of nearly 400 American sailors and the removal of the aircraft carrier USS *Bunker Hill* from the war gives testimony as to the loss of life that occurred with an effective kamikaze hit on a large ship. The possibility was vividly explored by Maxwell Taylor Kennedy, who wrote *Danger's Hour: The Story of the USS* Bunker Hill *and the Kamikaze Pilot Who Crippled Her*:

> The second half of the book tells what happened on the *Bunker Hill* after the planes hit the ship. Through extensive interviews and official reports, Kennedy reconstructs the attack and its aftermath, second by second. Just before the crash, Ogawa sent a final Morse code. 'I have found the enemy vessels .... Now, I am diving into the ship.' [8]

What is also telling is Kennedy's examination of the motivation of suicide pilots like Japanese kamikaze pilot Kiyoshi Ogawa. Intelligent, amusing, young and all too human, the book shows how thousands of like-minded young men would have rallied to the cause as the military leaders became more desperate.

Ogawa grew up in Gunma Prefecture and attended Waseda University in Tokyo. In the fall of 1943, he was drafted along with other liberal arts students from top universities. He entered the 14th Class of Naval Flight Reserve Students and received basic training at Takeyama Base near Yokosuka and flight training at air bases at Tsuchiura and Yatabe in Ibaraki Prefecture. He became part of the Kamikaze Special Attack Corps 7th Showa Squadron that sortied from Kanoya Air Base in southern Kyushu on 11 May 1945.

Kamikaze pilot Kiyoshi Ogawa in school uniform. With his wingman Seizo Yasunori, Ogawa rammed the USS *Bunker Hill* which took it out of action for the rest of the war and killed nearly 400 American sailors and aircrew. (Public domain)

Ogawa piloted the second bomb-carrying Zero fighter that crashed into *Bunker Hill*. This kamikaze attack killed 393 and wounded 264, one of the most significant numbers for those inflicted by any other Japanese suicide attack. The identity of Kiyoshi Ogawa as the pilot of the second

Zero fighter to hit *Bunker Hill* was determined from items taken from his remains by Robert Schock, a *Bunker Hill* crewman. Schock found a name tag with the Japanese characters for the rank of ensign, a broken aviator watch, and two photographs.[9] When Schock passed away, his grandson, Dax Berg, found Ogawa's possessions stored away in a box. The name tag, along with the date and time of the kamikaze attack on *Bunker Hill*, turned out to be the key to identification of Ogawa as the pilot. In March 2001, Ogawa's grandniece and her mother visited San Francisco to receive his items from Berg.[10]

As the kamikaze efforts intensified, so too did the development of more effective aircraft for defence. These too would have become suicide aircraft if they were too damaged to return to base. The Pacific War Research Society's analysis showed new aircraft – Raiden, Gekko, and Suisei – together with a four-engined bomber under development, the Renzan, and a rocket fighter plane, the Shusui.[11]

It was not just ships that were targets. The concept of a Japanese aircraft ramming an Allied one was developed. Sergeant Walter Odlin, an American Prisoner of War held in Tokyo, saw a massive raid of 25 May from the ground, with kamikaze aircraft used as a defence. 'The tiny planes (Bakas?) flew against the bombers and exploded, shattering into a thousand pieces. The bombers both burst into flames but remained intact while they came slowly down and crashed.' Twenty-six B-29 bombers were brought down in that raid, but mostly by anti-aircraft fire.[12]

The Ohka was deliberately developed as a one-way kamikaze aircraft, launched from a mothership aircraft, while others were variants of existing types such as the Zero or Val. A sortie was flown on 12 April with eight Betty bombers, which succeeded in launching six Ohka attack aircraft. In the only confirmed sinking of a vessel by an Ohka, one hit the destroyer USS *Mannert L Abele*. But five of the bombers were lost, and a sixth crashed on landing.[13]

A mission two days later saw all seven bombers launched lost. On the 16th an attack with six Bettys resulted in four losses.[14] Two B-29s, reports Hoyt, were destroyed by a Japanese fighter's act of *tai-atari* (self-ramming), which saw him hit one, and the resultant explosion set fire to another.[15]

New Japanese aircraft of significance in the defence of the Home Islands 1945–46

Aircraft name	Type/engines/ crew/variants	Armament	Number built	Comments
Mitsubishi Raiden Allied codename 'Jack'[16]	• Fighter • Single-engine • One-man • 6 variants	• 4 x 20 mm cannon	621	Poor visibility but excellent climb, firepower and performance.[17]
Nakajima[18] (Gekkou); Allied codename 'Irving'	• Night-fighter • Twin-engine • Two-man • 3 variants	• 2–3 20 mm cannon or • 2 x 551 lb bombs (kamikaze mode)	479	Couldn't match the height performance of later bombers, esp. B-29.[19]
Yokosuka[20] Suisei Allied codename 'Judy'	• Bomber, Dive • Single-engine • Two-man • 5 variants	• 3 rifle-calibre machineguns • 500/800kg bombs (design/ kamikaze)	2038	Poor engine reliability with insufficient crew and fuel protection.
Nakajima Renzan[21]	• Bomber, heavy • Four-engine • Seven-man • 1 variant	• 6 x 20 mm cannon • 5 x 13 mm machineguns • 8000 lb bombload	7	Never produced in quantity due to shortage of aluminum.
Mitsubishi Shusai[22]	• Fighter, rocket-propelled interceptor • One-engine • One-man • 5 variants	• 30 mm cannon	67	Navy On paper could outfly anything the Allies possessed. 3600 to be delivered by March 1946.
Mitsubishi Reppu[23][24]	• Fighter, 4-bladed propeller • Superchargers	• 2 x 20 mm cannon and 2 13.2 mm machine guns or • 4 x 20 mm cannon	8	Possibly capable of reaching B-29s. 8 prototypes built; production Oct 45.

Ohka suicide aircraft. (US Navy)

Aircraft carriers were a primary target of the kamikazes. *Danger's Hour* provides some useful data[25] on the larger carriers, with other information provided, as shown below, by Tony DiGiulian. Near misses and damage caused by the same and minor strikes are not included, but approximate another 50 percent of action.

Name	Date struck	KIA[26]	Result
Derived from Kennedy[27]			
USS *Franklin*	27/30 Oct 1944[28]	>700	Out of the war, according to Kennedy, but according to DiGiulian she returned to action. DeGiulan disputes the 700 men killed in this first strike, but notes 724 killed in a bomb strike on 19 March 1945. That strike indeed took her out of combat.[29]
USS *Intrepid*	24/25 Nov 1944[30]	11	Out of action 2.5 months
	16 Apr 1945	8	Out of action 3 months
	30 Oct 1944[31]	10	Operational immediately
USS *Ticonderoga*	22 Jan 1945[32]	143	Out of action 6 months[33]

Name	Date struck	KIA[26]	Result
USS *Saratoga*	21 Feb 1945	123	Out of the war
USS *Randolph*	11 Mar 1945	25	Out of action 1 month
USS *Enterprise*	5 Apr 1945	Nil	Out of action 1 month
	14 May 1945	14	Out of the war
USS *Hancock*	25 Nov 1944	15	Not out of action – 15 men KIA[34]
	7 Apr 1945	62	Out of action 3 months
USS *Bunker Hill*	11 May 1945	389	Out of the war
Derived from DiGiulian			
USS *Essex*	25 Nov 1944	15	Out of action 3 weeks
USS *Lexington*	5 Nov 1944	Nil	Out of action 4 weeks
USS *Belleau Wood*	30 Oct 1944	92	Out of action 3 months
USS *Cabot*	25 Nov 1945	62	Out of action 3 weeks
USS *Sangamon*	4 May 1945	36	Out of the war
USS *Suwanee*	25 Oct 1944	Nil	Operational immediately
	26 Oct 1944	150	Out of action 3 months
USS *Santee*	25 Oct 1944	16	Out of action 3 months. Other damage was inflicted by a submarine torpedo strike 16 minutes after the kamikaze, contributing significantly to the damage
USS *Manila Bay*	5 Jan 1945	14	Out of action 5 days
USS *Natoma Bay*	7 Jun 1945	1	Remained in action but required repairs
USS *St. Lo*	25 Oct 1944	126	Sunk
USS *Wake Island*	3 Apr 1945	Nil	Out of action 6 weeks
USS *White Plains*	25 Oct 1944	Nil	Out of action 3 months
USS *Kalinin Bay*	25 Oct 1944	5	Out of action 3 months

Name	Date struck	KIA[26]	Result
USS *Kitkun Bay*	25 Oct 1944	16	Out of action 2 months
	8 Jan 1945		Out of action 2 months
USS *Kadashan Bay*	8 Jan 1945	Nil	Out of action 3 months
USS *Marcus Island*	15 Dec 1944	Nil	Operational immediately
USS *Savo Island*	5 Jan 1945	Nil	Operational immediately
USS *Ommaney Bay*	4 Jan 1945	95	Sunk
USS *Lunga Point*	21 Feb 1945	Nil	Operational immediately
USS *Bismarck Sea*	21 Feb 1945	218	Sunk
USS *Salamaua*	13 Jan 1945	15	Out of action 3 months
HMS *Formidable*	4 May 1945	8	Operational next day
	9 May 1945	1[35]	Operational immediately
HMS *Illustrious*	6 Apr 1945	Nil	Out of the war, although damage was light. The strike coincided with intent to refit her.
HMS *Indefatigable*	1 Apr 1945	8	Operational immediately
HMS *Indomitable*	4 May 1945	Nil	Operational immediately
HMS *Victorious*	1 Apr 1945	4	Operational immediately
	9 May 1945		Operational after 2 days

The number of ships actually destroyed by kamikazes is difficult to determine. Two books – Inoguchi (1958)[36] with 34 ships given, and Warner (1982),[37] citing 57 ships sunk by special attack aircraft, are good sources. Tony DiGiulian's website *Kamikaze Damage to US and British Carriers* agrees with thirty-four.

However, an examination of other historical records by the author of the website *Kamikaze Images*, Bill Gordon, indicates that both of these lists do not have the correct number of ships sunk by kamikaze, and instead, with exhaustive analysis, suggests 47 ships as being correct. Gordon, in 2007, compared these with the listings of ships sunk at the websites of the US Naval Historical Center, and the American Merchant Marine at War.[38]

The effectiveness of the air kamikaze strikes would likely have killed around 100,000 Allied personnel in a conventional invasion. Harper suggests there were '200 concealed airstrips throughout Japan', supplementing the 70 regular airfields and 24 seaplane bases.[39] Frank estimates 10,000 aircraft, half of them kamikaze.[40] Weintraub suggests 8945 between Army and Navy, with 15 million gallons of fuel.[41] Arens agrees:

> ... the Sixth Army assessed that there were 5000 enemy combat planes of all types within range of intervention. In addition, an estimated 4000–5000 training planes could be used for kamikaze attacks. The Sixth Army also believed that the Japanese would fight the decisive battle on Kyushu, and commit all of their aircraft, primarily in kamikaze attacks. Upwards of 10,000 aircraft would be available to the Japanese to conduct an all-out suicide air offensive against the transport ships and landing craft. These attacks would be strengthened by the probable widespread use of the suicide-piloted rocket plane (BAKA), which was modeled after the German V-1 rocket bomb.

If we use one Okinawa figure of 200 aircraft killing 12,300 servicemen, with 1500 aircraft kamikaze strikes predicted for the Kyushu invasion, we can argue that 100 aircraft hitting their targets would kill 6125 personnel. This works out at 91,875 lives lost. We might round that up by 10 percent, given the greater intensity with which the Japanese would defend their homeland.[42]

A major failure of Allied intelligence concerned the Japanese capability for suicide attacks. In spite of countermeasures, the suicide attacks directed against the US task forces and transport areas would unquestionably have been serious and would have caused severe losses. The kamikaze attacks against the US fleet at Okinawa came after the aircraft flew more than 500 miles over open ocean. Many inexperienced pilots lost their way and never reached the American fleet.

Zero pilot Harada with the author in 2015. Many such regular aircrew members crossed over to become kamikaze in the final months of the Empire. (Photograph by Simon Loveday)

This great distance also allowed the fleet to receive early warning from picket ships and scramble fighters to engage the kamikazes. Bad weather in the target area also hampered the kamikaze pilots from acquiring their targets. With all of these difficulties, the Japanese ratio of 'planes launched' to 'planes successfully striking their targets' was one in nine. The Japanese flew 1840 'special-attack' planes during the battle for Okinawa. A ratio of one in nine would equate to approximately 202 planes striking their targets. The US Navy reported 192 ships hit by kamikaze planes during the battles for Okinawa; of these, 15 were sunk.[43] These figures concur with those thought reliable by Captain Fuchida in his interrogation post-war:

Q. Of the 900 that were expended in the Okinawa Area, how many hit their target?

A. Although it was widely publicised that 400 had been successful, I think that 200 would be more accurate figure.

Q. What percentage of hits did the JNAF expect in the Ketsu Operation?

A. We expected about the same percentage as during the Okinawa operation.[44]

An analysis from the Federation of American Scientists suggested a hit ratio of one in six or one in seven:

> Although the Japanese staff planned for a hit ratio of one in nine, many believed that they would be far more successful. The special attack aircraft would have to fly less than 100 miles to their target, with almost the entire distance spent over land masked by terrain. The Allied fleet would have very little warning time to intercept the aircraft. Anchored troop transports, just off the coast, would be easy targets as they unloaded their cargo. It is highly probable that the Japanese suicide attack hit ratio would have been higher, probably closer to one in six or one in seven. At these ratios, 1400 to 1600 kamikaze aircraft would have hit American ships.[45]

A different type of air kamikaze warrior was also demonstrated on Okinawa. In one successful attack, a two-engined transport, the sole survivor of a flight of five, evaded being shot down to skid to a belly-landing halt on Yontan Airfield in the centre of the island. Its occupants 'disgorged and scattered into the flight line lobbing grenades and incendiaries into parked planes. Seven aircraft were destroyed, 26 other damaged, and two fuel dumps' went up before the suicide raiders were killed.[46]

The enthusiasm with which the kamikaze personnel would have embraced their mission can be seen by the way they carried out attacks even as it was becoming obvious the war was over. On 12 August, Japanese attacks damaged a major US warship with a torpedo-bomber attack.[47] The next day 23 kamikaze aircraft were shot down during attacks.[48] On 15 August, a fight between 18 aircraft from HMS *Indefatigable* and 12 Zeros saw four of the Japanese aircraft shot down. One of the British pilots baled out, was captured, and executed that night, hours after the Emperor's surrender broadcast.[49]

Captain Mitsui Fuchida, who led the attacks on Pearl Harbour and Darwin, reported that 1000 naval kamikazes were going to be used in defence of the mainland. There were 500 of each of the navy's aircraft at Kyushu and in Tokyo, with 300 in Hokkaido and 200 in Shikoku. Fuchida, being a naval man, did not know (or did not say) precisely where the Army aircraft were deployed, expect that they were 'similarly' but reported on the same number being available to his armed force comrades.[50] The kamikazes would have been armed with 800-kilogram weapons.[51]

There were also '2500 remaining combat aircraft which would be used during Ketsu operations for search, night torpedo, and air cover', according to Fuchida. We can safely surmise that those that were not shot down in combat, or in a state of disrepair, would be used as kamikazes.

Interrogation of the Chief of Staff of the First Air Fleet throughout the Philippine Campaign reported that approximately one-sixth of all kamikaze planes used in the Philippines hit their target, and the Japanese estimate of the Okinawa figure was approximately one-ninth.

One Navy officer, interrogated post-war, thought 'about 2/3 of the planes would be thrown into an attack on Kyushu'. The plan was to use Kamikaze attacks primarily at twilight or on bright moonlight nights, utilising Shiragiku, Zero fighters and Willow types of planes, without pathfinder aircraft. After the Allied landings on the beaches, the plan was to wait until the very last moment, until 'the American forces were dispersed as little as possible and thus inflict a greater amount of damage'.[52]

Troop transports would have been the primary target rather than carriers, although the kamikaze pilots preferred the latter. Commander Yamaguchi, from August 1944 to January 1945, Operations Officer on the Staff of Vice Admiral Fukudome, CinC Second Air Fleet (Formosa), said in his interrogation to the question: 'On the approach to Lingayen, we noticed that some pilots still preferred to attack carriers rather than transports':

A. Although orders were definite that they should attack transports first and always, sometimes temptation was too great when the pilot sighted a carrier and he would violate orders to the distress of his command. We tried to persuade them of the importance of attacking the transports again and again.

Q. Was a Kamikaze pilot given a greater promotion for successful attack on one type of ship over another?

A. There is no difference in merit given to the pilots according to the ships they attacked; they were treated the same.

Q. We understood at one time that for hitting an aircraft carrier, the pilot would be promoted two grades, for another ship one grade – is that not correct?

A. There was a case like that in the beginning of the campaign, sometime in October. The pilot who sank a carrier got [a] two-grade promotion because that was [a] main target at that time. That system of two-grade promotions tempted them later on, even though [the] situation had changed.[53]

Conclusion

Summing up, it therefore seems there would have been intensive use of kamikaze aircraft in an invasion of the Home Islands, with a heavy death count inflicted on the Allies' landing forces of around 100,000 lives lost.

CHAPTER EIGHT
SEA KAMIKAZE FORCES

Overview: In this chapter, we appraise the type and number of suicide boats, submarines and divers used by the Japanese forces. Would they have been effective?

The air concept of kamikaze was developed to be used against (preferably) the larger ships of any Allied force, such as battleships, battle cruisers, aircraft carriers and troopships. Bombers too were targets, as outlined previously. But suicide boats, submarines, and 'frogmen' were devised for closer attack against incoming assault craft, for example. The larger the target, the better the general concept.

Kaitens mounted on a mother submarine during a parade of the ship's company. (Public domain)

There is a degree of confusion about different types of suicide boats used by the Japanese forces. There were only two types of suicide boats in actual usage. There were another five in design. The general name was 'shinyo', which translates as 'ocean shakers'.[1]

Part of the confusion lay in the numbering system. The two in production were Type 1 and Type 5.[2] Types 2, 3, 6, 7, and 8 were in design.[3] The Type 4 title was not used apparently because of a superstitious avoidance of the pronunciation of 'shi', which sounds a little like the Japanese word for 'death'.

The two types in production were designed as follows:

Name	Length	Crew	Speed	Propulsion	Armament
Type 1	5.1 m[4]	One-man	23 knots[5]	Single/inboard	• 270 kg bow charge • 2 x 12 cm stern-firing rockets (AA/anti-ship)
Type 5	6.5 m	Two-man	25 knots	Two/inboard	• 270 kg bow charge

Other slight differences between the two were that the Type 5 was designated as a 'division leader' vessel and carried radio. By the end of the war, the Type 8 was in production, but not actually used, although it is surmised it would have been in any 'conventional' attack. Its design was:

Name	Length	Crew	Speed	Propulsion	Armament
Type 8	8.0 m	Three-man	23 knots	Three/inboard	• 2 x 8 cm torpedoes • 2 x 12 cm stern-firing rockets (AA/anti-ship) • 1 x 13 mm forward-firing machinegun

The Type 8 was not designated as a suicide weapon. Instead, it was a 'squadron' leader, also carrying radio, which would lead several 'divisions'. (The naming is confusing – a 'squadron' refers to 'aircraft' but it used to be a cavalry term, while a 'division' is a very large Army formation of around 25,000 men.)

The idea behind the Type 1 was to drive the vessel straight into the side of the target ship. Lashing (securing) of the controls was possible to allow the operator to dive over the side, but such escape was not planned for, the better to enable efficient targeting. The charge could be fired in any one of three ways, including via impact.

The Shinyos would be driven by middle school boys aged 15–16 years old. According to the US's investigation post-war, it was apparently the case that there was an ample supply of volunteer pilots. This was because they were given 'special privileges, early responsibility, fast promotion and the promise of a monetary reward to the volunteer's parents'. This last benefit was probably in the event of a successful strike.

The boats were grouped in their divisions along the coast of Japan (presumably the southern coast, although most reports do not say); carried on motherships, and in 'bomb-proof cases' for transport. Harper suggests that there were '98 secret Shinyo bases'.[6] Plans for a carrier ship to be entitled *Junyo* were made, although this was for transport of the attack boats rather than a combined ship/boat strike.

Suicide tactics, notes Hoyt, were in use in Okinawa, where soldiers from small boats climbed aboard moored ships and went rampaging with swords until cut down. And in land battles, soldiers flung themselves under tanks with explosive charges.[7] It is unknown whether the small vessels employed in the former were Shinyos without their explosives fitted.

There are difficulties in wartime in determining which vessels approaching a warship at high speed are suicide boats. Any small fast boat approaching a warship close to the coast of Japan would have been thought suspect and fired upon, probably leading to the quick destruction and sinking of it, and therefore a lack of knowledge as to whether it was in fact a genuine suicide craft.

Skates estimates that 2000 of these boats would have been ready for the defence of Kyushu.[8] One Internet discussion site estimates more: 'These suicide boats were produced in great number, 6200 for the Navy and 3000 for the Army.'[9]

One account suggests that during the 88-day Okinawa campaign, almost 700 suicide boats supported by about 7000 troops sank two American ships and damaged five, and probably damaged another.10 If so that would be a relatively poor return for the amount of lives lost.

Harper reports a Shinyo attack on 30 August, in which the defending British naval force sunk three and bombed their shore base, causing heavy casualties.[11] Suicide boats are to this day reported as being active in the defence of the fortress island of Corregidor, but little is said of their victories, if any.[12]

Model of a Shinyo attack boat with driver and machinegun in Yasukuni Shrine Museum, Tokyo. (Author photo)

Imperial Japanese Army fast attack boats

Designated 'Maru-ni' (meaning 'liaison boats'), these vessels operated on the principle of dropping one or two depth charges in the vicinity of the target and speeding away.

Name	Length	Crew	Speed	Propulsion	Armament
Maru-ni	4 m approx.	One-man	30 knots	Single/inboard	• 2 x 120 kg depth charge

In the invasion of the Luzon area of the Philippines in January 1945, these vessels were likely used in a number of attacks against primarily US ships. The most serious of these was an attack against auxiliary transport *War Hawk*, which killed 61 men,[13] and an attack against Landing Craft Support, Large, *3-26* in February, which killed 76 onboard personnel. Several other incidents including some inflicting severe damage on ships were reported. However, the combined army and navy attack vessels lost around 1100 men in this period, although accidents and attacks onshore from Allied assets were included in this. James Fahey, a sailor who kept a diary during his four years in the Pacific, noted that they always attacked at night.[14]

According to Captain Tsuezo Wachi, commander of a unit responsible for the defence of the southern half of Kyushu, there were 'about 600' of these craft hidden in 'small ports and other vantage points'. There were also about 100 'kaiten-type human torpedoes' and 'about 60 2-man submarines'. Most significantly, Wachi was of the opinion that 'We were absolutely confident that with this force we could sink about 200 American transports.'[15]

Imperial Japanese Navy Fukuryu suicide frogmen

According to the Yasukuni Shrine Museum in Tokyo, the Navy was developing ideas, tactics and equipment for a squad of suicide frogmen. The Japanese name for them was Fukuryu, meaning 'Crouching Dragon'. Wearing breathing sets, these men would be waiting in shallow water to destroy enemy landing craft. Their weapon was an explosive on the end of a bamboo pole, which would be brought sharply into contact with the underside of the enemy boat hull.[16] The diver would have died almost instantly once the explosive was detonated, from a combination of explosive force and their breathing set failing.

Given breathing sets were in their infancy, the use of suicide frogmen would have been a dubious proposition, with problems relating to breathing longevity, given the attacker would have needed to be in position for some hours. Getting the frogmen into position unseen would have been another problem. Once the possibility of frogmen attack would have been known by the Allies, a simple counter-measure would have been to lob grenades into the water ahead of the landing craft once shallow depths were reached.

Model of a Fukuryo Tokko Taiinzo diver in Yasukuni Shrine Museum, Tokyo. (Author photo)

Tadamasa Iwai, who trained in the technique, outlined how the diver:

… breathed oxygen gas … from two oxygen bottles settled on his back. Exhaled breath was blown into the absorbing (purifying) box on his back through a rubber tube, being deprived of carbonic acid here the purified oxygen was sent into the helmet and breathed again.

When the oxygen for inhaling was consumed to a certain extent, it was supplied from the bottles on the back by controlling a supplying valve. In the absorbing box there were thin sticks of soda hydroxide, which played [the] role of absorbent of carbonic acid contained in the exhaled breath.

The diver must avoid inhaling carbonic acid gas contained in his own exhaled breath. So he must inhale through [the] nose and exhale into the mouthpiece attached inside of the helmet sticking his mouth to it. Inhaling through [the] nose and exhaling through [the] mouth into the mouthpiece was the most important way of breathing for the diver. If he does not observe this rule he will soon fall unconscious or, in the worst case, go to death.

The problems of breathing air as opposed to oxygen were well understood, as given here in an awkward translation:

- It allows to stay longer in the water.

- It prevents caisson disease ['the bends' whereby joint failure, unconsciousness and death could be caused by the absorption of nitrogen into the blood].

- It makes Fukuryu diver unfindable as he need not discharge each exhaled breath into water.

Tadamasa Iwai went on to describe the difficulties with the equipment:

The special diving suit for Fukuryu was considerably heavy, as the helmet, its holder around the neck and two oxygen bottles were of iron. Moreover to the suit belonged an absorbing box, various metal fittings and rubber tubes etc. They were settled almost all on his back. So the diver put on lead sandals and attached a lead ballast on his abdomen in order to lower the center of gravity. Therefore the diver carried a load as heavy as about 60 kg (160 lb) altogether according to my memory. This weight made it hard to walk on land and the diver was liberated from the difficulty only in water.

The diver must always hold a posture bending forward in water as heavy things were all on his back, or he was turned over just as a tortoise flipped over and, once he fell into such position, it was almost impossible to restore normal posture and work in some way or other.

The Fukuryu diver, wearing such special suit, carried in his hand a bamboo rod with a small-sized mine at its top. The mine had a horn made of glass and covered by rubber at the top detonating on contact. This special mine was developed only for Fukuryu-tactics. But we were not given the mine for practical use but the one only for exercise.

The new device was not, however, a success, according to the Museum, which is silent on whether any of the frogmen were ever deployed. It cites 'mechanical logistical problems' and says that 'many Imperial Navy sailors perished as a result of the unsuccessful experiments' of this new attack weapon. Tadamasa Iwai recalled: 'I also fell unconscious during exercise in the water and had a narrow escape from death.'

The frogmen themselves would have caused little damage because of the inherent inabilities of their situation. They were basically men breathing underwater holding an explosive up on a stick. How would they have been deployed without being seen by surveilling aircraft and targeted? Once the concept of frogmen became known, how would they defend against artillery rounds hitting the immediate sea in front of the beach? Given they would have had only an hour or so of air, how would they have been replaced?

The author's own extensive experience of scuba diving suggests the suicide divers would have been more of a danger to themselves than the enemy. Even modern divers, with much lighter, streamlined and effective equipment, would find it difficult to use such an attack method. Limitations to visibility underwater suggests that the diver would have had a difficult time sighting the assault craft in time and detonating the explosive quickly, and explosives are not very effective underwater. Even depth charges weighing much more than that envisaged for the diver in this situation were not effective against steel submarine hulls unless detonated extremely close to the target.

However, there are some unverified attacks – sources for the information are not given – which state that on 8 January 1945, the infantry landing craft *LCI (G) 404* was damaged by suicide swimmers in Yoo Passage, Palaus (sic). On 10 February, Japanese suicide swimmers attempted an attack upon the survey ship *AGS-2* in Schonian Harbor in the same location.[17]

One interesting aspect of the experiment is the way the Imperial forces were diverted by such possibilities. Although a new weapon would have been welcome, how much in the way of men, materiel and money were expended on such an idea? The personnel would in hindsight been better used as air kamikaze fighters.

Imperial Japanese Navy Kaiten and Kairyu suicide submarines

Kairyu and Kaiten submarines should not be confused with the various midget submarine craft that were employed by the Imperial Japanese Navy. These specialised in covert assaults such as those made on Pearl Harbor, and Sydney, Australia.

The expectation of those boats was that due to their small size they could penetrate defences bigger submarines could not. For example, in the case of Sydney, the three attacking midget submarines went around the end of a defensive harbour boom net, which a larger submarine could not have done. In such assaults the submarine was intent on attack via torpedo and then withdrawal and recovery by a mother submarine.

There is confusion as to the names of these other small submarine types. The first – the Kaiten – was simply a modified Type 93 torpedo with a one-man pilot. It was a suicide craft designed for a 'one-shot' short mission. Japanese Special Attack naval officer Tadamasa Iwai notes that 'the word 'Kaiten' means 'Revolution of Heaven' and the name was adopted perhaps hoping [for a] complete recovery of the unfavourable war situation.[18]

The aft half of a kaiten after recovery by US forces at Ulithi Atoll in 1945. The forward section, including warhead, tanks and crew compartment is missing. (US Navy)

Kaitens

Tadamasa Iwai describes the characteristics of the kaiten as follows:

Kaiten torpedo consisted of two parts: the hind part of 93-type torpedo (the part with an air flask, a fuel flask, an engine, fins and double propellers turning to reverse directions) and a big shell with a diameter of one metre added to it, which contained upper and lower hatches, controlling device, a seat for pilot, a small-sized periscope, an auxiliary air flask and an explosive charge at the top.

Total length was about 15 metres .... Every part was made watertight, of course.

It ran underwater at 30 knots per an hour (sic) with the same engine as the original 93-type torpedo. The explosive charge loaded at the top weighed as much as 1.6 tons (about 3500 lb) and its explosive power was enormous enough to send any huge battleship to the bottom within one minute. [19]

Iwai went on to comment on the adverse characteristics; the inevitable death of the pilot, and the method of launch from a mother submarine:

Kaiten torpedo had controllability owing to the embarkation of man. But it inherited some defects from the original: it was impossible to go back and to re-set the engine which once stopped, because the engine for original torpedo was converted intact to it: though the travelling direction could be changed, the rudders worked ineffectively and its turning radius was as large as about 200 metres (about 183 yards), as they were small and installed before the propellers.

Anyway the controllability of Kaiten must have raised its accuracy rate in theory. But, in fact, in most of the cases, attacking results could not be identified. And its hit must inevitably bring death to the pilot on board. There was no escaping device.

Kaiten torpedo could not be shot out from [a] torpedo tube like the normal one, as its size was too large. So it must be launched from the deck of a submarine, which had been loaded with it. (Usually one submarine was loaded on its deck with 4–6 Kaiten torpedoes). Only after [the] announcement of [the] beginning of [the] 'Kaiten battle' the pilot got on it, the lower hatch was closed and then it was liberated.

Tadamasa Iwai was still eloquent in 2015, describing how the kaitens were launched:

In those last few months of the war, pilots would wait on a submarine until an enemy warship came into sight. They would then squeeze into a manned torpedo and pull the hatches over their heads, before being launched toward the target.

When I first saw a human torpedo, I shuddered with the thought that this was going to be my coffin. It was a 15-metre-long iron stick. The cockpit was tiny and not fit for humans.[20]

Kairyus

The Kairyu refers to several different models of small two-man genuine manoeuverable underwater craft. (The following text corrects sources that have confused the two names.)

In the case of kaitens, there was an overall design of, as the American examination put it, 'a long range torpedo which hits the enemy ship without fail due to the steering by the pilot who gets into the torpedo'. The pilots were trained men who had volunteered, again with the encouragement of rewards as well as patriotism.

Kaitens were designed to be stored in target areas for use when necessary, and in Japan's final Home Island defence distributed along the coast, preferably in cave bases facing away from the sea, probably to negate naval gunfire attacks. The standard attack procedure was to approach a target submerged with periscope navigation, and for the final run, dive to perhaps five metres. To get the kaitens closer to their target, the design was made so that as many as six could be carried on the casing of a mother submarine. The pilot could enter the kaiten while the mother submarine was submerged, thus adding to the covert nature of the assault.

In the case of the kairyus, four types were developed, with characteristics as below:

Type	Length	Breadth	Speed/range	Warhead
I	14.7 m	100 cm		1550 kg on two, 250-mm charge
Designed for 100-m dives, but only capable of 60, the Type 1 could be launched submerged from mother submarines.			12/78 k 20/43 k 30/23 k	One of these is on display at the Yasukuni Shrine Museum in Tokyo.

2	16.5 m	135 cm	20/83 k	1500 kg on 2000-mm charge
Hydrogen-peroxide powered, about 200 units constructed, but never fault-free.			30/50 k	
			40/25k	
4	16.5 m	135 cm	20/62k	1800 kg on 2000-mm charge
Kerosene/oxygen powered, which allowed a heavier warhead.			30/38 k	
			40/27k	300kg on 1125-mm charge
10	9 m	70 cm	7/3.5 k	

Probably built in the last stages of the war, as sufficient batteries were available to allow this short-range weapon a possibility.

Of all of the four variants, only the Type 1 seems to have been a successful mass-produced design. One authoritative source reports 330 of the Type 1; does not give a figure for Type 2; 'about 50' of the Type 4, and is silent on a Type 10 total. That gives a total of about 600 kairyus produced.[21] John Skates estimates only 177 kairyus, however, but then confuses them with others, citing 393 'small submarines' surrendered at the war's end, which would give about 600 available.[22]

The suicide submarine is not widely studied, and there is some confusion in its design as to manning. A comprehensive US Navy's report was made post-war. It specifies the four types were all one-man. The report offers diagrams of all four, showing one man driving each vessel. The confusion was caused, according to the US Navy, because the design for Type 2 was burnt at the end of the war. Their reconstruction of the plans were from the memories of an engineer R Nagano, who designed Engine Number 6 for the Type 2 variant.

Nihon Kaigun, the most comprehensive study of the Imperial Japanese Navy known to the author, specifies that Type 2 was a two-man design.[23] Given there are four surviving two-man types still available for inspection, there is no doubt that a two-man model, the kairyu, or 'sea dragon', developed.[24]

Although some photographs exist showing kairyus deploying, it seems they had little success in attack. One possible achievement may have been against the USS *Underhill,* a destroyer escorting a troopship convoy transiting between Okinawa and the Philippines on 24 July 1945. She was attacked by kairyus launched from *I-53*, and one impacted the ship forward of the waist, almost cutting it in two in the resultant explosion. One hundred and twenty-two of the ship's company of 190 died. [25]

Apart from that, the well-researched account *The Sacred Warriors: Japan's Suicide Legions* confirms the sinking by kairyus of the tanker *Mississinewa* on 20 November 1944, with the loss of 50 men. The merchant vessel *Canada Victory* is cited by Toland as having been sunk.[26] The suicide submarines may have also accounted for another three other ships damaged – one being a troop transport, and two being merchant vessels.[27]

Another attack may have occurred in the Philippines, in January 1945, in an action confused by two score of Army suicide boats. A two-man submarine – how it was known to be operated as such is unclear – was supposedly sighted in an attack on the USS *Belknap*, a destroyer.[28]

On 12 August, according to Harper, kairyus sunk the US submarine *Bonefish*, as well as the destroyer USS *Callaghan*, and the destroyer escort USS *Underhill*.[29]

Defence effectiveness

It is very difficult to estimate the success the varying types of Japanese small submarines would have had. But studies of what became later known as 'swarm' attacks in naval warfare, a methodology developed by Soviet, Iraqi, and Iranian forces, show that there is a small amount of 'leakage' in such situations. In other words, although you on a defending ship may be able to destroy a very large percentage – perhaps even as high as 90 percent – of the oncoming swarm of attack vessels, if only 10 percent get through, then they have a result that is disastrous for you as the recipient.

In terms of frogmen attacking landing craft, there would have been little success for the Japanese.

Conclusion

Some of the above defence techniques have an air of ridiculousness – and desperation – about them. The suicide diver is a particularly foolish technique. It would have been better to concentrate on the most effective forms of attack and use such personnel there.

Sea kamikaze operations would have produced little to slow an Allied conventional advance. Nevertheless, they would have had to be accounted for and would have produced some lessening of the assaults as a result. Once their attack characteristics would have been analysed and absorbed, they would have been wiped out wholesale.

CHAPTER NINE
LAND FORCES

Overview: In this chapter, we study troop strengths and capabilities on both sides, with some analysis of Allied sea and land assaults. We also analyse Japanese civilians as defenders, as well as the timeline and composition of a conventional assault, together with the aircraft carrier fleet composition. The structure of a Japanese land defence is discussed, and a scenario of an attack is sketched out. It is on land that the Japanese would have been effective, not in terms of stopping the Allies, but in terms of inflicting significant loss.

Even if a conventional invasion was to be the method of subduing Japan, there was no certainty that it was going to be a success. This seems to have escaped the proponents of a 'no-nuclear attack' option.

One problem would have been less combat-experienced troops rather than more. The effective end of the war in Europe, if not the immediate end of the troop presence there, brought an immediate claim for release from the theatre of an enormous number of American troops. As many as 72 percent of Americans expected a partial mobilisation at least, given one poll. The remaining 28 percent wanted even more than that: they wanted a defined number of military personnel returned home. So Congress, composed of politicians sensitively attuned to their electorates, demanded a reduction in the Army of one million men, from its then total of over seven million.[1]

This was no simple reduction by numbers. It meant a radical reduction in fighting troops: the combat arms of the armies of the United States, the attrition of the armour, infantry, and artillery components of the forces, the men who would actually go in to take the ground away from the enemy, and hold it. The big guns of naval battleships, battle cruisers and cruisers would be of much use, and the new weapon of capital ship airpower even more so, given its better range. They could pulverise the ground; destroy above-ground defences, and generally deny logistical support to the Japanese, especially where they had invested islands. But ships and airpower were not the troops that would have been needed.

A member of a Marine patrol on Saipan found this family of Japs hiding in a hillside cave. The mother, four children and a dog, took shelter from the fierce fighting in that area. (Cpl. Angus Robertson, June 21, 1944)

As Iowa Jima, Saipan, Okinawa, and many other islands had shown, painfully and with the loss of lives and equipment, only the combat arm of the infantry could take and hold the ground. That was what was going to have to happen to make the Japanese capitulate. Otherwise, a Japanese armed force could hold the mountainous terrain of the Home Islands for years. Over 75 percent of Japan is not level. Such ground would be of enormous advantage to the defenders.

The United States would have provided the bulk of the attack forces. It had the biggest logistical capabilities, and its forces were the primary power in the Pacific. British naval assets were also fighting there, along with its Dominion navies of Canada, Australia, New Zealand, and units of its colonial assets such as India. But the United States was the emerging 'superpower', to use a word not then invented. For example, it was able to muster 26 aircraft carriers for a Pacific invasion, as opposed to six from the Royal Navy – Britain's Empire being the reigning superpower up until World War II.

So it would have been with dismay that the US planners of a conventional assault viewed the destruction of the very forces that would provide success across the beachheads and beyond. Using a system known as Adjusted Service Rating, individual servicemen's scores were calculated: 85 gave anyone the right to be discharged. A month was given to commands to sort their adjustments. The result was catastrophic. As Frank shows, the 28th Division, to use one example, showed a turnover of 20 percent of its men and 46 percent of its officers. The 804th Tank Destroyer Battalion rotated 50 percent of its people; the 122nd Signal Radio Intelligence Company, 95 percent. The 45th Infantry Division reported that 83 percent of its personnel was eligible for a return home.[2]

The overall morale in the armies of the Allies is difficult to ascertain. As the great Napoleon noted, it is as three to one. The war had gone on for years; unimaginable casualties had resulted – most of the afterwards-calculated figure of 60 million had already died. Now would come warfare against an enemy of unbelievable ferocity, bravery, resolution and determination. Meanwhile, 37,500 hospital beds were being set up in Manila for Japanese invasion casualties.[3] Was a conventional assault even possible given such circumstances? There was certainly no clamouring for the fight. At least 72 percent of Americans in one survey wanted a partial demobilisation. The remaining 28 percent did not want less – they wanted more troops returned. The US Congress insisted that at least a million men be returned home.[4]

The situation in the rest of the Allied forces was no better. Robert P Newman cites an occasion in January 1945 when out of 15,600 Canadians destined for overseas duty, some 6300 deserted.[5] In the United Kingdom, the war had centred on defeating Germany, and victory had been proclaimed in May. There was little taste for a similar struggle in the Pacific, and little understanding of that part of the world. Most UK people had never travelled to the far-flung parts of the British Empire, and the thought of UK servicemen and women serving there had little support and little understanding of the techniques and training required. Most British people, for that matter, had no knowledge that Australia had been heavily bombed in its north for two years, with 207 air missions conducted by Japan over the northern landmass of that country, some involving scores of bombers at a time.[6]

An air raid drill in Japan during World War II. Note the primitive ladders. (Public domain)

Not that invasion was ever thought of as an easy solution. In the pre-war years, under the name War Plan Orange, US planners had war-gamed operations against Japan. The resolution of the defenders – of what was presumed by then – would be a Japanese empire had not been underestimated. Using a seaborne attrition scenario, the establishment of forward bases had been assumed, but the planners had hesitated at a conventional assault. One 1922 study had thought it offered 'almost no prospect of success'; another 'extremely doubtful' given the limited capacity of transporting war materials against a Japan that was fighting from its means of production; and the War College looked at the Japanese 'steep and soaked' terrain with trepidation.[7]

The Japanese defence strategy, in their own scenarios, would have nearly three million men at its disposal. The plan would not aim at preventing a landing, recognising the strength of the Allied bombardment, but it would aim to destroy any beachhead force. It would also summon all able-bodied civilians, regardless of gender, to act as suicide troops. A series of publications, such as the National Resistance Manual, began to promulgate the plan.[8]

Japanese troop strengths

The amount of Japanese forces within the main target area is difficult to calculate. Diplomat Kase noted that the Army had two million men in the Home Islands, and 'some eight thousand planes' from the combined forces of the Army and Navy.[9]

Frank estimates 2.9 million men in the homeland area. He cites ULTRA decrypts as showing 14 Japanese Army divisions, as well as tank and infantry brigades – at least 680,000 strong in southern Kyushu. Figuring in the militia, the three local prefectures contained 3.8 million adults. If only one in ten died, a lower loss rate than Okinawa, then total Japanese fatalities would have come to 580,000 to 630,000.[10] Hoyt suggests '2.5 million soldiers on duty in the homeland.'[11] Toland cites 53 infantry divisions, and 25 brigades – a total of 2,350,000 troops. These would be backed up by four million defence civilians, 'a special garrison force of 250,000', and a civilian militia of 28 million.[12] General Sweeney, the pilot of the Nagasaki B-29 A-bomber, suggested there were 'two and one half million soldiers and four million civilian military employees preparing for the invasion force'.[13]

There would also have been those Japanese forces and government personnel in the lands already held by Japan. These would have constituted a force that would have had to be contained. The *Demobilisation and Disarmament of the Japanese Armed Forces Reports* of General MacArthur, stated that: 'The overseas forces at the close of the war consisted of approximately 3,450,000 service personnel and over 3,000,000 civilians.'[14]

Organic defenders

The fighting during a conventional assault was envisaged by both sides as taking place at Kyushu and southern Shikoku, and then into the inland and the Japan Sea areas. Coastal fortifications would repel some of the invasion force with a stand-and-die defence. Counterattack regiments would assault any Allied force moving forward, intermingling to negate some of the enemy's superior artillery and air firepower. Close-quarter combat would be sought. More transportation facilities, to allow the rapid movement forward of shock troops, would have been constructed by that time, largely by civilians.

The battle was envisaged as being primarily against Allied tanks, and comprehensive suicide tactics were adopted from the Japanese forces' successful use in Okinawa, where they had been responsible for destroying 221 tanks, or 57 percent of the American force.[15] Japanese armour would have suffered the same disadvantage as the attackers: Japan is no tank country, so probably the best positioning of the Japanese units would have been as semi-mobile artillery, perhaps deploying the same concept of concealed guns in caves that were used on some of the Pacific islands. In mid-1945, Japanese tank strength in the Home Islands was 2970 units. These were divided into two divisions, six brigades, seven independent regiments, and several smaller units.[16]

These plans were by no means simply on paper. The movement of vast bodies of troops was being carried out in 1945, and frantic effort went into the construction of coastal fortifications, tunnels, caves, roads and layered defensive fields of progressive strength back from the beaches. Preparation was often carried out at night, to deny the surveillance of reconnaissance aircraft, and work was put into deception equipment and facilities. One post-war analysis of what had been carried out in the Kyushu area found:

> ... hundreds of caves, artillery ports in the cliffs and prepared installations to concentrate both heavy and light fire on the

road and paralleling railroad .... Underground installations were not confined to supply and ammunition, they had caves for everything, C.P.'s mess and housing, vehicles and even farmers had their safety caves .... Inside ... were many concrete individual rifle strongpoints, a fight right in thru the plants, to the death.[17]

I have stood on the beaches of Kyushu, driven the twisting roads through its almost-all mountainous terrain, alighted from the car and stood beside the narrow winding highways beside the sea, and imagined from a soldier's viewpoint what it would be like to take such land. Many of the emplaced defence points can still be seen. I have seen artillery, armour and airpower at work in a modern war, and experienced the difficulties of carrying out co-ordinated attacks with infantry, armour, airpower and a logistics tail. It is not a perfect practice now, and in 1945, it was even less so. In Kyushu, the advantage would have definitely been with the Japanese, and they would have inflicted much punishment on the Allied forces. In particular, the attitude of 'an enemy tank or gun destroyed is worth the suicide of a Japanese defender' would have worked for them.

The inland seas and mountainous terrain would have worked extremely well to Japan's advantage. James Fahey assessed this when his cruiser USS *Montpelier* was tasked to go into the inland seas of Japan as part of the Occupation Force, through the sea the Allies would have sailed on their drive to Tokyo from after taking the Kyushu Peninsula:

It is 240 miles from Wakayama to Hiro. All day long we sailed through the Inland Sea. Land could be seen on both sides of us at all times. The Inland Sea is about 35 miles wide. I never saw so many islands. One right after the other on both sides of us. I imagine the japs have gone on most of the islands. These islands are all very high. It would have been suicide if we ever had to come in here and fight for them, island by island. We never would have gotten in. There must be hundreds of islands in the Inland Sea. It is like a fortress guarding the main island of Japan.[18]

Cliffs near Ibusuki constitute formidable barriers. The topography of the Kyushu Peninsula offered only limited lodgement possibilities for the Allies. (Author photo)

The geographical advantage in Japan's peninsula would have been all with the defenders. Given cave defences described as above, they would have been largely impervious to initial assaults by naval gun, and aerial bombing and rocket attacks. Of course, some would have died, but it would have been among those caught in the open here and there by chance. The attackers could not have pounded the entire seaboard with gunfire unceasingly for weeks without eventually landing their own armour, artillery and infantry. Sooner or later the fight would have become soldier to soldier. What would have happened then?

Fighting forces drawn from the civilian population

Every able member of Japan's population, of what was often said to be around 100, but was in reality 72 million people, would have been mustered to the cause. Foreign Ministry official Kase described the preparation of civilians for combat with some despair:

> ... the disheartened nation reluctantly prepared for the worst.

As there were no guns or swords to arm them with, they were told to improvise spears out of sharpened bamboo sticks! Men and women were herded together and compelled to drill with these primitive weapons morning and evening.[19]

In her personal account of being in Hiroshima, high-school-age girl Junko Morimoto noted that 'Everyone had to spend their summer holidays doing military exercises.'[20] Another girl's story gave more detail:

Every household has a bamboo spear posted near the door, and Do-oh, her classmates, and thousands of other students participated in combat training, on how to use these spears to attack enemy soldiers, despite how ridiculous this seemed to those who understood that they would be shot before they could even get close.[21]

Suzuki's cabinet, on 12 April 1945, the day of Roosevelt's death, authorised the organisation of a Volunteer Army of men from 15 to 55 years, and women from 17 to 45 for the mainland battle.[22] Later, this age limit was extended for the men to 60 years, and around that date the cabinet was shown some of the weaponry: 'muzzle-loading rifles and bamboo sticks cut into spears stacked beside bows and arrows from feudal times'.[23] Kase noted a law passed on 22 June 1945 that entitled the 'National Volunteer Fighting Corps Bill'. It was modeled on the Volkswehr ('People's Army') concept of Nazi Germany. All adult males were to be in military service. The females were to work under the Army or in factories. Kase phrased it as: 'The entire country thus became a military barracks.'[24]

Such use of civilians had been seen in the defence of Okinawa: 'One group of enthusiastic high school students were trained to fight: 750 of them were formed into special Blood and Iron for the Emperor duty units and trained to infiltrate enemy lines and carry on guerilla warfare.'[25] These local forces were thought to have numbered 17,700 in the Boeitai, or Home Guard, with another 750 in youth groups. Together with engineer units, there were 'more than 23,000 Okinawan men, women and children ... formally mobilised for the defence of the island.'[26]

Japanese home defence-training in 1945. (Public domain)

The defence of Okinawa was largely seen as having been effective in inflicting heavy losses on the Allies. Such losses were part of the strategic thinking of enacting so heavy a price that Japan could exact favourable conditions for a negotiated surrender. So rather than the High Command having been put off continuing the war through seeing the Okinawa losses, it was rather a spur for *further* continuation. If civilian defenders could be made to exact a shocking price for the Allies at Okinawa, then they would certainly do so in the Home Islands. Surely, such thinking went, the Allies would balk at such a price being exacted on their armed forces, and then they would grant Japan favourable terms.

The lesson of Okinawa was slowly and painfully learnt, but in many respects, if planning for a conventional invasion continued, and if it had happened, it would have showed the lesson had not been learnt at all.

An inspection of the three ridge lines where the Japanese held the Americans on Okinawa is instructive. I have walked this ground: the terrain is absolutely appalling from an attacker's perspective: steep, sheer and able to be mined into caves to be used by the defenders.

It renders advancing armour largely impotent, negates much of the advantages of air attack, and forced the US forces to use their infantry in what was to be a most bloody and costly assault.

Over several months, the Japanese compelled the Americans to come at them into what was a mincing machine, for if the island was to be used as the nearest operational air base to the Home Islands, there could not be a guerrilla force left in the south of Okinawa while air operations were carried out from the north. This is the grand strategy that would have been followed on the Home Islands: force the Allies to come at the defenders *not* so they could have been defeated, but so that Conditional Surrender could have been exacted, rather than the Unconditional Surrender the Japanese feared. And to this end every man, woman and child would have served.

Harper describes a National Volunteer Combat Force, which wasn't volunteer at all, but pressed into service all males ages between 17 and 42 who weren't already in uniform. They were put into a compulsory service force of 28 million personnel. They 'drilled with ancient rifles, swords, bamboo spears, axes, sickles and other agricultural implements'. Harper details crude pistols that fired bolts, and the making of Molotov cocktails, and hydrocyanic acid bombs. (The first is a combustible liquid, like petrol, in a bottle with a rag fuse; the second is a bottle filled with acid and a reacting base such as drain cleaner. For the latter, shake the bottle hard, wait and throw.) Karate and judo classes were part of the preparation, and these included training for women too. [27]

General Sweeney, the pilot of the Nagasaki B-29 A-bomber, said:

The People's Volunteer Corps pressed into service every able-bodied civilian: man, woman and child. This mass of 32 million would supplement the two and one half million soldiers and four million civilian military employees preparing for the invasion force. All of Japan had become an armed camp, all of its population combatants.[28]

The old, the very young, and women began learning to drill and use primitive weapons as the pike[29] and such complicated ones such as explosives. [30] Japanese schoolgirls learnt to use rifles. Japanese women learnt sharpshooting so they could harass Allied troops from the mountains. The concept of 'satchel charges' was taught, where the user hurled oneself under an enemy vehicle and detonated it.[31] Dr Shuntaro Hida, working at the Army Hospital in Hiroshima, later recalled some of the details. Ironically, one of his tasks was to educate his medical orderlies into the techniques of becoming suicide bombers. 'The soldiers were trained to strap bombs to their bodies and throw themselves against the tanks. At the military hospital we had to teach this.'[32]

The Japanese employed booby traps routinely as they retreated. Sailor James Fahey saw the results of one when the wounded were brought on board his ship USS *Montpelier*:

> One of our crewmen came across a wire and pulled it. A mine exploded. One of our party was killed while three others were badly wounded. I was near the quarterdeck when they were brought aboard on stretchers. The one that was killed had a large hole in his chest. He lived a few minutes after the explosion.[33]

Private First Class EB Sledge, author of the memoir *With the Old Breed at Peleliu and Okinawa*, observed that the fighting grew 'more vicious the closer we got to Japan', with the carnage of Iwo Jima and Okinawa worse than what had been seen before. He pointed out that what the Allies had experienced in fighting the Japanese on the Pacific islands caused the Allies to formulate some very definite opinions that a conventional invasion would be disastrous carnage. 'It would shock the American public and the world. [Every Japanese] soldier, civilian, woman, and child would fight to the death with whatever weapons they had, rifle, grenade, or bamboo spear.'[34]

Such knowledge of the forces ready to resist the invasion would have hardened the hearts and attitudes of the invasion forces. The intelligence officer of the US Fifth Air Force declared on 21 July 1945, that 'the entire population of Japan is a proper military target', and he added emphatically, 'there are no civilians in Japan'.[35]

The resolve of the Japanese people to die is, however, not well catalogued. There had been little to show that they were not willing to do what the military caste told them to. How well would they fight? It is hard to know. But Charles Munoz saw at firsthand post-war what one Japanese mother thought of the country's determination to have her son die:

> During the Korean War I sailed as radio officer on several munitions ships to Korea. Usually we'd make a stop at a US base in Japan.
>
> During a port stay in Kure, I took the train and spent two days in Hiroshima. Aside from the destroyed building that was preserved as a monument, I saw no signs of the damage that had been done, though I didn't look for any: Hiroshima was the only oriental city I've visited where the avenues were wide and straight.
>
> I had dinner as the guest of a Japanese family, and the damage that had been done to them was evident. Their house had been saved by being in a valley; they spoke of how the blast had moved across the higher land on both sides and (with sad giggles) the grandmother had been on that high land. I didn't press for details.
>
> The 'brother' of the house was a young man exactly as old as I was. (I may have been 25 or so at the time.) Unexpectedly, he wore a black kimono and did not sit at [the] table with us. I saw [a] few men wearing what I think of as Japanese clothing when I was there, and of course I'm not sure that kimono is the proper term. Anyhow, it was a full-length gown. He sat off in a corner of the room staring at me through the meal. After dinner, his mother showed me through their scrapbook of photographs.
>
> He had been a kamikaze pilot.
>
> When it came time for him to make his flight, he had been hospitalised with tuberculosis. His mother showed me photographs of him in his flight gear. In some of the pictures

the officers wore sashes. The sashes had Japanese flags (at least, the 'meatball') on them. In every picture, his mother had cut out the flag.[36]

The US Marines inch forward on Peleliu in the Caroline Islands. (Photo by PFC John P Smith, USMC)

But as an alternative to what that mother thought, Yoshia Katsuji described how he felt, aged 13 in 1945, about the training and indoctrination. 'We thought Japan would win for sure. We had to endure until we won. That's how it was. Everyone wanted to fight in the war. We longed to. We were educated this way starting in elementary school. We were brainwashed, so we didn't think it was possible for us to lose.' For more than a year, Yoshida's classes had been cancelled; instead, he had dug air raid shelters, joined bucket brigades, made bamboo spears, and participated in drills to use them to fight the enemy. [37]

And in Okinawa, the Japanese military had already shown they were prepared to force the civilian conscripted militia to fight. Edward Drea details that not only were the locals forced to carry ammunition, work as nurses and bring up rations, but they were ruthlessly executed if they did not do so, or if they were suspected of being 'spies' or for disobeying orders. In one incident, more than 300 villagers were coerced into committing suicide rather than surrender.[38] Faced with heavy losses, and civilians who would rather suicide than surrender, surely the Allied war machine would hesitate, and then stop.

The capabilities of the civilian forces

The point can certainly be made that a muzzle-loading rifle will certainly kill someone, as will a bow and arrow, or even a pike. But the deployment of these weapons, in the hands of Japan's hastily gathered militia, needs a small word of explanation. A number of aspects would count negatively against such a Japanese defence.

First, even given equal training and morale on both sides – aspects to which we shall return – a single-shot firearm is outclassed by a magazine-fed, repeating action firearm in the same way a Model T Ford is inferior to a modern motorcar. The assault rifles that would have been utilised by the Allied forces would have been the M1 carbine and the .303 Lee-Enfield, both capable of firing 20 or more aimed shots a minute. By comparison, a muzzle-loaded firearm could fire around one shot a minute, and a breech-loading single-shot weapon – in trained hands around 10 shots a minute. Many Allied troops also would have been utilising light and heavy machine guns, and they would have been well equipped with grenades and mortars capable of firing short range bombs.

Second, the Allied troops would have been veterans of the Pacific and European wars. By mid-1945, the armed forces from the Allied coalition of nations had been welded into capable machines, and they had learnt the hard way what worked and what didn't. Many would have been through the island-hopping campaign of the Pacific, or the streets of Europe where they had forced back the German army mile by bloody mile. As soldiers, they were hardened and capable. The Japanese civilian 'militia', by comparison, would have been learning on the job, and would have been experiencing assaults not just by infantry for the first time but from artillery and air attack.

What would have been the motivation of the Japanese militia forces? Pride in their country of course, or even fear itself, which as a motivator should not be underestimated. Guy Sajer summed it up in World War II after some years of combat as an infantryman in the Wermacht:

> ... most of us were resigned to death – a resignation which often created the most glorious heroes of the war. Simple cowards or pacifists, who had been opposed to Hitler from the start, often saved their lives and the lives of many others in a delirium of terror provoked by the accident of an overwhelming situation .... We fought from simple fear, which was our motivating power. The idea of death, even when we accepted it, made us howl with powerless rage. We fought for reasons which are perhaps shameful, but are, in the end, stronger than any doctrine. We fought for ourselves, so that we wouldn't die in holes filled with mud and snow; we fought like rats, which do not hesitate to spring with all their teeth bared when cornered ....[39]

If the Allied soldiers were resigned to the job, but realistic about it, how would they compare to the Japanese civilian-soldiers in combat. The Japanese probably would have been brave, even suicidally so, given the proximity of their comrades – a powerful motivator in not retreating. There would have been the usual incompetence in battle at least initially: these new combatants would have been 'freezing' on the trigger; shutting their eyes when firing, putting their head down and keeping it there – all of the usual initial behaviours of many in combat situations for the first time. But that is not to say they would have fled *en masse*. There would likely have been 'battle police' stationed at intervals: regular soldiers whose job it was to mete out death for anyone trying to flee. That may seem shocking, but it was regular practice in many countries' forces in World War II.[40]

What the beaches might have looked like. Australians in an American assault boat at the Battle of Balikpapan. The US combat cameraman standing up, and the bulldozer of the Seabees on the beach indicate a landing being consolidated. (Public domain)

The civilian forces would not have been deployed into conventional infantry attack formations. They would have been defensively placed. On the mainland, the Japanese would have had an adaption of their successful plan for the defence of Peleliu and Iwo Jima. This was to deny the Allies the location of a front line, and to infest instead every possible defence locale, thus rendering the Allied overwhelming artillery firepower a measure of negation. Marine EB Sledge, who served at both Peleliu and Okinawa explained:

> Peleliu also was important to the remainder of the Marines' war because of the changes in Japanese tactics encountered there.

The Japanese abandoned their conventional all-out effort at defending the beach in favour of a complex defence based upon mutually supporting, fortified positions in caves and pillboxes extending deeply into the interior of the island ....

In earlier battles, the Japanese had exhausted their forces in banzai charges against the marines once the later had firmly established a beachhead. The Marines slaughtered the wildly charging Japanese by the thousands. Not a single banzai charge had been successful for the Japanese in previous campaigns.[41]

What the Japanese defenders would have received. Artillery men of C Battery, 90th Field Artillery, US Army, lay down a barrage on troublesome Japanese artillery positions in Balete Pass, Luzon, in the Philippines, on April 19, 1945. (US Army)

Sledge goes on to describe how the Japanese, instead, did not establish a main defence line now, which could have been simply pounded to bits by the Marines' organic artillery and the supporting guns of the Navy, and the American aircraft. Instead, the defenders were dug into caves, some small ones holding only two soldiers and others large holding hundreds. This proved so successful on Peleliu, the Marines took 'twice as many casualties' as they had on Tarawa. And this was the same defence employed on Iwo Jima. The Japanese Home Islands' terrain is the same; however, instead of a few score miles of it, the fighting would have been up through the Kyushu Peninsula for hundreds of miles towards Tokyo, and then in a second landing from Tokyo Bay.

Japanese troop capabilities

The presence of experienced permanent Japanese soldiers would have bolstered the defence immeasurably. While surrender was mostly not an option for the Japanese, there were occasions when they broke and ran – at least, in the case of the Army, in one Marine's opinion, but he also held that their Marine Corps was as tough as America's own: 'Their Marines were well equipped and would fight to the bitter end. The Japanese Army broke under pressure, but not their Marines – when we met head on it became like running into a brick wall, neither side gave an inch.'[42]

The Japanese Marines were indeed tough troops. The Marines who Robert Leckie fought with in the final year of the war took on the Japanese when they were probably at their most determined. Even when it was obvious that a unit was broken, its soldiers would still not surrender, and the Americans exterminated them. Robert Leckie's Marine comrades found that 'they all resisted, and they were all destroyed, bayoneted for the most part …'.[43] Such men placed throughout the defensive network of the Japanese on the Home Islands would have heightened the resolve of those who were inexperienced.

Even by the final few months of the war, the shattered Japanese armies possessed soldiers who were not surrendering quietly, even when it was apparent to the lowliest infantryman the cause was lost.

The later-author and then British soldier George MacDonald Fraser found this out when he was attacked by a soldier 'who came howling out of a thicket near the Sittang, full of spite and fury, in that first week of August. He was half-starved and near-naked, and his only weapon was a bamboo stake, but he was in no mood to surrender'.[44]

The incoming forces taking Japanese positions in World War II quickly adopted to new tactics in the face of this level of resistance. Japanese in a hospital were given no chance to surrender, because some held grenades under their blankets.[45] On Tinian Island, where it was thought that there were Japanese soldiers in caves, they were, in some areas, targeted with loudspeaker broadcasts urging them to surrender. Individual caves were given a call from outside by Marines, and if there was no response, the cave was sealed.[46]

The Japanese defenders would not have existed in organised conditions: eating in mess halls; sleeping in barracks, or even receiving organised support. Instead, they would have existed in haphazard conditions: sleeping at their posts and eating whatever they could. The endurance of the Japanese people would have been a major factor in their support – they were perhaps the most determined people on Earth in World War II. In New Guinea, in January 1943, despite being in hopeless positions, Japanese soldiers 'actually charged forward to a defiant, faster finish'.[47] Australian forces were shocked by their resolve, even finding partially consumed human bodies as early as October 1942.[48] The practice was caused by desperate men at the end of an ineffective supply system: combat soldiers in some circumstances were existing on less than 500 calories a day.

They would resort to a universally shunned practice if that meant survival so they could fight on. Paul Ham notes several incidents of the Japanese eating Australian flesh in Kokoda and that it was widespread.[49] Ulrich Strauss, who studied the Japanese concept of surrender, concludes that cannibalism was caused by extreme conditions in the field.[50] An Australian soldier answering a questionnaire under the initials of 'HMW' said he saw 'two cases of cannibalism by the Japanese in the area, one involving the body of a Jap, and Australian bodies in the other case'.[51]

Australian naval officer Marsden Hordern said of his time in New Guinea that he had heard second-hand stories of the practice. He met an Australian soldier who told of one of his mates shot in a forward position; when the body was reached half an hour later it had been substantially stripped of flesh.[52] Hordern later tells of the trial of a Japanese lieutenant after the war who admitted to cannibalism and asked to be shot as a penalty. American soldier Peter Bezich, fighting in New Guinea, said he came across two instances of it, with the Japanese taking meat from their own.[53] But there could be confusion: two natives from the Rabaul area, who the Japanese had been using as carriers, admitted to Australia soldiers that a recent incident where a cannibalistically mutilated soldier had been found and had in fact been caused by themselves.[54]

The national willingness to die for the Emperor rather than be captured would have figured significantly in the defence of the Home Islands. Surrendering as a prisoner would have been out of the question, with everyone surrounded by others determined to fight. Allied officer Peter Young organised a five-pound reward for a 'prisoner-taking', such was the difficulty of taking one alive: when a Japanese soldier so-captured recovered consciousness, he struggled so much he swallowed his gag. Even wounded, the Japanese would have fought on. Young later walked across through positions where a fierce battle had raged and the Japanese had lost. He commented that 'I could hardly move a step without treading on a dead Jap', and that the dead had mostly taken two or three wounds each: 'they had to be very thoroughly slain'.[55]

American soldier Louis Maravelas said of the Japanese he fought:

> ... they were simply stupid. They sacrificed their own men needlessly, for no purpose at all. During a battle along the Matanikau, three or four were straggling towards us as though they were going to surrender. There must have been a dozen of us with a bead on them. Sure enough, one bent over and there was a carbine or submachine gun slung on his back that a comrade tried to grab. We shot them down instantly .... They did this type of thing so many times. It got to the point where

we took no prisoners. It wasn't a written order, but a way to survive. No one should take a chance to take a guy prisoner who might kill him.[56]

The general Japanese feelings on surrender were further illustrated by the actions of the soldiers defending an atoll 75 miles south east of Tarawa. Their commander, addressing them with sword in one hand and pistol in another, accidentally shot himself in the head. And so, as Derrick Wright tells us, 'The distraught troops, unable to make any decisions without their commander, had dug their own graves and killed themselves ….'[57]

The author in front of a cave on the reverse slope of the initial Japanese defence ridge on Okinawa. (Photo by Kaylene Anderson)

At sea, the attitude was the same. The submarine *Wahoo* was 'mooned' by Japanese survivors in the water – they exposed their backsides to the surfaced submarine, insulting their victor, and refusing to be captured. The Commanding Officer of the USN submarine *Flasher* tried to entice aboard a dozen survivors of a small freighter which they had sunk – only two took up the offer, the rest refusing to move from the upturned keel of their vessel. The two who came aboard turned out to be captured Chinese, who the Japanese had been using as servants.[58] When the submarine USS *Tinosa* came across 17 Japanese military members 'in a variety of uniforms' in a lifeboat, they all refused to board the vessel, lying face down in the open boat, some eventually being taken by force for intelligence purposes, and the rest abandoned.[59]

No Japanese officer – commissioned by command of the Emperor – defending the Home Islands, would have surrendered. On Iwo Jima, the Japanese General Kuribayashi was sent a message, carried by two Japanese prisoners, advising that 'his position was now hopeless and he could surrender with honour'.[60] The note reached him, as had another previously, and Radio Tokyo by then was broadcasting that the island was fully penetrated by US Marines. Nevertheless, he refused to surrender and killed himself.

Wearing a parade uniform and carrying a sword, a Japanese officer in New Guinea, with his position overrun, challenged the advancing Australian troops. He 'went whoosh with his sword, and he carved all the bits of the side of the palm fronds', inviting the soldiers to take him on, one presumes, with their bayonets. He was given a count of ten to surrender and then shot.[61]

Lesser-ranked soldiers in the same tactical situation showed the same spirit as elsewhere: Lieutenant Doug McClean observed: 'They seemed to want to die and we were delighted to oblige them. They didn't give in, they didn't surrender and therefore there is no point in saying we showed them mercy.'[62] LM Opie thought 'they were ready to die; when we overran their positions, their personal papers had been laid on the edge of their weapon pits' so they could be identified when dead.[63]

Then again, there was certainly plenty of aggression shown towards prisoners. Towards the end of the war, Cam Bennett, leading a company of the Australian Army, noted that in the rare event of taking a prisoner it was difficult to get them taken to the rear alive. 'It was essential to send some of them back with a good reliable NCO or they would be shot by their guards while attempting to escape' (so the guards said).[64] Enough of the attackers of the Japanese mainland would have seen their friends killed or wounded, and therefore why would feelings be any calmer in late 1945 and beyond?

A Japanese assault was repulsed in late 1942 in New Guinea, by an Australian force that had been underestimated in numbers. The Japanese retreated, and the Australian followed. While a sizeable portion got away, a large number were run to earth near the village of Gorari. The Australian forces surrounded the area and – after some exchanges of fire and a few intermittent night incidents – the two sides settled down to an uneasy calm. At dawn, the Australians went in at the charge, surprising many Japanese having breakfast. All were killed, with the Japanese fighting hard, although overwhelmed. Five hundred and eighty bodies of the enemy were later counted.[65]

Flight deck of USS *Essex* in WWII, date unknown. Over 30 carriers were ready to strike Japan by August 1945. (US Navy)

Later, at Gona, Japanese troops whose positions were taken after artillery fire were shot down 'as they fled along the beach or swam wildly out to sea'.[66] Every Japanese defending there died – around 1000 of them.[67]

In summary, a land assault would have seen no quarter given from both sides. There seems little reason to doubt extremely high fatality rates would have resulted for the Japanese.

Allied troop capabilities and tactics

Maritime assault force

Any Allied attack force would have been almost in its entirety a maritime assault group. At its centre, it would have comprised aircraft carriers from the United States and from British Empire forces. This latter component probably would have centred around six carriers:

> The fighting core of the BPF was the 1st Aircraft carrier Squadron (1 ACS), commanded by Rear Admiral Sir Philip Vian, which included all six of the Illustrious class armoured carriers in 1945, although not all were operational at any one time. The fleet included King George V class battleships, light cruisers and destroyers in growing numbers, and it was arguably the most powerful British fleet ever deployed in the pre-nuclear era.[68]

But the majority of the fleet would have been from the United States. In May 1945, there were 26 fleet carriers available – an enormous organisation of massive firepower.[69] (The United States in the 21st century operates around 12, albeit much more powerful, carriers.) The aircraft carriers would have been the biggest then in operation; there was also a smaller version, sometimes known as a 'jeep' carrier, used for convoy escort purposes. Thirty-two large aircraft carriers would have mustered around 3000 aircraft. However, the carriers would not be enough: the taking of the Kyushu peninsula was essential for the establishment of land bases, which would allow the supply, operation and maintenance of thousands more aircraft, and the basing of ships, essential for taking the rest of the Home Islands.

To support the carriers at sea meant that the operation alongside them was a vast protective armada. This consisted firstly of 'big-gun' vessels, which were now becoming obsolete, as the carrier aircraft far outranged them because it was able to punch a bomb, rocket and gun attack against a land target such as the Home Islands at a distance of hundreds of miles from the ships, as opposed to scores of miles for the battleships' big artillery.

The big gun ships, which included battle cruisers – faster, less armoured, but still powerful, were primarily in universal naval use to engage in fleet actions such as World War I's Jutland. Japan by now was largely divested of such big ships: vessels such as the *Yamato*, with her 18-inch gun armament, the mightiest ever seen, were being negated in their role by aerial attack. In any case, the *Yamato*, along with her sister vessel *Musashi*, were now lost to the Japanese and used in suicidal efforts to keep the Allies at bay.

But the battleships were also capable of firing at aerial intruders with considerable firepower. The lessons of not being able to protect themselves were learnt earlier in the war with the loss of ships such as *Repulse*, *Prince of Wales*, the *Bismarck*, and scores of lesser warships insufficiently gunned to be able to efficiently shoot down their flying tormentors.

Smaller warships would have joined in the air defence screen, but were also equipped to hunt down any surface warships left of the Japanese Navy, and their submarines too. The capability of such submarines should not be forgotten or dismissed. Significantly although unknown to the war effort at large, the heavy cruiser USS *Indianapolis*, after a voyage carrying parts for one of the two A-weapons, had been sunk by the IJN submarine *I-58* on 30 July, which resulted in the loss of over 800 lives. Japanese submarines would have proved a dangerous if not large threat, due to most of them having been sunk[70] by this stage, and also due to the strength of the Allied anti-submarine force.

There would, however, be large losses of life in any such attacks. The IJN submarine *I-58* launched a torpedo attack on the *Indianapolis* on 30 July 1945. Japanese submarines were still a dangerous if not substantial threat, due to most of them having been sunk by this stage, and because of the strength of the Allied anti-submarine force.[71] On the day of the attack, there were no screening destroyers to guard the cruiser, and the *Indianapolis* was not following a 'zig-zag' course, as was often the practice for ships in threatened waters.

The ship sank quickly. Of 1196 men on board, approximately 300 went down with the ship. The remainder were left with no lifeboats and with little food or water. (Warships did not carry lifeboats as did commercial vessels, but relied on the ship's boats and fitted life rafts for survival.) The ship was not missed, and by the time the survivors were spotted by accident four days later, only 316 men were still alive.[72] Such submarine attacks during a Home Islands assault would be commensurately damaging.

The carriers operated with a huge logistical tail that carried not only vital aircraft fuel, although the flat-tops carried much themselves, but tonnes of food, aircraft and ship parts, machine shops, facilities for the injured and sick, intelligence staff, and so on. These ships also facilitated the constant movement of aircrew too pressured to continue – the wisdom of rotating such people had been recognised – and allowed the arrival of replacement aircrew and aircraft to be facilitated.

Artillery assault on the Home Islands

Any landings on the mainland would have been preceded by an enormous ship artillery attack. The artillery attack would have resembled Okinawa's, but would it have worked? Attacking that last great fortress of the Japanese:

> The Navy was brought in to help. At five-forty the next morning six battleships, six cruisers, and eight destroyers began bombarding the five-mile defence complex extending across the island.

> Twenty minutes later, 27 battalions of artillery – 324 pieces in all – sounded off, digging up front-line positions before lifting 500 yards to the rear. At six-thirty the artillery lowered, splattering the front lines for another ten minutes.

It was the greatest single concentration of artillery in Pacific warfare – 19,000 shells .... Incredibly, the unprecedented bombardment left the Japanese relatively intact, and though all three units attacked aggressively, all three were thrown back.[73]

What the defenders would have received first. The USS Pennsylvania blasts shore defenses preparatory to the invasion of Guam July 20, 1944. (US Navy Photo, originally published in a double page spread)

At this point, 27,226 rounds of five-inch or larger calibre shells had carpeted Okinawa. The effect appeared devastating, but the main line of defence was still almost intact, although initial judgment thought the assault effective.[74] Even the more experienced news reporters were initially fooled. '"We were on Okinawa an hour and a half after H-hour, without being shot at, and hadn't even gotten our feet wet," reported the GIs' favourite correspondent, Ernie Pyle. Okinawa was a piece of cake.' [75] Ironically, Pyle later died, shot by a sniper, on the island. The campaign to take the island took weeks, and saw the loss of thousands of Allied lives. The Japanese would have fought just as fiercely for the mainland.

Sooner or later, though, any initial naval bombardment against the Home Islands would have had to lift, to allow the Higgins boats, Buffaloes, and other amphibious vessels to take soldiers ashore. The amount of ordnance expended can also relate to the strategic need, and to the composition of one's own forces. Once ashore, the essence would have been one of speed. The assault on Europe from 1944, by the Allies, was marked by knowledge that Germany could not escape the trap they were in, and therefore materiel was the key to the game, not expending infantry lives where one could avoid it. This cautious approach is not always the best: General Patton's speed in attack is often more preferable to General Hodges' caution.

But the knowledge was there that the Allies were, as Professor Sir Michael Howard – both military historian and combat veteran – later put it, they were 'fighting the best professionals in the business'. General Slim was using the same characteristics in assault in late 1943. Offensive operations were:

> ... carefully staged, ably led, and as I was always careful to ensure, in greatly preponderating strength. We attacked a Japanese *company* [author emphasis] with brigades fully supported by artillery and aircraft, *platoon* posts by battalions.[76]

Note here the massive overkill, which is what would have also faced Japanese positions in the mainland. A company is measured in the low hundreds of men – a brigade in the thousands; a platoon is scores of men; a battalion in hundreds. Note too that Slim was hitting the enemy not merely with his infantry, which would have gone in as secondary forces, but primarily with his artillery and aircraft, which would not have sought to 'soften up' the enemy but to totally destroy them, so that the valuable personnel of the infantry would merely have had to walk in and take the ground.

Slim goes on to relate how a visiting staff officer of high rank once asked whether this tactic was like using a steam hammer to crack a nut. Slim's reply was that he did not care if there was nothing left of the enemy position when he had finished with it.

The nature of much of the weaponry used does not allow too much discrimination in targeting. As one World War II soldier put it: 'When you're an artillery man and you help to fire shells – at that time I guess at nine or ten miles away – you're not really conscious of what destruction you're creating.' Another thought given that suggested that warfare was perhaps more civilised in older times when the firepower wasn't available to kill so indiscriminately: 'Many soldiers, particularly artillerymen and fliers, had to kill innocent women and children – non-combatants. Seems to me in a moral sense there's been a great deterioration in modern war.'[77]

The overkill characteristic was being adopted all through the Allied armies of the latter stages of World War II. The German Army, still dangerous and possessed of immense tactical skill, fought hard for every inch of ground, and was superb in counter-attack. So the Allies used their superior artillery and airpower before committing their infantry. Sir Michael Howard, both a military historian and a veteran of combat against the Wehrmacht, later said: 'We blasted our way into Europe with a minimum of finesse and a maximum of high explosive.'[78]

Canadian soldiers meeting up with Americans in 1945 discussed their approaches towards advancing. One of the Canadians commented that the Americans 'admitted their policy was to blast the objective with airplanes and artillery, and if even so much as a single Spandau replied, to blast it again, before going in'.[79]

Any conventional attack against Japan would have had to look like that, particularly as by now the non-use of the atomic weapons would have been a known factor in the Allied forces. President Truman's enemies would have been criticising him for not using them, and would have been saying: 'Look, this is your fault – US lives are being lost simply because you would not use these new bombs because they are too brutal.' The possibility of nuclear weapons being used in a conventional assault also seems to have been little considered by analysts of the situation. The United States would have possessed several by the time of the Home Islands invasion. Using one or more against identified strongholds would have been demanded, both politically and militarily. Both Barton Bernstein and Marc Gallicchio have written on this. The tactical use of weapons was thought to be feasible as little was known of the radioactivity problem. One scenario called for the use of nine in the Kyushu area; three of them would have been dropped in the path of the three army corps envisaged for initial landings.[80]

There does not seem to exist a comprehensive single military assessment of whether Japan could indeed be conventionally assaulted with success, apart from two studies that are post-conflict, the United States Strategic Bombing Survey, and a study by RF Ennis for the Strategic Policy Section.[81] [82] Gar Alperovitz concluded: 'Not a shred of serious deliberative work concerning options and decisions appears in any Joint Chiefs record.'[83] In other words, the Allies would simply have gone ahead and done it: there was no concept now – with impetus, bitterness, realism, and logic triumphing – of the war being stopped without forcing Japanese surrender.

Infantry force composition

The composition of the initial landing force is confused, a mish-mash of documentation left over after the war, neither finalised or complete – understandable in that the war stopped abruptly. According to James Jones, 13 divisions were scheduled to land in the mainland by November 1945, and ultimately 16 divisions were scheduled for Honshu in March 1946.[84] Skates cites '582,560 troops', almost three times as many. [85] A starting date for what constituted an invasion would not have been as precise as D-Day. Fussell points out that the pre-invasion artillery bombardments had already started by July 1945:

> And the invasion was going to take place: there's no question about that. It was not theoretical or merely rumoured in order to scare the Japanese. By 10 July 1945, the pre-landing naval and aerial bombardment of the coast had begun, and the battleships *Iowa, Missouri, Wisconsin*, and *King George V* were steaming up and down the coast, softening it up with their sixteen-inch shells.[86]

Jones observed that the forthcoming invasion of Kyushu 'was well into its collecting and stockpiling stages before the war ended'.[87] Saipan was designated a main ammunition and supply base for the invasion; visitors today can still see some of the assembled materials.[88] 'The assault troops were chosen and already in training,' Jones reminds his readers, and he illuminates by the light of experience what this meant:

What it must have been like to some old-timer buck sergeant or staff sergeant who had been through Guadalcanal or Bougainville or the Philippines, to stand on some beach and watch this huge war machine beginning to stir and move all around him and know that he very likely had survived this far only to fall dead on the dirt of Japan's Home Islands, hardly bears thinking about. [89]

Infantry force tactics

Marine sergeant William Manchester reflected on the US forces' growing capabilities in amphibious assault as the war progressed. But this was accompanied by a better understanding by the Japanese of how to fight against the waterborne enemy.

Manchester participated in early landings, and eventually was present at Guam in mid-1944. At the end of the attack and the defeat of the Japanese: 'Tokyo was beginning to learn the lesson of Biak. Though the Nipponese were losing the war, they vowed to kill as many of the foe as possible before falling themselves. Thus the war's greatest slaughters lay in the future.'[90] Quoting Japanese orders, Manchester explains the US forces from Iwo Jima onwards would be allowed 'to land in full' and 'lured into a position where they cannot receive cover and support from naval and aerial bombardment'.[91]

These tactics were as used by the German army in retreat in 1944–45. Gene Garrison was an infantry soldier in that campaign: 'The Germans usually allowed the lead element to pass, then sniped at the trucks loaded with troops. Any snipers discovered by the GIs weren't given a chance to surrender.'[92] On another occasion he describes how 'a 15-year-old kid' allowed two jeeps and a half-track to go by his concealed position before firing a Panzerfaust at a US tank-destroyer. The youth was shot instinctively by the gunner in the next vehicle.[93]

Williams Manchester's thinking on the forthcoming invasion is well worth repeating in detail:

Iwo was declared secure on March 16 and the operation officially completed ten days later, but heavy ground fighting continued, with the Marines taking another 3885 casualties before GIs arrived to garrison the island. Even then, the soldiers had to spend another two months mopping up. It was depressing; the closer we came to Japan, the more tenacious the defenders were. No one wanted to talk about, or even think about, what would happen when we invaded their Home Islands. [94]

They meant to make the conquest of Iwo so costly that the Americans would recoil from the thought of invading their homeland. They knew the island could only be taken by infantrymen, the U.S. warships' 21,926 shells and the six weeks of B-24 bombing didn't touch them; it merely rearranged the volcanic ash overhead and gave the invaders dangerous illusions of easy pickings. [95]

On Peleliu, the Japanese had changed tactics. Manchester explains:

Everyone was waiting for the banzai charge, which had ended other battles. Slowly they grasped the enemy's new tactics. A Marine company would scale a bluff unmolested; then the Japanese would open up on three sides with infantry fire, mortars, and antitank guns, killing the Americans or throwing them to their death on the floor of the gorge below. [96]

Skates, however, sees the tactical engagement differently. He argues the Japanese would not have allowed a beachhead to be established, although he sees the argument of pulling the Allied enemy in close enough to neutralise effective artillery and aircraft support.[97]

However, given the fact that the Allies were determined and well resourced, they would have eventually been able to make lodgments in strength. What would the ensuing fighting have looked like?

The Kyushu 'Coronet' invasion would have comprised a force of 750,000 men. After four months, the 'Olympic' invasion, timed for March 1946, would utilise a force of 1,800,000 men from America and the British Commonwealth to assault the Tokyo area.[98] The Allied landings would not have seen a battalion taking on a regularly entrenched force, but rather Japanese people everywhere that could be concealed, attacking with all sort of weapons, big and small. A 'front line' would have been impossible to define or understand. In some places, fierce fighting would have taken place; however, in other places, there would have been very little fighting. The previous battles on the Pacific Islands are an example.

On Peleliu Island, EB Sledge's unit of Marines fired at Japanese who were walking and running away from the American position. Some of them were swimming in the sea, trying to escape further along the beaches. Urged on by their NCOs, the Marines fired until they had killed all of the Japanese.[99] When a Japanese bunker was cleared, several enemy soldiers raced out and were ruthlessly shot down, Sledge commented: 'We felt not pity for them but exulted over their fate. We had been shot at and shelled too much and had lost too many friends to have compassion for the enemy when we had him cornered.'[100]

This was similar practice to what had been seen in Europe. In the heat of battle after D-Day, a fight with grenades and machine guns and rifles between some Americans and Germans saw three German infantry start to run: they were all shot down, and one who was wounded and fell, calling 'Help! Help', was machine-gunned.[101] No Japanese combatant would have been spared. Civilians now becoming quasi-military would have been shot in their hundreds of thousands.

The Japanese suicide tactics would have meant 'reconnaissance by fire' or instant pulverising of whatever looked like an enemy position: trees, cave sites, even roads, for human mines would be used, as experienced by General Slim's forces in South-East Asia:

A Japanese soldier with a 100-kilo aircraft bomb between his knees, holding a large stone poised above the fuse would crouch in a foxhole. When the attacking tank passed over the almost invisible hole, he would drop the stone then bomb, man, and, it was hoped, [the] tank would all go up together. The device was not very effective and accounted for more Japanese than tanks.[102]

The interior's steep valleys would have seen any 1945 bridges destroyed in the path of the Allies (Author photo)

It is hardly likely that the Allied troops would have been able to disengage from killing Japanese civilians as combatants, or potential combatants, if a conventional assault had gone ahead. There were plenty of other similar examples in World War II.

Once civilians as a group take up arms, the enemy routinely assumes all are possible combatants, and they are treated as any other army. This, of course, means that movement – any movement – draws fire. German army soldier Henry Metelmann's Panzer squadron was attacked by partisans as they entered a Russian village, and a tanker was badly injured. So, 'from then on they had shot at everything that moved'.[103] On 1 August 1944, the Polish Resistance launched its effort to dislodge its German occupier. Two thousand five hundred of its fighters died on that day; 35,000 civilians in the first week. Max Hastings tells us of the savagery of the fighting: 'wounded were machine-gunned. Prisoners were hurled from the windows of apartment buildings. Polish women and children were used as human shields for the advance of German troops'.[104] The struggle was eventually lost by the defenders with immense cost.

Where there was a possibility of fire being taken from what are purportedly civilian infrastructure, the oncoming commanders behaved with instinctive reactions, as they always did when under assault by the enemy. Response in as massive a form as could be arranged was poured onto the target. The surviving population was usually well aware that they had better not be identified as combatants, or sheltering combatants, in any way.

There may have been some 'Rules of Engagement' devised for the incoming Allied forces in the attack on the Home Islands. However, it is doubtful they would have been followed. In Europe, they were tried with varying results. Accidents took place because attacking fire was poured into possible shelters for the enemy. Henry Metelmann's crew in his Panzer did just that by advancing towards a Russian village, and then they found they had killed a 12-year-old girl who had been out collecting apples.[105]

On another occasion, a group of teenage girls came running out of buildings ahead of Metalmann's advancing soldiers. The sudden movement attracted machine-gunfire – 'had they walked, none of us would have taken the slightest notice' commented the young German soldier – and two were killed.[106] What would have happened to the Japanese children not old enough to fight does not bear thinking about. But their fate would have been terrible – with their carers gone they would have been reduced to struggling for survival in the ruins. And any movement would have drawn fire.

There may have been some attempts by the Japanese populace to surrender. It would likely be found, as in Europe, that these were doomed to fail. Guy Sajer's section of the German army in the Ukraine found that partisans were infiltrating crowds of refugees. 'At a given moment, they would shoot some of our men in the back, sowing general confusion. These manoeuvres were supposed to crack our self-control, and provoke us to acts of reprisal, which would then turn the refugees against us.'[107]

The Allies would have taken months to prepare their troops to make a conventional assault. This in itself would have caused Allied casualties. Not all would have been combat-hardened veterans. Live-fire exercises would have resulted in deaths. Sometimes this would have involved scores of fatalities. In Exercise Tiger, one of a series of large-scale rehearsals for the D-Day Normandy invasion, at Slapton Sands in Britain's Devon, 946 American servicemen died.[108] Aircraft operations in World War II saw more aviators die from training, test and ferry flights, than combat. The USAAF saw 14,903 personnel killed during the war to aircraft mishap, and during 1943, for every plane lost to combat, six were lost in accidents.[109]

The possible use of the USSR is discussed in a later chapter, but here we must presume their troops would have been incorporated into an invasion. No common command network would have been available so that Russian troops could be included in the tactical network of the amphibious assaults. Drawing on D-Day and Operation Zipper experience, the Allies would have assigned separate sectors to the Russians so they were to be involved only in their sectors. Major difficulties would have been encountered though in providing ship artillery support to troops when and after they landed.

Maintaining the 'edge' on the infantry forces, held at sea, would have proved extremely difficult, if not impossible. Realising that the preparation would take months, the Allies would have formed forward bases in the South Korean peninsula to take advantage of practising in terrain resembling that of Kyushu's.[110]

The war would have continued in Japanese-held areas around South-East Asia and China. There the Allies would have probably tried switching to containment and holding operations, taking no further Japanese territory in an effort to minimise casualties. This practice, by the stage of the war that was concentrating on pushing towards the Home Islands, was fairly standard. For example, on the island of New Britain, the 5th Australian Division was containing 70,000 Japanese troops concentrated around Rabaul, 'content to patrol … and let the large Japanese garrison wither on the vine'.[111]

However, Japanese forces would have likely taken non-action as a sign of weakness and gained an ascendency in morale. They would have begun to conduct forays from their held territories in an effort to gain inflict casualties. Conversely, Allied forces' morale would decline. To maintain some surprise elements, the Allied commanders would not have signalled their timetable or strategy. Troop commanders would have been unable to tell their forces when and how they would be directly attacking Japan, but nor would forces be told that they would be returning to their home countries. Discontented and resultant poor behaviour would have risen.

Sickness would have taken a massive toll of Allied military personnel. For example, from May to August 1945, the Australians, making slow progress in Wewak, lost 1500 in battle during that time, but had casualties from sickness of over 16,000. [112]

One aspect often forgotten is the battle rhythm of the Pacific War already achieved. The war had reached a pace whereby operations were being carried out on an enormous scale. They now could not be stopped. We move further on to examine that in a further chapter, but first we will take the precaution of examining whether Japan had any alternatives in its armoury. Were there any 'wonder weapons' to save them – the equivalent or perhaps even more deadly than Hitler's V2 rockets?

Conclusion

The conventional assault on the Home Islands would have been long and bloody. The advantage would have lain heavily with the defenders, given the terrain. The attacking forces would have seen their armour and artillery deprived of many of the advantages they would have had in Europe. Airpower, although overwhelming, would have also found the terrain difficult to attack. The bravery and tenacity of the Japanese would have been high. Due to this and the Allies' disadvantages, the attackers would have used high explosives in enormous amounts rather than attack by infantry. The death toll among the Japanese would have been enormous.

CHAPTER TEN

ALTERNATIVE DEFENCES – WEREWOLF, CHEMICAL AND BIOLOGICAL WARFARE OPERATIONS

Overview: In this chapter, we discuss what a continued land struggle would have looked like. What of 'stay-behind' operations such as werewolf and guerilla operations? Would and could Japan have deployed chemical and biological warfare operations? Did Japan's nuclear bomb efforts constitute a credible threat to the Allies?

Werewolf operations

The werewolf, or 'stay behind', operations envisaged in Nazi Germany as the Allies advanced following D-Day were not planned with such detail in Japan. For one, the nation state itself had not seen its home territory entered, as had Germany, with the armed forces of three countries – Britain, United States and USSR – making inroads firstly across the country's borders and then racing towards Berlin.

Inducting thousands of personnel forcibly into organisations such as the Hitler Youth, the Germans, chiefly under Nazi architect Albert Speer, dominated by Hitler, planned a 'scorched earth' policy. This was to be embarked upon to leave the German nation as a vast smoking wasteland where nothing of value was envisaged left standing to give comfort to the Allied invader.

So fierce was the policy that Speer protested, envisaging nothing left which would see the German people surviving the war. Hitler's attitude was that he cared nothing for the people, as they had failed to live up to his dream and thereby denied themselves success. Secretly, Speer began to deny his boss's orders.[1]

With a conventional invasion of the Home Islands beginning in late 1945, however, it is highly likely that Japanese commanders would have devised guerilla operations to combat the Allied forces. They would have realised that they would be operating on a weakened defensive against superior logistics. The quotation 'amateurs talk tactics, professionals study logistics', often attributed to General Bradley, has been well understood by professional military people for millennia. The Japanese would have realised they would have been overwhelmed by the enormous war machine that the Allies would have brought to their shores. The Japanese would have been low on food, and their ability to manufacture the essentials of war was being reduced by the day. A steady aerial bombing campaign would have lowered their ability to make ammunition, small arms, heavier anti-tank and anti-air weapons, and even manufacture clothing for the oncoming Japanese winter.

An ideal Japanese World War II guerilla strategy would have been to operate from caves. (See the previous description of those prepared in the Kyushu peninsula.) Seventy-five percent of Japan is not level ground, and the mountains and hills offer enormous facility to any guerrilla forces. Incoming armour would have found the terrain difficult, and artillery would have been difficult to deploy. One problem for the Allies would have been that although they could strike with airpower and artillery where guerillas could be identified, they could not simply attack all possible terrain; their resources would not have allowed that, and besides, blasting caves did not necessarily mean killing those deep inside.

Chemical warfare

It has been alleged that Japan employed poison gas bombs in the Wusung-Shanghai campaign at the beginning of the Second Sino-Japanese war in August 1937.[2] The main research for chemical weapons development was carried out by a unit called the Kwantung Army Technical Testing Department (later referred to as Manchuria Unit 516).[3] Together with the more notorious biological warfare units described below, the staffing for these research facilities was considerable: by 1939, some 10,045 personnel were employed.[4]

There has been work carried out on disposal of Japanese World War II chemical weapons in the years since the war. One report names the stockpiles as enormous: 'Chinese scholars say there are at least two million pieces, whereas Japan says the number should be about 700,000.'[5] Various news items are not specific about the nature of the weapons, apart from mustard gas, which reportedly killed at least one man in recent times, although unspecified fatalities from other weapons have been reported.

Chemical warfare was not used extensively in World War II, partly as it had been found ineffective in World War I. Containing and deploying the chemicals had been difficult and dangerous. The wind was usually a necessary factor, to blow the chemicals towards the enemy. If the wind changed, however, it could impact your own troops. In general, it had not been found worth the effort.[6] But as a last ditch weapon it offered possibilities. There is every reason to suppose Japan would have used whatever stockpiles it had. It would have caused a considerable check to the Allies; their military did not routinely carry and prepare for chemical warfare, as had been the case in the previous world war.

Biological warfare

Frank details biological warfare experiments carried out from 1932, largely under the command of military doctor Shiro Ishii, who headed the by-now infamous Unit 731, which had its main research station near Harbin. Although thousands died in gruesome circumstances in research conducted to develop biological agents, the Japanese capabilities attained by 1945 were capable enough to utilise in defence. Frank names – citing the leading authority on the subject, Sheldon H Harris – various usages of biological agents, one of which was responsible for the deaths of probably 30,000 Soviet soldiers due to plague-infested mice.[7]

Other writers[8] assert that bubonic plague was spread by aircraft at Changte, Hunan in November 1941, and five other occasions, at least three of them by aircraft distribution. Another article lists attacks from 1940–42 carried out in cities along the Chang River.[9] It goes into detail about an assault on the city of Ningbo on 27 October 1940, using what was described as a 'heavy bomber' to distribute plague fleas.

A further assault was described as having taken place in 'the fall of 1941. One of the targets was the city of Changde, about 1000 kilometres east of Shanghai in the Chinese interior'. This killed less than ten people.

A disaster using cholera bacteria is also portrayed, caused by Japanese troops overrunning an area where biological warfare had been used against Chinese troops:

> ... the attacks resulted in more than 10,000 casualties. It has also been reported that some victims contracted dysentery and the plague. More than 1700 soldiers died, mostly from cholera. This would have been considered a great success for the Ishii group, but for the fact that all of the victims were Japanese soldiers. [10]

The fatality number was thought to be conservative, having been reduced by the Japanese to minimise the bad news. But the incident bought to an end such use of bio-weapons, in such a fashion, and the effort turned instead into trying to deliver them by artillery shell. This proved inconclusive, and such was the state of the program when the war ended.

There was some thought among US authorities about the possibility of bio-weapons being received by the balloon attack on the west America coast between September 1944 and the end of the war. One of these balloons, which carried explosives, killed a pregnant women and six children when one, which had impacted the ground, exploded. By the end of the program, no biological or chemical weapons had been delivered.[11]

Toland notes that the Okinawa land commander, Lieutenant General Mitsuru Ushijima, trained a small special force of 750 'enthusiastic high school students', who were 'formed into special Blood and Iron for the Emperor duty units and trained to infiltrate enemy lines and carry out guerilla warfare'.[12]

Members of an American Engineer Aviation Battalion remove parts from a Japanese cyclotron in the Nishina Laboratory, Tokyo, 4 Dec 1945. (AP Photo Julian C Wilson)

A Japanese A-bomb?

Japan was pursuing the development of atomic weapons in World War II. The sources for this information are difficult to obtain, and may be exaggerated. However, a good summative account of their projects may be found in *Japan's Secret War: Japan's race against time to build its own atomic bomb*, by Robert K Wilcox.

Published in 1985, and then reissued with updates in 1995, Wilcox's book is well researched. It is journalistic in style, which doesn't detract from its value, but nevertheless it is written to provoke interest and even controversy. It starts with its most startling claim: that Japan exploded – in 1945, on the north Korean mainland, which it then controlled – its own atomic weapon.

Wilcox first learnt, he says, of the successful test from an article, published in the summer of 1946, written by a correspondent for *Life* magazine. The journalist learnt of the information from a Japanese officer who had provided security for the project. The test device, sent off on a 'robot launch' on 10 August, had produced a 'fireball' of around 1000 yards after it was triggered, destroying test watercraft around it.[13] But the technology had arrived too late, and the Russian invasion down the peninsula overran the production site, with many scientists captured, and the equipment was either destroyed or taken by the USSR. Japan surrendered five days later.

The book takes us then exhaustively through the Japanese invention of the atomic technology, which had been separately developed by both the Army and the Navy before they joined forces on the project. The Navy had wanted to use it for aircraft 'fission' kamikaze weapons – Japan, like America, did not operate a separate air force in World War II – and the Army had another nuclear weapons project.

Nuclear engineer Yoichi Yamamoto commented decades after the war that if the atomic bombs had not been dropped 'millions more [from both sides] would have died. Japan was preparing to defend the homeland at all costs .... As terrible as they were, the American bombs averted an even worse bloodbath'.[14] He has 'vigorously defended the American dropping of the bomb. When they are at war, countries do what they must'.[15] (There also seems to have been a book published by Yamamoto, entitled *The Truth Regarding the Japanese-made Atomic Bomb*, but it was possibly only a small-print run edition in 1976.[16])

The Allies had made sure Germany's moves towards a nuclear weapon, which they were growing to fear as their own expertise also increased, was lessened in capability by armed attacks. In Norway, heavy water facilities, which would provide moderating material for any nuclear reaction, were attacked with bombing and sabotage. The Office of Strategic Services, the forerunner of the CIA, formed a group known as 'Alsos', to track and if necessary destroy any components of a nuclear program. Ironically, it was under the command of General Leslie Groves, who would head up the Manhattan Project, whose name translated as 'alsos' in Greek.[17]

By 1945, Japan had started to develop multiple strategies for uranium enrichment. A thermal diffusion device at a research institute known as RIKEN, near Tokyo, was destroyed by Allied bombings. Blueprints for turbine-based centrifuges, including one scheduled for completion in August 1945, were found post-war at Kyoto University. The major obstacle to enrichment, however, was uranium procurement. Missions were sent to various parts of Asia, even to Mongolia and Burma, without finding useful uranium ore. On this front, there was some co-operation between the Axis powers: in 1945, as Germany was falling to the Allies, a U-boat loaded with uranium was dispatched to Japan. Allied naval forces captured the submarine before it arrived, but the amount of uranium being transported was not enough to make a bomb.[18]

Wilcox notes that the OSS had a 'report about "stories" of an atomic discharge to be used against [Allied] aircraft.' Then:

> ... a few months later Alsos mission headquarters ran into a report about a scientist standing before the Japanese House of Peers and announcing that 'he is succeeding in his research for a thing so powerful that it would require very little potential energy to destroy an enemy fleet within a few moments. The reference was clearly an atomic bomb, according to a sheet I found at the National Archives' Navy and old Army Branch. Alsos, which, of course, was created to determine what progress the Germans had made on a bomb, had headed it 'quite a coincidence'.[19]

Their nuclear weapon was detonated following years of research in which Japan pursued, on a much smaller scale, the atomic experiments then being conducted in the United States, and to a lesser extent, in other Allied countries, and in Germany, Japan's Axis ally. Ironically, between 1901 and 1932, a third of Nobel Prizes had gone to German scientists, of whom a quarter were Jewish, and nearly all of these were forced to leave the country because of the anti-Jewish actions of Nazi Germany. If these escapes had not been made, the war's outcome may well have been Germany acquiring a nuclear weapon before any other country.

As it was, German scientists over-estimated the amount of enriched U-235 needed to produce a bomb, requiring at least a ton rather than the 56 kilograms the United States used, and they misunderstood the role of the moderating material.[20] They also were spending vast amounts of resources pursuing other 'wonder weapons', which would turn the tide of the war for them, such as the V2 rockets and jet aircraft.

Historian Mark Walker asserts they did not see the possibilities of nuclear experiments as leading to overwhelmingly capable devices: 'the Germans did not believe that nuclear weapons could influence the outcome of the war, or that such weapons could be realised in the near future ...'.[21]

Returning to Japan, as its Home Islands were relentlessly attacked, the Japanese moved their experiments, which by then they were sure would produce an effective weapon, away from the targeted areas. Physicist Yoshio Nishina, for example, was conducting atomic bomb experiments at a Tokyo laboratory.[22] New areas were set up in caves on the north Korean peninsula, near the location of Konan – their name for Hungnam.

In 1949, researcher Chitoshi Yanaga admitted that when news about Hiroshima leaked through to them 'Japanese scientists knew immediately that it was the atomic bomb, for they too had been working on for years'. In the two weeks between Japan's surrender and the arrival of US occupation forces, much of the evidence of this work was deliberately destroyed.[23]

One clear piece of evidence that suggests no atomic test took place though is that many, many people would have been required to a) move the nuclear weapon facility to Korea, and b) set up the test. In the intervening years, none of these people have come forward to say they took part in the experiment. The conclusion to be drawn between further nuclear weapon tests in the 1950s and beyond, and what these workers would have known about, is irrefutable. The absence of such people coming forward must be a significant factor in dismissing the claim that the Japanese work had reached to such a level.

But then again, there is a process known as 'reverse-engineering', whereby you have seen someone do something scientifically possible, so therefore you know it can be done; therefore you just have to figure out how. It cuts experimental time down by a big factor. So, if the Japanese had some knowledge of the Manhattan Project they could have made considerable progress in a short time. And the first attack at Hiroshima would have given the Japanese nuclear scientists a tremendous amount of knowledge in a short time. With some irony, if the Japanese had not surrendered they may have been able to assemble their own bomb and eventually use it as part of the Home Islands defence.

Indeed, according to some, there is evidence of this. Nuclear physicist Dr Asada commented:

> I was requested to report my observations [on Hiroshima] to the Naval Technological Institute .... The audience were all admirals. I reported to them that it was an atomic bomb and that there was no means of coping with this weapon. The conclusion made at that time by the naval authorities was indeed horrible. It was to isolate all the Japanese physicists in the caves at Nagano prefecture and to have them produce a bomb .... The Navy had no intention to surrender.[24]

For example, they could have surmised from it being delivered by vertical attack that it was in a bomb inside a known bomber. Therefore it could not be bigger than the bomb bay of a B-29, the biggest around. So they may have concluded that the trigger device was possibly inside the bomb. In fact, the 'gun' bomb in simple terms was that – basically two pieces of U-235 slammed together. As Hiroshima exploded at height, and this was known by them, the trigger could have been a 'gun type' – and so they would try to duplicate that.

In another example, weight is a big problem with A weapons, as the materials they use are very dense. *Enola Gay* only just made it off the runway by some accounts, although possibly these are exaggerated. If the Japanese surmised a B-29 was necessary, they probably would surmise conclusions about the weight. Therefore you need 'X' quantity of uranium to make it and not a much bigger amount, which is what they had been working with.

They may have therefore concluded with certainty that they didn't have to just have uranium. They also needed to change its atomic weight from the original to U-235. But they may have concluded they didn't have enough centrifuges.

However, if: a) they had enough electricity, which apparently they did on the Korean peninsula; b) they had a lot of uranium; c) they had enriched some in the centrifuges; then they would have made an effort. They may have made a small lab 'fizz bomb' - a gram of uranium banged into another. The explosion could have destroyed a laboratory and killed some technicians; ergo: use more next time and move to a safe distance. This to an extent is what happened with the Trinity test bomb the Americans made.

Japan probably didn't realise how much material it needed, as Jake Adelstein suggests:

> When the nation surrendered, the occupying US forces discovered just five cyclotrons, devices that speed up atoms in order to separate isotopes that can then be used for a bomb. US atomic facilities in New Mexico, by comparison, contained hundreds of separators operating day and night to produce just four bombs.[25]

If the Japanese had succeeded in making a bomb, then how would they have delivered it? They would have known that a heavy bomb needed a B-29, but they didn't have such aircraft. So they would have still had a problem in how to deliver such a weapon to the target. Little Boy was about 5000 kg and three metres in length. The Japanese would not have been as efficient in their device. Theirs would at least have been about the size of a medium truck, and would have weighed at least 15,000kg.

So it's not the A-bomb, it's how to 'weaponise it', to use the modern word. Lacking a modern delivery system, one alternative could have been to use the weapon rather like a mine: conceal it and detonate it when the Allied invaders moved over it.

Of interest to the theme of this book – that the Japanese were fortunate to have been attacked with the A-weapons rather than conventionally invaded – is the scenario that if the attacks had not been made, then the Japanese nuclear scientists would indeed have quickly moved to accelerate their work. Utilising the reverse engineering approach, they may well have been able to build nuclear bombs and use them in the defence of the Home Islands. It would have been the ultimate irony if this had happened.

Conclusion

The Japanese likely possessed little in the way of effective battlefield weapons other than what they had already deployed. Ironically though, a conventional invasion would have meant they would have been more likely, rather than less likely, to be used.

CHAPTER ELEVEN
THE IMPERATIVES OF 'BATTLE RHYTHM'

Overview: In this chapter, we look at whether the A-bomb effort was a possibility, not a certainty. Even the successful test gave no guarantee that a bomb could be dropped from an aircraft. The war was a huge machine, moving along inexorably towards an invasion of Japan. It could not stop and wait for anything. A comparison with D-Day and a small monetary analysis are also included.

Many veterans of the Pacific post-war would have wondered why they had to suffer through an Okinawa when the successful test at Alamogordo New Mexico, on 16 July came just a few days after the island was declared secure. Surely the carnage on Okinawa could have been delayed until late summer to let such envisioned weapons convince the Japanese of the futility of prolonging the war.[1]

The continuation of the war, even in a state of maintaining a holding pattern while waiting for the Japanese to come to a realisation of their position, would have meant the maintenance, on station, of tens of thousands of aircraft and thousands of vessels big and small. One of the overlooked factors of keeping such a force active in the Pacific would have been the steady deaths of many personnel by accident.

In fact, this is an overlooked factor of this military campaign: more deaths were encountered by *accident* than from *combat*. To look at United States Army Air Force losses is instructive. For every one plane lost to enemy action, six more were lost to misadventure.[2] These accidents were inevitable, given the intensity of operations and the equipment of the time. Aircraft of the 1940s were simply not as safe as those of the time this book was written more than 70 years later. They did not have Global Positioning System navigation, for example, and getting lost was always a possibility. Bomber navigators worked their position through dead reckoning – star plotting through astrodomes when flying at night, and some crude electronics. Mechanical and electronic systems did not have triple redundancies as they do today. Crew training was measured in weeks rather than years.

A B-29 crew, wearing their lifejackets, listens to their commander before take-off from Guam. (USAAF)

Aircrews were also pushing their airframes and engines to the limits in order to maximise effect. Charles Sweeney described one typical accident that took place in front of him:

A steady flow of B-29s from the 313th were taking off in the darkness on the strips below. I saw an airplane struggling to lift off with its full load of fuel and bombs. It didn't make it. The burning aviation fuel and exploding napalm-filled bombs sent plumes of flame and smoke billowing up into the sky.[3]

The scale of the forces involved also meant huge casualty figures. In the USAAF, 35,946 personnel died in World War II in non-battle accidents. [4] Given military propensity for an assault force to grow to the maximum allowable by time before it is committed, and the enormous scale therefore of Coronet and Olympic, how many thousand more would have died simply from accident alone? There was no lessening of the tempo – until Japan surrendered. After the Hiroshima bomb had been dropped, for example, 'Even on the home front the war's toll escalated, as when Major Richard Bong, 25, testing the new P-80 Shooting Star jet, crashed at Lockheed's airport ....'[5]

The reality of the European situation, with its war collapsing, also precluded massively the continuation of the war by conventional means. As Franks shows by lengthy analysis, the people of the United States were demanding what today would be called in future conflicts a 'peace dividend'. It was not merely a case of switching armed forces *en masse* from Europe to the Pacific theatre. The war was different there. It was fought from island bases, and from aircraft carrier battle groups, not over a continental landmass. The Japanese enemy was not the Wehrmacht, not nearly so professional and capable in some ways, but differently equipped and possessed of different techniques, imbued through and through with steely resolve. The Germans gave up where it was sensible and logical – the Japanese fought to the last man, even when no material gain was apparent. The Japanese terrain, once landed upon, was different: most of it was inclined, sometimes very steeply, and the open country tank techniques of North Africa and Europe would not be possible in the Home Islands.

Moreover, the citizens of the United States would not settle for the protracted engagements that had followed D-Day. At least 72 percent of Americans in one survey wanted a partial demobilisation. The remaining 28 percent did not want less – they wanted more troops returned to the States. Congress insisted that at least a million men be returned home.[6] A quick result was being demanded by the nation, which had the most Allied combatants in the Pacific.

This could be hardly surprising. Paul Fussell has suggested that the abiding rationale for the war in the United States was to go home. He puts together a convincing argument that centred around slogans, propaganda, and indeed the overriding persuasion among the fighting troops to get the job done, get the war over, and return to civilian life. Instead, the reality of having to continue the war for probably a year and half more was being posited.

Certainly the frontline troops who carried out the Okinawa assault assumed the Japanese would fight to the last man in defence of the Home Islands. EB Sledge thought:

> We were resigned only to the fact that the Japanese would fight to total extinction on Okinawa, as they had elsewhere, and that Japan would have to be invaded with the same gruesome results. [7] The new pattern of defence in depth and no banzai charges that the Japanese had tried on the 1st Marine Division at Peleliu was repeated on Iwo Jima. When that island was declared secured on 16 March, the cost to the three Marine Divisions that fought there sounded like our Peleliu casualties magnified three times.[8]

In the United States homeland there was a strong argument for finalisation and a return to normal life. For example, the children's book titled *John's Book* was produced, which showed a young reader their father flying the 'big planes'. His purpose in doing this is to win the war, so he can 'come home and have fun with John'.[9]

A poster showed a US pilot holding up three fingers to signify the three Zero fighters he has downed – an interesting suggestion implying all pilots habitually shot down this many enemy aircraft on a flight, which surely would have ended the war years earlier if it had been true. The text explains that the pilot is now 'three long steps nearer the front porch of his home – nearer the girl who's waiting'. [10]

Airborne All the Way. (Public domain)

Anti-Japan poster. (Office for Emergency Management. Office of War Information. Domestic Operations Branch. Bureau of Special Services)

Buy New Victory Bonds WWII poster. (Public domain)

Greyhound Bus Poster, WWII. (Public domain)

Greyhound Bus Poster WWII. (Public domain)

Greyhound I'll be home for Xmas. (Public domain)

Overtly advice to mail home safely, but implicitly sending the message of the woman at home you were fighting for. (US Army)

Throw Everything into the Fight. (Public domain)

There were plenty of other such posters. The Greyhound bus line played on the idea, with a small boy and a loving wife greeting a uniformed serviceman in front of a Christmas tree. Outside the window can be seen the Greyhound bus that dropped him home. Another shows the letters 'USA' in which can be seen iconic scenic pictures of the home country, with a soldier proclaiming 'I fought for this ... one day I'm going to see it and enjoy all of it.' Another urges the purchase of War Bonds to ensure the 'Highways will be Happy Ways again'.

These were social expectations as well, and to match them there were political imperatives. Truman thought there was a 'need for speed in the Pacific and expressed the fear of famine in Europe that might lead to chaos'. But this would be dependent on the United States being able to turn its economic might into that area of focus rather than attacking Japan.[11] A petition argued: 'are we to go on shedding American blood when we have a means to speed victory? No! If we can save a handful of American lives, then let us use this weapon – now!'[12] As Len Giovannitti and Fred Freed put it: 'If a quick end to the war would save American lives, it was only slightly less crucial that it might also save Europe.'[13]

Time was against them. The early pace of the war in the Pacific was very slow:

> During the one year since the launching in 1942 of Pacific counter-offensive at Guadalcanal and on New Guinea, the total westward advance had totaled less than two hundred miles. 'At [this] rate,' one journalist snidely observed ... 'we would get to Tokyo in 1960'.[14]

Several committees were formed to consider various problems of using the atomic bombs, but the most organised and vociferous was called the Committee of Social and Political Implications. It soon became known as the Franck committee after its chairman.[15] The Committee felt: 'If the United States were to be the first to release this new means of indiscriminate destruction upon mankind, she would sacrifice public support throughout the world.'[16]

Conversely, as news of the atomic weapons spread among those in the Manhattan Project, and among those who had seen the successful desert test, and within the Allies in general, the need for speed became a major driver. British leader Churchill thought that there 'never was a moment's discussion as to whether the atomic bomb should be used or not'.[17] Physicist Robert R Wilson compared the program to a boxing match, where one of the boxers had instinctively known through the match when the right moment would be reached for a knockout blow, but they were then asked not to deliver it.[18]

The alternative to air attack – and hopefully a quick end to the war – would have been massive. An invasion of the Japanese mainland would have taken an enormous armed host to be assembled to successfully land a beachhead on the Japanese coast. The conventional wisdom is that to attack an entrenched prepared enemy demands a four to one advantage in terms of personnel numbers. Where would the amphibious force have come from? Would it be American, kept at a peak of readiness with constant training? Would a sustained starvation policy have worked? Would the enemy be so weakened that they would have quickly succumbed?

The Allies had been through this before, and they knew the enormous effort that a conventional attack would have needed once more. On D-Day, the Allies landed around 156,000 troops in Normandy. The American forces landed numbered 73,000: 23,250 on Utah Beach, 34,250 on Omaha Beach, and 15,500 airborne troops. In the British and Canadian sector, 83,115 troops were landed (61,715 of them British): 24,970 on Gold Beach, 21,400 on Juno Beach, 28,845 on Sword Beach, and 7900 airborne troops.

Nearly twelve thousand – 11,590 – aircraft were available to support the landings. On D-Day, Allied aircraft flew 14,674 sorties, and 127 were lost. In the airborne landings on both flanks of the beaches, 2395 aircraft and 867 gliders of the RAF and USAAF were used on D-Day.

Operation Neptune, in support of D-Day, involved huge naval forces, including 6939 vessels: 1213 naval combat ships, 4126 landing ships and landing craft, 736 ancillary craft and 864 merchant vessels. Some 195,700 personnel were assigned to Operation Neptune: 52,889

US, 112,824 British, and 4988 from other Allied countries. By the end of 11 June (D+5), 326,547 troops, 54,186 vehicles and 104,428 tons of supplies had been landed on the beaches.[19]

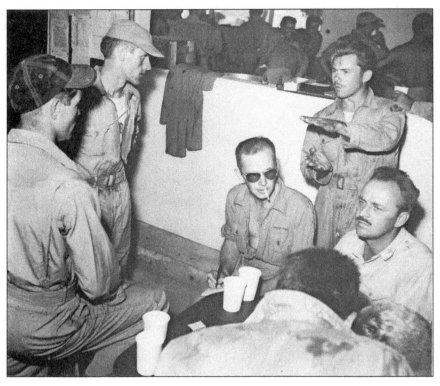

P-51 Mustang pilots discuss their tactics after returning from a mission escorting the bombers. Standing and demonstrating how he attacked is Lieutenant Frank Garcia. (USAAF)

The Pacific War moving into a conventional assault was seeing an even bigger buildup of forces. For example, more than 30 aircraft carriers were deployed by mid-1945. More and more forces would have seen further build up. The monetary cost was also enormous; *Enola Gay* pilot Colonel Paul Tibbits estimated 'seven billion dollars a month'.[20]

By comparison, the Manhattan Project had cost $2 billion to date. A comparison with modern dollars is very difficult, but in 1973 dollars the entire Apollo Moon missions were reported to the US Congress as being $25.4US billion,[21] a program that had taken double the number of years of the World War II effort, for four months worth of dollars, even without adjusting for inflation. To suppose the Allied countries would continue to pour their economic life into the war without it moving forward to achieve its aim is unrealistic in the extreme.

Conclusion

The settlement of the Pacific War was moving inexorably to a conclusion. It could not be stopped. It had to progress one way or the other.

CHAPTER TWELVE

DEMONSTRATIONS AND LEAFLET DROPS – WAS JAPAN EFFECTIVELY WARNED?

Overview: In this chapter, we look at whether Japan was sufficiently warned? Could a demonstration of an explosion have convinced the Japanese to surrender? Were more than two atomic weapons available?

Before the first A-bombing, leaflets were dropped across Japan. On the city of Hiroshima, the first target, 720,000 leaflets were dropped two days prior to the atomic strike. They warned (as the Potsdam Declaration had promised) of the 'inevitable and complete destruction of the Japanese armed forces and just as inevitably the utter devastation of the Japanese homeland'. [1] [2] [3]

The first A-bombing did not bring the war to an end, nor did an Allied propaganda campaign, post the initial strike, of informing the Japanese people of what happened. On 8–9 August, American aircrafts dropped new leaflets across Japan.

They read:

We are in possession of the most destructive explosive ever devised by man. A single one of our newly developed atomic bombs is actually the equivalent in explosive power to what 2000 of our giant B-29s can carry on a single mission. This awful fact is one for you to ponder and we solemnly assure you it is grimly accurate. We have just begun to use this weapon against your homeland. If you still have any doubts, make inquiry as to what happened to Hiroshima when just one atomic bomb fell on that city.[4]

Front side of OWI notice #2106, dubbed the "LeMay bombing leaflet," which was delivered to Hiroshima, Nagasaki, and 33 other Japanese cities on 1 August. (CIA photo)

Allied radio stations transmitted a similar message to Japan every 15 minutes.[5] By 9 August, more than five million leaflets had been dropped. Further leaflets gave warning of further bombing, even to the extent of naming the cities to be targeted:

> Read this carefully as it may save your life or the life of a relative or friend. In the next few days, some or all of the cities named on the reverse side will be destroyed by American bombs. These cities contain military installations and workshops or factories, which produce military goods. We are determined to destroy all of the tools of the military clique, which they are using to prolong this useless war. But, unfortunately, bombs have no eyes. So, in accordance with America's humanitarian policies, the American Air Force, which does not wish to injure innocent people, now gives you warning to evacuate the cities named and save your lives.
>
> America is not fighting the Japanese people but is fighting the military clique, which has enslaved the Japanese people. The peace which America will bring will free the people from the oppression of the military clique and mean the emergence of a new and better Japan. You can restore peace by demanding new and good leaders who will end the war. We cannot promise that only these cities will be among those attacked but some or all of them will be, so heed this warning and evacuate these cities immediately.[6]

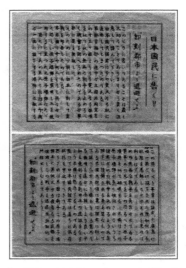

Japanese prisoners helped turn out leaflets and newspapers on OWI's presses on Saipan. (CIA)

Leaflet AB11 with information on the Hiroshima bomb and a warning to civilians to petition the Emperor to surrender was dropped over Japan beginning on August 9, by the 509th Composite Group on the bombing mission. (Nagasaki Atomic Bomb Museum)

Loading OWI leaflets for transport to the US air field on Saipan, 1945. (CIA)

Leaflets written 'in Japanese with the full text of the government's conditional surrender offer of 10 August, along with Byrnes' response' were dropped by B-29 on 14 August.[7] Some of them even ended up in the Imperial Palace gardens in Tokyo. They carried more than just the consequence of ignoring them – the military propaganda had been so effective that almost all of the military did not know of any thoughts of surrender.[8] But the leaflets and broadcasts had little effect. For example, there was no mass revolution, or even the suggestions of civilian unrest. Even after the dropping of the first A-weapon, as Kase put it:

> … the authorities tried to drown out the powerful enemy broadcasts … but these broadcasts in excellent Japanese exercised a great influence on the minds of the people. When it became no longer possible to suppress the truth, the Army attempted to minimise the destructive power of the bomb.[9]

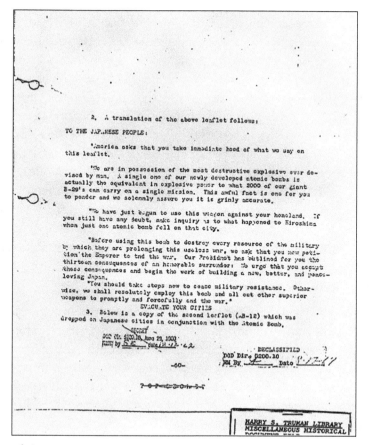

Leaflet translation.

A demonstration bomb?

The concept of giving a warning by means of a demonstration blast was widely canvassed in the United States high command. It met with both support and opposition. The Army's General Marshall stressed: 'It's no good warning them. If you warn them there's no surprise. And the only way to produce shock is surprise.'[10]

The Secretary of State, Stimson, believed the use of the bomb might well shorten the war, particularly if the shock value and the devastating effect of it could be demonstrated under optimum conditions. He was aware of the Scientific Panel's opinion, and particularly bomb designer Oppenheimer's thoughts that the bomb would not impress the Japanese if demonstrated on a desolate area. He considered a bombed-out city a poor target with which to give the Japanese the psychological blow necessary to induce surrender. Stimson felt that if the bomb were badly used so its power was not clearly understood by the Japanese, it would have the adverse effect of strengthening their resolve to continue the war in the belief they would get more suitable terms than unconditional surrender.[11]

Oppenheimer did not feel qualified to question the intelligence reports he had been given. He had been told 'that an invasion was planned. It would be necessary and it would be terribly costly'. He accepted this analysis and persuaded others to accept it. And in the last analysis, Oppenheimer, whose influence on his colleagues was enormous, fully endorsed the use of the bomb: 'On the whole, you are inclined to think if it was needed to put an end to the war and had a chance of so doing, we thought that was the right thing to do.'[12]

Oppenheimer later remembered: 'It was not that we said a test isn't feasible, we said we didn't think we could recommend one that was likely to induce surrender.'[13] Byrnes noted:

> I told the President of the final decision of the Interim Committee (to use the bomb on Japan without warning.) Mr Truman told me he had been giving serious thought to the subject for many days, having been informed as to the investigation of the committee and the consideration of alternative plans, and that with reluctance he had to agree that he could think of no alternative and found himself in accord.[14]

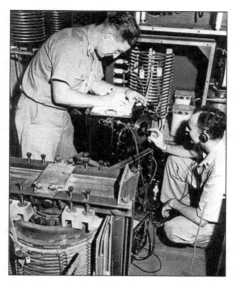

OWI personnel adjusting the KSAI radio transmitter to new frequencies to avoid jamming by Japan. (Central Intelligence Agency)

The recollection of the demonstration discussion from American physicist Arthur Compton is worth reproducing in full:

> At the luncheon following the morning meeting, I was seated at Mr. Stimson's left. In the course of the conversation I asked the Secretary whether it might not be possible to arrange a nonmilitary demonstration of the bomb in such a manner that the Japanese would be so impressed that they would see the uselessness of continuing the war. The Secretary opened this question for general discussion by those at the table.

> Various possibilities were brought forward. One after the other it seemed necessary that they should be discarded. It was evident that everyone would suspect trickery. If a bomb were exploded in Japan with previous notice, the Japanese airpower was still adequate to give serious interference.

> An atomic bomb was an intricate device, still in the developmental stage. Its operation would be far from routine. If during the final adjustments of the bomb the Japanese defenders should

attack, a faulty move might easily result in some kind of failure. Such an end to an advertised demonstration of power would be much worse that if the attempt had not been made.

It was now evident that when the time came for the bombs to be used we should have only one of them available, followed afterwards by others at all-too-long intervals. We could not afford the chance that one of them might be a dud.

If the test were made on some neutral territory, it was hard to believe that Japan's determined and fanatical military men would be impressed. If such an open test were made first and failed to bring surrender, the chance would be gone to give the shock of surprise that proved so effective. On the contrary, it would make the Japanese ready to interfere with an atomic attack if they could.

Though the possibility of a demonstration that would not destroy human lives was attractive, no one could suggest a way in which it could be made so convincing that it would be likely to stop the war.[15]

Some scientists seemed to have wanted it both ways: to bring an end to the war, but at the same time to appear if not pacifist in their outlook then at least not bloodthirsty. Oppenheimer appeared to hold immense sway over his colleagues, and in the end it may be that he moved many:

One hundred and fifty members of the Chicago laboratory may have signed a petition, which was claimed by Arthur Compton in his book *Atomic Quest* to show that '87 percent voted for the [bomb's] military use'. This is disputed by Giovannitti and Freed, who suggest it was more that '46 percent voted for a military demonstration'.[16]

Any demonstration of the bomb had attendant difficulties: it might fail to detonate, inspiring the Japanese to fight on; the aircraft carrying it might be attacked, and the bomb lost in a crash. The demonstration blast zone might well be assaulted deliberately before the triggering of the A-weapon, with the intention being to destroy it before its capabilities were shown. There could even be the placement of some Allied prisoners of war in a proposed demonstration site.

Stimson wrote:

> I felt that to extract a genuine surrender from the Emperor and his military advisers, there must be administered a tremendous shock which would carry convincing proof of our power to destroy the Empire. Such an effective shock would save many times the number of lives, both American and Japanese, than it would cost.[17]

> Nothing would be more damaging to our effort to obtain surrender than a warning or a demonstration followed by a dud – and that is a real possibility. Furthermore we have no bombs to waste, and it is vital that a sufficient effect be obtained quickly with the few we have.[18]

This is critical to an understanding of the need for victory quickly, or at least to move ahead steadily, as touched upon in the previous chapter discussing 'battle rhythm'. And using one bomb on a demonstration would have meant there would only have been one left. The possibility of further nuclear weapons being available is somewhat obscure, but it was likely measured in months rather than weeks. Groves was of the opinion[19] another could have been available within August 1945; Colonel LE Seeman of the Manhattan Project thought 'at least seven bombs' would probably be ready[20] for use by the end of October; Tibbets of the *Enola Gay* suggested a third bomb would not have been ready until September.[21] Whatever the case, it would have been illogical and foolhardy to use one of the two available weapons as a demonstration.

Stimson ... abhorred the terrible fire-bomb raids on Japanese cities that took such a heavy loss of lives and at the same time he did not believe that victory could be quickly achieved through airpower alone; he searched for a way to induce a Japanese surrender before an invasion was necessary to conquer Japan at the estimated cost of half a million casualties.[22]

The cover of a vinyl record, advising that the purchaser will be able to hear the sounds of approaching Allied bombers, thus enabling them to take cover quickly. (Public domain)

In 1947, 'The implications of this possible error of judgment were clear to him. Only on this question did he later believe that history might find the United States, by its delay in stating its position, had prolonged the war.'[23] But as he had concluded at the time, Stimson was of the opinion: 'We all feel some way should be found of inducing Japan to yield without a fight to the finish.'[24]

Conclusion

Japan was indeed suitably warned of the A-bombs both before the first attack and after it. A demonstration blast would been both foolhardy and dangerous.

CHAPTER THIRTEEN
THE RUSSIAN OPTION

Overview: In this chapter, we question whether the Russians entering the war would have caused the Japanese to surrender? What were their capabilities in any invasion of the Home Islands?

The entry into the war against Japan by the Soviet Union – which had until its declaration on 9 August 1945 refrained from combat action – has been cited by many as a significant factor in causing the Japanese to surrender. It is seized upon by those who wish to attack the United States for the A-bombs, but the significance of the USSR's usefulness is often expanded beyond logic.

In his autobiography *Journey to the Missouri*, World War II Foreign Ministry official Toshikazu Kase gives a lively but anguished account of the situation regarding the USSR, and in particular Japan's attitude to the country. He notes the feasibility of the four nations of Germany, Italy, USSR and Japan, bound by geography as well as militaristic outlook, combining to achieve victory. Then, of course, Germany attacked Russia and the concept disappeared. But with Japan at peace with the USSR in early 1945, the Soviet possible role in staving off defeat was an entertained possibility.[1]

Frank makes the point that the entry wholesale of the USSR into conventional combat would have meant even more deaths, and we can safely surmise this would have been by the many hundreds of thousands, given the size of the armies involved.[2] He suggests the experience between Russian and Japanese troops on the mainland is instructive. The Russians, thrusting into the Hokkaido area, killed around 400,000 Japanese.[3]

There has been an eagerness of some historians to see the Russian military possibilities as being a definitive and more positive outcome than that posited by the atomic weapons. This has led to some glossing over of the facts and even, according to some critics, of a willingness to manipulate the evidence. For example, Robert James Maddox criticises Gar Alperovitz for his use of ellipses in his referencing. In one example, Alper omits one word – 'had'. But this is said to change the meaning.

Here is the original quotation:

> Molotov had sent for Ambassador Harriman on 8 August and announced to him that the Soviet Union would consider itself at war with Japan as of 9 August. This move did not surprise us. Our dropping of the atomic bomb on Japan had forced Russia to reconsider her position in the Far East.

Alperovitz reproduced this in his *Atomic Diplomacy* as: 'Our dropping of the atomic bomb on Japan ... forced Russia to reconsider her position in the Far East.' The rewording is revealed in Robert James Maddox's essay 'Gar Alperovitz – Godfather of Hiroshima Revisionism' in *Hiroshima in History – the Myths of Revisionism*.[4] The slight rewording makes it look as if the Americans deliberately used the atomic bomb attacks to force Russia into a diplomatic position favourable to the United States.

Similarly, Sheldon Garon has argued that the atomic bombings were not necessary, as Japan was going to surrender anyway, and it was the USSR that was pivotal. He:

> ... attributes Japan's delayed surrender to military intransigence and diplomatic incompetence, a dithering that subjected Japan to needless devastation.

> Finally, it was the Soviet entry into the war and the atomic bombings that precipitated a hasty surrender. But it was overdue because the signs of defeat, including a devastating series of setbacks on the home front, had been gathering for some time: endless fire bombings, growing shortages of food due to the United States blockade 'Operation Starvation,' bereaved families and the subversion of people voting with their feet. There was

no appetite for suffering the fate of the Nazis or subjecting the nation to more nightmarish ruination.[5]

Garon discounts the notion that the Japanese would have fought to the last possible combatant. He:

> … observes that the Germans fought like samurai, sacrificing all even when they knew it was for a losing cause. While much is made of Japanese authorities training women and children to resist US invaders with bamboo staves, Garon notes that none ever did so. In contrast, Germany took desperate measures, resorting to full mobilisation and deploying these untrained conscripts to battlefields where many died or were injured.

A line of Russian heavy IS-2 tanks advance, passing some refugees. The IS-2 first saw service in early 1944 and were involved in the Battle for Berlin. (Public domain)

This is a specious argument, however. No invader ever landed on the Home Islands, so this is hardly a comparison. The Germans knew full well from their World War I experience about the feasibility of defending their homelands. To dismiss the willingness of the

Japanese to die in combat is to dismiss the evidence of the rate at which their armies did indeed die: to a level of over 90 percent, as has been shown.

It is also to discount the unthinking obedience with which the Japanese civilians acted, for example on Okinawa.

On a converse note, it is instructive to observe the lack of assassination attempts upon the Emperor and other senior leaders – perhaps three pre-war – compared to over 40 attempts made against the life of Hitler by Germans, including his own troops. In addition, the Germans hardly employed a scorched earth policy despite Hitler's orders to do so. His Minister for Armaments, Albert Speer, defied these orders in the final months of the war, reasoning that to go ahead with them would have meant the deaths of huge numbers of Germans from starvation, and eventually, from the rigors of winter.[6]

Diplomat Kase was asked by journalists who entered Japan with the Occupation forces whether it was the USSR's war opening against Japan, or the A-bomb attacks, which had been responsible for the surrender. He answered that he thought the Japanese would have surrendered eventually anyway – but both facilitated it. 'Without them, the Army might still have tried to prolong resistance.'[7] Then again, other Japanese scholars have seen a twin cause, as Saburo Ienaga says: 'The twin shocks of the atomic bombings and the Soviet declaration of war broke the stalemate in Tokyo.'[8] Similarly, J Samuel Walker, for example, argues that it was a combination of the atomic attacks and the USSR's declaration of war that brought about the Japanese surrender.[9]

Many people argue that the Russian entry into the war would have bought about a collapse of Japan's determination to fight on. Citing a 1946 study, Alperovitz suggests that Japan's leaders just needed a pretext to bring about surrender.[10] Russia's entry would 'almost certainly' have allowed such leaders to dominate the 'die-hard Army Group' that was pressing for the country to fight on. Documents are cited by Alperovitz to show how the United States wanted Russia's participation in the Pacific theatre. Saburo Ienaga quotes the thoughts of HMS Blackett, who he argues 'questioned why America has to employ the bomb so hastily. If the primary objective was to save American lives, Washington could have deferred both the bomb and an invasion of Japan until the Soviet offensive had run its course'.[11]

Such arguments focus on the political rather than the military factors, and therefore miss the point.

Russia's entry would have been a reasonable factor militarily, giving help but not a solution to the Allied quest for victory. Their entry to the war would have eventually expelled Japanese troops from the mainland Asian holdings in the north, although Japanese resistance would have been as fierce as their efforts anywhere else. Of interest to this book's theme is the certainty that this would have brought about many more deaths on both sides, the Japanese no doubt fighting with their usual tenacity, and the Russians with the commissar-driven brutality which had made them such a tough opponent for the Germans. So the entry of the USSR may well have killed more Japanese rather than less, and more of Japan's opponents than less.

The Russian entry to the war would indeed have lessened Japanese morale, an important factor in maintaining troop capability. The Russian entry would certainly have tied up Japanese units. However, Russia's military capabilities would not have proved decisive or even significant. In all of these areas, however, supporters such as Alperovitz and Ienaga do not assess the *military* factors.

For example, Russia had no aircraft carriers, and showed little signs within the war of developing such a versatile weapon, which was one of the main three factors in bringing Japan to its knees, the others being heavy bomber attacks and submarine operations.[12]

Soviet Russia is actually thought by some to have been completing the carrier *Krasnaya Znamya* in 1945, a 60-aircraft ship of 22,000 tons. Laid down in Leningrad in 1939, she is said to have been completed by 1945. A second hull named *Voroshilov* may have been begun, and a small seaplane carrier named *Stalin* may have also existed. None of these were known to be anywhere near operational – it is worth noting that mere completion of the ships was worthless unless naval air units could be embarked and used. The skillsets necessary, such as taking off and landing on a carrier, take years for a navy to develop. The Russian Navy was composed of several battleships, cruisers, and a host of smaller vessels such as destroyers, and around 100 submarines, many of the latter small and their abilities doubtful.

Alperovitz gives the USSR naval forces two lines: 'US control of the seas made it obvious that Russia would not have the power to share in the actual occupation of Japan if the United States chose otherwise.'[13] 'Control of the seas' has nothing to with it. If Russia had wanted to participate in an amphibious assault it would have had to ask for transport and gunfire support from American and British naval units.

The Allied carriers – there were several British aircraft carriers fighting in the Pacific, apart from the stronger American strength – were carrying out land-strike missions against Japanese airfield and targets of value. Moreover, they were the main factor in decimating the Japanese fighter presence, which allowed more capable bomber penetration of Japanese airspace and the bomber destruction of its cities. There were no Russian carriers.

Russia had nothing significant[14] in the long-range bomber capability, which was represented by the four-engined B-29 and Lancaster heavy bombers of the Allied effort. Although, as shown elsewhere in this study, the B-29s were having considerable success pounding Japanese cities into ruins, the Lancasters of the British-led effort were concentrating on attacking the European cities. With the end of German resistance following Hitler's suicide on 30 April 1945, that heavy bomber assault (and thousands of other small bombers) would have been eventually switched to attacking Japan, although it would have been months before basing with all of the necessary support was arranged. Russian land-based medium bombing could have operated from the Korean peninsula, but it would have been chaotic indeed incorporating it into the Allied Order of Battle and its operational philosophies, given the language difficulties.

In the area of amphibious assault, the USSR's capabilities were minimal. A D-Day style attack on the Kyushu peninsula, with the USSR given say one landing zone out of five, would have required close co-operation with the other friendly forces to provide the troopships and landing craft to launch the attack, for the Russians had nothing in strength of the former.

Therefore, it follows they could not have operated such vessels if offered them, for the operation of heavy lift shipping and the deployment of troops into small shallow-draught boats for a landing was a specialised operation that the United States, Britain, and Canada had developed expertise in well before they landed on the five beaches at Normandy. Once ashore, the troops of the spearhead need immediate support in terms of their equipment, ammunition, food, accommodation provision, and so on. If the Russians had been involved, the language problems in all of this would have proved not just insurmountable but disastrous if tried.

There is some evidence the Russians were willing to try small amphibious landings, but their experience in the latter years of the war suggests they were less than competent in their operation:

> Unlike their Western allies, the Soviets lacked specialised boats for amphibious landings on defended beaches. But under Project Hula, the United States secretly transferred 149 ships to the Soviet Navy through Cold Bay, Alaska – and trained 12,000 Soviet personnel how to operate them. This included 30 Landing Craft Infantry: 48-metre-long shallow-draft vessels capable of depositing 200 troops directly onto an unprepared beach.[15]

Fighting indeed took place between the Soviets and the Japanese on 17 August 1945, with the former coming off the worse. Sources vary, but it appears the Soviet Army and Navy combined lost around 800 dead and over 1400 wounded in the Battle of Shumshu, compared to 370 Japanese dead and 700 wounded. However, by this time, Japanese command orders to surrender were coming through, and they were obeyed. The Soviets gained a strategic victory, but their material loss is indicative of how they would have fared in amphibious warfare had the conflict not ended.

Russia had no submarine fleet of the United States' capability, which was already strangling Japan's sea supplies and troop movements.[16] The US fleet was doing a very capable job of this already, and when it was joined by other US naval elements even more pressure was applied. In fact, allocating separate patrol areas for the USSR would have lengthened the war: communications between the Allies would have been extended, weakened areas exposed, and Japanese abilities to exploit these increased.

In none of these areas of carrier strike, amphibious landings, long-range bombing, or submarine attack was Russia capable of inflicting more than minimal damage on the Japanese Empire. The USSR's formidable armies were land-based, and centred around infantry, armour, artillery, and close-range air support. All four of these capabilities would have needed sea support to move to a Japanese mainland attack. That support would have had to be supplied by the other Allied countries, who would already have been moving their own forces into position.

While Russian land forces would have been politically welcome, by no means would their entry to the war have been decisive or even useful. In fact, as with the submarine concept, integrating the USSR presence into the Allied Pacific Order of Battle would have been a delaying factor. In fact, it is notable that initial planning for Operation Coronet was centred by the US planners around their own forces only, even though 'the British, Canadians, Australians and French all desired to field ground forces'. Problems in equipment compatibility, supply, and in tactical doctrine were all envisaged.[17]

Although Japanese morale would have been impacted by the entry of a traditional enemy such as the Russians into the conflict, it is difficult to assess how much of a factor this would have been for Japanese troops. The frontline soldiers were not supplied with news of home in the way that Allied soldiers were via radio and newspapers. The Japanese had triumphed over the Russians in 1905 in a famous and formidable victory. In World War I, Russia and Japan, while not joining hands in the way US and British Empire Forces had done, had fought on the same side. The Japanese probably did not fear the Russians as much as the Germans did.

Despite all of these factors – generally ignored – supporters of a Russian involvement in mid-1945 as an alternative to the use of the

A-weapons, generally skirt around the edges of what such participation would have meant.

The basic line seems to run as follows: the United States knew that Russia would join the war against Japan; however, they were not keen for this to happen. The reasons for this are varied: primarily, the Americans wanted to awe the Russians by the use of the bombs to scare them off post-World War II expansion. If that had happened, Japan would have collapsed, the A-weapons would therefore not have been needed, and the Americans would have been morally culpable for using them.

So we are given selective phrases and words from the opponents of the US's operations to condemn them. Alperovitz's study, for example, glosses over the reality of the situation. Quotations from various sources are used ambiguously. For example, the Joint Intelligence Committee's 'Within the year'[18] is used, and 'Surrender might follow fairly quickly'[19] and 'By the autumn of 1945'.[20]

Over several chapters, the alternative to using the A-weapons is argued: that Russian involvement would have led to the collapse of the Japanese Empire, without the destruction of two cities and massive civilian loss of life. But nothing definitive in terms of a timeline is argued, and as will be later shown, with fatalities in the Pacific War of hundreds of thousands a month occurring, to say that time was of the essence would be the understatement of the 20th century.

Ienaga argues that 'The Red Army was smashing through Manchuria before the United States could reach Japan, a situation not to the liking of the American military.' But what does this mean? The Soviets, as shown above, could not reach the Home Islands with an invasion force. What aspects of this did the American military not like, and why?[21]

A carefully selected series of Alperovitz's sources basically seem intent simply on blackening President Truman's name. The involvement of the Russians would be slowed down – for example, by the postponement of the Potsdam conference from June to July. The British Prime Minister would be induced to agree to this because Truman 'didn't want to go to Potsdam and meet Stalin until he knew the exact outcome of the tests … [because] the United States would be in a far stronger position once the bomb had been tested.'[22]

Alperovitz concludes one chapter of this diatribe by suggesting there are hidden documents that will continue to support this theory:

> If the pattern of occasional but regular documentary finds of the last century continues, it would not be surprising were the Hopkins and Davies missions one day to be illuminated as fully and clearly as have the once equally puzzling reasons for the president's decision to postpone his meeting with Stalin.[23]

What is not examined is the possibility of a more logical approach in the matter of timing in the management of the war. That is, that the Americans, as well as the many countries alongside them in the Pacific War, were concerned for combat to be brought to a halt as quickly as possible.

Conclusion

The involvement of the USSR as an instrument to bring about Japanese surrender is usually cited in a generalist way that takes little account of the inadequacies of the Russian forces to be useful in a conventional invasion. Indeed, their involvement would have seen many more casualties on the Allied side being received.

REVENGE AS A MOTIVATOR – PEARL HARBOR, BATAAN AND OKINAWA

The opinions of veterans considered

Overview: *In the chapter, we discuss whether the use of the A-bombs was inevitable once the Manhattan Project began? Was there any turning back from Unconditional Surrender once details of the treatment of prisoners of war in instances such as the Bataan Death March – seeing the deaths of around 2000 US military – leaked out? The reactions of Allied personnel to the bombings are sketched to provide a contrast to the later chapters that show the rejection of the necessity of the A-bombings.*

While dismissing the involvement of the Soviet Union as a means of ending the war, and not using the A-bombs, it must be acknowledged that there was an element of revenge in the Allied assault on the Home islands.

An opinion poll carried out in the United States in December 1944 asked ordinary Americans: 'What do you think we should do with Japan as a country after the war?' One in three people answered that Japan should cease to exist as a country. More than one in eight said that all the Japanese should be killed. US soldiers felt even more strongly. In an opinion poll in 1943, half of US soldiers polled said that all Japanese soldiers would have to be killed before there was peace.[1]

American troops in the Philippines celebrate the long-awaited news that Japan has, finally, unconditionally, surrendered in August 1945. (US Navy)

Bataan, and beyond

Journalist William T Laurence flew on the mission that dropped a second atom bomb, on the city of Nagasaki, on 9 August 1945. In an article in the *New York Times* three weeks after the event, he described his feelings as had looked down on the city about to be destroyed. 'Does one feel pity or compassion for the poor devils about to die? Not when one thinks of Pearl Harbor and the Bataan Death March.'[2]

The pressure the United States would have been under to avenge the deaths of other countries' prisoners must also be understood. In January 1945, Japanese forces had killed around 100,000 Filipino civilians in the defence of Manila.[3] Sixty thousand Koreans died working as slave labourers in Japan.[4] To expect any nations suffering such levels of loss to be merciful to Japan is to misunderstand human nature. The United States was fighting across the Pacific and relied on its allies, both formal and informal, for basing and support, as well as participation. For example, Australia was a major base for US activities, but the Australians were suffering the most proportionally from POW losses.

Country	Total POWs	POW deaths	Death rate (%)
Britain	50,016	12,433	24.8%
Holland	37,000	8500	22.9%
Australia	21,726	7412	34.1%
United States	21,580	7107	32.9%
Canada	1691	273	16.1%
New Zealand	121	31	25.6%
Total	132,134	35,756	27.1%[5]

Japan had not signed the Geneva Convention of 1929, which provided some rulings on the treatment of prisoners taken in war. However, Japan had signed the Hague Conventions of 1899 and 1907, and so it had signified agreement to the concept that prisoners did have rights and should be treated in an internationally agreed fashion.

As the war progressed, the situation of POWs held by Japan became more prominent. Manhattan Project leader Groves was of the opinion when there were reservations against too much gratitude that: 'I was not thinking so much of those casualties as I was about the men who had made the Bataan death march.'[6] A compiler of *An Oral History of the War Years in America* observed:

I distrust people who speak of the [atom] bombings today as an atrocity they strongly opposed in 1945 ... I don't believe them. At the time, virtually everyone was delighted that we dropped the bombs, not only because they shortened the war and saved thousands of American lives but also because the 'Japs' deserved it for the terrible things they had done to our boys at Pearl Harbor, Bataan, Guadalcanal, and all the way through the Pacific.[7]

Japanese POW camps in the war routinely used Allied prisoners as a source of labour, unlike those in the European theatre. Where they thought it necessary, the Japanese moved such labour forces, often through walking them, to more useful locations. The Bataan-forced march of prisoners was undertaken in April 1942. Around 76,000 prisoners were compelled to march approximately 105 kilometers to further imprisonment, and along the way many died or were executed. It is thought 28,500 Filipino and 2000 US personnel died during the march and afterwards.[8]

Treatment of prisoners such as that meted out at Bataan was not isolated. Forced marches, incurring high death counts for the unfortunate prisoners compelled to undertake them, are plentiful in Pacific World War II history. The lesser-known 'Sandakan Death Marches', for example, saw the deaths of 2394 Australian and around 750 British POWs in the Borneo region.[9]

Such treatment of the POWs meant for harbored revenge. Laurens Van Der Post was a prisoner in a Japanese camp:

> More and more people see the horror ... out of context. They tend to see increasingly as an act of history in which we alone were the villains. I have been amazed to observe how in some extraordinary kind of way my own Japanese friends do not seem to feel that they had done anything themselves to provoke us into inflicting Hiroshima ... on them, and how increasingly incurious they are about their own part in the war.[10]

John Falconer, a POW in Japan, saw Hiroshima shortly after the attack and described the destruction as 'beautiful':

> First there were trees. Then the leaves were missing. As you got closer, branches were missing. Closer still, the trunks were gone and then, as you got in the middle [of the blast zone] there was nothing. Nothing! It was beautiful. I realised this was what had ended the war. It meant we didn't have to go hungry any longer, or go without medical treatment. I was so insensitive to anyone else's human needs and suffering. I know it's not right to say it was beautiful because it really wasn't. But I believed the end probably justified the means.[11]

Pearl Harbor - propaganda poster. (Public domain)

President Truman raised the 'murder of our prisoners of war' as a motivating factor in his decisions in a letter to the Federal Council of Churches in Christ shortly after the second bombing.[12] Truman's attitude has to be understood from another point of view too. Once the secret was out that the A-bombs were available, he had no choice. If he didn't use them then the next president would – and so on. No population stands by and lets thousands of its people die and be seriously wounded every week on the basis of 'our new weapons are too nasty'.

By the later stages of the war, the brutality that prisoners of the Japanese would face, and the prospect of death in captivity, was so high that B-29 atomic aircrew carried cyanide capsules in case the aircraft came down and they faced capture.[13] So not only the normal hazards of warfare had to be faced, but the unusual and different – compared to the European theatre – had to be prepared for, and endured.

As a measure of understanding how the A-bombings were judged by the serving troops, some opinions have been collected, which are shown below. These opinions are not offered as a 'grab bag' of random military personnel's individual opinions, but as the assessments of experts. Personnel who had been fighting in the Pacific should have their judgments treated as being backed by experience, considered calculation, and weighted by being of more worth than military employed elsewhere in World War II. The Asian theatres were a lot different to those of Europe or Africa or the Atlantic, and should be treated as such.

RAF armourer CR Coleman: 'But for the atomic bombs, I don't think we'd have stood a cat in hell's chance. We would have been murdered in the biggest massacre of the war. They would have annihilated the lot of us.' [14] [15]

Enola Gay pilot Paul Tibbets: 'Despite the number of people we killed, we saved multiple numbers over that from being in a war, and being killed, on America's side, on the Japanese side.' [16]

Photographer W Eugene Smith's picture of a Marine drinking from his canteen during 1944's Battle of Saipan is as iconic a war picture as any ever made. (USMC)

RAAF Flight Lieutenant SE Armstrong compared the invasion to what he had seen in the island-hopping attacks: 'Every hill on every island, and there are many, had hidden roll out fire then roll back in under vines medium size howitzers on them.' [17]

Charles Munoz, aircrew member, recalled where he was when the news came through:

Truman's 11 am announcement of the atom-bombing of Hiroshima came when I was on a train, going home for my first leave from the navy, so I didn't hear of it until we reached Grand Central station in New York that afternoon. I suppose there were newspapers being hawked loudly in the station, but I really don't remember. My squadron, night-flying navy torpedo bombers, was training for an invasion of Japan, which all of us knew was coming up in the future. We even had heard that our carrier was to be the *Antietam*.

I was still on that short leave when the Japanese gave up. I remember happiness in the house, of course, but, at 18, I remember the feeling of the young man in Faulkner's *Soldier's Pay*: They had stopped the war on me.[18]

President Truman was on board the ship *Augusta*, dining with some of the crew, when he was told the news of the successful attack. He read the message and then said he wanted to talk to some of the crew. He told them 'of a powerful new bomb', which was 'greeted by them with great applause, not [because of] the suffering of people but because they believed, as all of us believed, it would bring about a quicker ending of the war'.[19]

US Marine 'Slim' Manchester remembered: 'You think of the lives which would have been lost in an invasion of Japan's Home Islands – a staggering number of American lives, but millions more of Japanese – and you thank God for the atomic bomb.'[20]

Rex Pullen was a gunner on HMAS *Armidale*, an Australian corvette that was sunk by Japanese aircraft, who then strafed the survivors in the water. He was vehement in his reaction: 'The A-bomb!! That should have been dropped much earlier. The Jap law – the only one they knew about – strike first and talk later.'[21]

Paul Fussell, a 21-year-old American second lieutenant: 'When the bombs dropped and news began to circulate that ... we would not be obliged to run up the beaches near Tokyo ... we cried with relief and joy. We were going to live. We were going to grow up to adulthood after all.'[22] Fussell later wrote in *From Thank God for the Atom Bomb and Other Essays*: 'If around division headquarters some of the people [J. Glenn] Gray talked to felt ashamed [of the US use of atomic bombs], down in the rifle companies no one did, despite Gray's assertions.'[23]

Fussell wrote later:

When the atom bomb ended the war, I was in the 45th Infantry Division, which had been through the European war so thoroughly that it had needed to be reconstituted two or three times. We were in a staging area near Rheims, ready to be shipped back across the United States for refresher training at Fort Lewis, Washington, and then sent on for final preparation in the Philippines.

My division, like most of the ones transferred from Europe, was to take part in the invasion of Honshu. (The earlier landing on Kyushu was to be carried out by the 700,000 infantry already in the Pacific, those with whom James Jones has sympathised.)

I was a 21-year-old second lieutenant of infantry leading a rifle platoon. Although still officially fit for combat, in the German war I had already been wounded in the back and the leg badly enough to be adjudged, after the war, 40 percent disabled. But even if my leg buckled and I fell to the ground whenever I jumped out of the back of a truck, and even if the very idea of more combat made me breathe in gasps and shake all over, my condition was held to be adequate for the next act.

When the atom bombs were dropped and news began to circulate that 'Operation Olympic' would not, after all, be necessary, when we learnt to our astonishment that we would not be obliged in a few months to rush up the beaches near Tokyo assault-firing while being machine-gunned, mortared, and shelled, for all the practiced phlegm of our tough facades, we broke down and cried with relief and joy. We were going to live. We were going to grow to adulthood after all. The killing was all going to be over, and peace was actually going to be the state of things.[24]

Pilots aboard a US Navy aircraft carrier receive last minute instructions before taking off to attack industrial, and military installations in Tokyo. February 17, 1945. (US Navy)

Historians Robert Jay Lifton and Greg Mitchell describe the overall feeling:

> Most Americans recognised immediately that the new bomb would shorten the war. No one felt more grateful than soldiers in the Pacific. 'We whooped and yelled like mad, we downed all the beer we'd been stashing away,' one later recalled. 'We shot bullets into the air and danced between the tent rows, because this meant maybe we were going to live, and not as cripples.'[25]

'We were playing a lottery,' John Ciardi, a bomber pilot in the Pacific (later a poet), recalled. 'A certain number of planes had to be lost. You were just hoping that by blind chance yours would not be. When news of the atom bomb came – we didn't know what it was – we won the lottery. Hey, we're gonna get out of here!' With Japan's surrender, the bomb appeared to fulfill its promise as the winning weapon. 'Thank God for the atomic bomb' a serviceman from Mississippi wrote in *Life* magazine. William Styron, then a Marine officer slated to lead a rifle platoon in the invasion, would recall that he felt 'ecstatic' to have 'an almost tactile burden of insecurity and dread' lifted from his shoulders.[26] For James Fahey, he simply wrote in his diary: 'This was the happiest day of our lives.'[27]

When Sledge's US Marine unit heard the news:

> With quiet disbelief coupled with an indescribable sense of relief. We thought the Japanese would never surrender. Many refused to believe it .... Sitting in stunned silence, we remembered our dead. So many dead. So many maimed. So many bright futures consigned to the ashes of the past. So many dreams lost in the madness that had engulfed us. Except for a few widely scattered shouts of joy, the survivors of the abyss sat hollow-eyed and silent, trying to comprehend a world without war. [28]

Frank in *Downfall* summarises up the feeling within the US military community as being: 'Millions of American servicemen believed that they personally had their lives spared by the bombs.'[29] An American publication, *The New Republic*, used the headline: 'Thank God for the Atomic Bomb.'[30]

Major John E Moynihan, the Public Relations Officer for the atomic attacks, wrote on the Little Boy bomb the words 'No white cross for Stevie' in reference to the impact this would have on his young son back in America.[31] The 'white cross' was that which he, Major Moynihan, would have received had he died.

British Army officer, and later journalist and author, George MacDonald Fraser later reminisced: 'Like everyone else, we were glad it was over, brought to sudden devastating stop by those two bombs that fell on Japan ... we did not know what the immediate effect of those bombs had been on their targets, and we didn't much care ... our country had been hammered mercilessly from the sky and so had Germany ... we were not going to lose sleep because the Japanese homeland had taken its turn.'[32]

Royal Australian Navy communications rating Gordon Johnson was serving in Townsville at the time, when three telegraphists came back from a task and told them their job was finished – the war was over. Johnson didn't believe them and sent them back to complete their job; he remembers they were all later pleased but a bit shocked at the enormous power of the new weapons. Johnson's brother Keith was a staff officer to Commodore Buchanan. Keith was sent to visit the bombing areas; he later died of radiation poisoning.[33]

Aircrew were grimly enthusiastic, perhaps realising that their involvement would have been doubly dangerous – both in the combat element and simply in the reality of flying at the time. Bomber wireless operator/gunner Brian Winspear thought: 'Wacko! This'll teach the bastards.'[34] Spitfire pilot Lysle Roberts was serving in the Pacific at the time. He remembers: 'Everyone was elated. If we hadn't done what we did, you can almost say we would still be fighting.'[35]

James Vernon, flying Hellcat fighters off aircraft carriers near Japan, recalled that when he and his shipmates heard of the atomic strike on Hiroshima: 'Reports of its devastating effects made us feel certain that the war would be over within hours.' His ship celebrated: 'High-class booze that had been jealously guarded for months surfaced in our rooms; celebrations continued until the early hours of the morning.' However, their celebration was dampened considerably by news their aggressive and dangerous flying would continue until a formal surrender: 'On the schedule were combat air patrols and strikes against targets ....'[36]

The "Fellow who lighted the fuse" cartoon by Carey Orr, capturing popular attitudes towards the A-weapon use at the time. (*Chicago Tribune*, August 8, 1945)

Navigator of the *Enola Gay*, Theodore Van Kirk, was of the opinion: 'I thought: Thank God the war is over and I don't have to get shot at anymore. I can go home.'[37] Later in an interview with the *New York Times* on the 50th anniversary of the raid, he recalled 'a sense of relief,' because he said he sensed the devastating bombing would be a turning point to finally bring the war to a close.[38] Spitfire pilot Nat Gould, later to be a Lieutenant Commander on board HMS *Implacable*. 'Bloody good job! I wish we'd killed more of them.'[39]

The assault would have been amphibious, as least in its initial stages. Marine office William Styron, who would have led a rifle platoon in the invasion, said he felt 'ecstatic' to have a burden of 'insecurity and dread' lifted from his shoulders.[40] Austin Aria, a veteran of the Okinawa campaign, thought:

> We hated the Japs, but nobody had the slightest desire to go there and fight them because the one thing we knew was that we'd all be killed. I mean we really knew it. I never used to think that, I used to say the Japs would never get me. But there was no question about the mainland. How the hell are you going to storm a country where women and children, everybody would be fighting you? Of course we'd have won eventually, but I don't think anybody who hasn't actually seen the Japanese fight can have any idea of what it would have cost.[41]

Ground troops were prosaic. Geoff Brown's grandfather, John Walter Arthur Brown, was serving in New Guinea in the Australian Army when word came through of the dropping of the A-bombs and the Japanese surrender. A married man with five children, he recalled thinking: 'It was a dirty, stinking job, it looked like finishing, and we could all go home.'[42]

Charles Miller wrote:

> When the war ended, my dad was on an APD going to a temporary station in Attu. He was slated for carrier duty during and after the invasion.

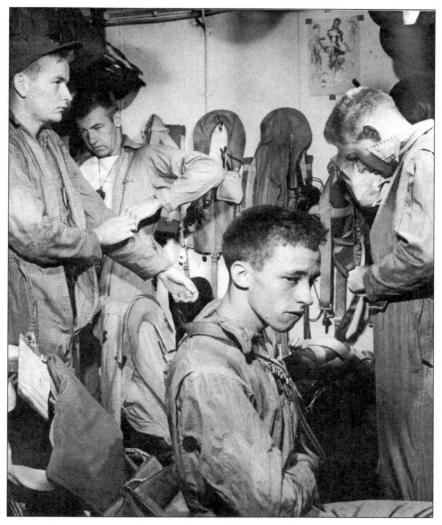

Veteran aircrewmen put on flight gear on board their aircraft carrier for a strike against Manila. Sober faces show they know what they are up against. (Photo by Lieutenant Wayne Miller, USNR. US Navy Photo)

Many years later, we toured the USS *Missouri* at Pearl Harbor. In those days, there was a little loudspeaker above the surrender deck. The speaker played an endless loop of MacArthur's surrender statement. When we got to the surrender deck, Dad recited along with it, word for word, still burnt in his memory after more than 55 years.

After they both said, 'These proceedings are closed,' Dad turned to me. 'When I first heard that.' A pause, voice breaking. 'I knew I could live to be twenty one.'[43]

Army Maritime Services soldier John Moyle was in Moratai preparing for further invasion of Japanese territory. He later said, 'I thought it was justification. There was only one way to call it quits. Probably a matter of who did it first.'[44]

British Army infantryman George MacDonald Fraser recalled at that time: 'There was certainly no moralising, no feeling at all of the guilt which some thinkers nowadays seem to want to attach to the bombing of Hiroshima and Nagasaki.'[45] But he goes on to say that it was certainly barbaric, but implies then again so was all of the war, and even surmises that maybe he and the section of infantry he led would not have dropped the bomb if they knew the destruction it would have caused – because 'that is the kind of men they were'.[46]

Rotter cites a Gallup poll of August 1985, which found an 85 percent approval rating for the use of the bombs, and a later Roper poll, which found 53.5 percent thought the attacks had been 'just right', with 23 percent more wishing the military had dropped more weapons.[47]

Of interest is that some Japanese, who later wrote about their experiences, saw the atomic weapons as having saved their country. Fighter pilot Yasuo Kuwahara, already notified that he would become a kamikaze pilot, later wrote:

> More than ten years later I learnt that on 8 August 1945, I was to have been part of a final desperation assault, involving thousands of men and planes – all that remained. The great besom of destruction that had swept away so many of my countrymen at Hiroshima had saved me.[48]

Finally, there were about 300,000 Allied prisoners of war in captivity by 1945. The orders for their 'disposal' once the invasion began had already been drafted. The relief they must have felt put all others in the shade.

Conclusion

The reaction of these serving in the Pacific was widespread and universal: thankfulness and relief. It is telling that in all of the accounts of Pacific warfare this author has read, not one serving person said they regretted the use of the atomic weapons.

CHAPTER FIFTEEN
THE ACTUAL AND POSSIBLE DEATHS OF POWS AS A FACTOR

Overview: In this chapter, we discuss the grim fatality rate that would have continued to decimate the POWs if the war had continued. Around 300,000 prisoners were held by the Japanese. But it would not have been the routine bad treatment that would have seen them all die – an execution order would have been put into effect the moment an invasion of the Home Islands started.

Although the Japanese took prisoners all across their new-found Empire, they treated them far more brutally than did other nations of the Axis countries. If you were captured by the Japanese in World War II, you stood a fair chance of dying, and you would certainly be mistreated, not only through not being fed or imprisoned properly, but by being beaten or tortured. As the war intensified, it became clearer to those imprisoned that their fate was of little concern to their captors; in fact, they were an inconvenience likely to be disposed of.

John Fletcher-Cooke, a POW, believed that: 'Few, if any, POWs would have got out of Japan alive if the atomic bombs had not been dropped on Hiroshima and Nagasaki.' He added: 'If the Allies had been forced to make an opposed landing, the Japanese would have undoubtedly have liquefied the POWs, if for no other reason than to guard them and feed them would have interfered with the task of repelling the invaders.'[1] Fletcher-Cooke argued that the A-bombs saved the lives of tens of thousands of POWs, as well as hundreds of thousands of Allied servicemen and 'millions of Japanese', for they would have fought on, he thought, if commanded by the Emperor, 'literally, have fought to the last man'.[2]

Allied prisoners of war cheer their rescuers, as the US Navy arrives at the Omori prison camp in late August 1945. (US Navy)

Fletcher-Cooke's number of POWs given above was on the conservative side. It turned out that 'Allied POWs and internees in Japanese hands turned out to be nearly 300,000, of whom 140,000 were caught up in the new turmoil in Java.'[3] A steady invasion would also have meant the end of all of these POWs in a systematic series of executions. Already, 35 percent of POWs were dying – a grim figure compared to those captured by the Germans during the war, with 0.9

percent there losing their lives. One analysis states: 'Of the 140,000 Americans held by the Japanese, 34 percent – 47,000 – would die in captivity.' [4] 'Of 22,376 Australian prisoners of war captured by the Japanese, 8,031 died – 36 percent of those held.'[5]

Frank details some of the fates of those interned by the Japanese during the war when prisoners were executed as reprisals after bombing raids: 22 were killed in the Gilbert Islands; 90 were bayoneted in Ballale; 96 were machinegunned in Wake, and 150 were murdered in Palawan. Such casual executions were by no means rare. They were inflicted, on the whole, by the Japanese Army and its Korean guards. The Navy, by comparison, treated prisoners it took humanely. Some of this may have been to do with their recognition of the unfortunate circumstances those survivors of a crippled or sinking ship found themselves: mariners who by no fault of their own were unable to fight on. The Army seemed instead to treat its prisoners, at least in part, with brutality because they perceived them as not having fought to their utmost.

Concerning the Imperial Japanese Navy, for cases of being treated well after battle, one only has to look at the stories of the sinking of HMAS *Perth*. One of the survivors of *Perth* later wrote:

> The Japanese sailors were curious as to our nationality but treated the Australian and American sailors kindly with eye drops for oil blindness and water and dry biscuits. Our oil-covered clothing was taken away and replaced with new white cotton loin cloths ....[6]

In another incident, naval officer Sam Falle gives an account of his rescue after HMS *Encounter* was sunk along with HMS *Exeter* and USS *Pope* on 1 March 1942 in the second Battle of the Java Sea:

> It must have been about midday, for the sun was vertical and we were just south of the equator. About 200 yards away we thought we saw a Japanese destroyer. Was she a mirage? We all saw her, so perhaps she was real, but our first emotion was not joy or relief, for we expected to be machine-gunned.

There was a great bustle aboard that ship, but the main armament was trained fore and aft, and there was no sign of machine guns. The ship's sailors were lowering rope-ladders all along the side of the ship. They were smiling small brown men in their floppy white sun-hats and too-long khaki shorts.

The ship came closer. We caught hold of the rope-ladders and managed to clamber aboard. We were covered with oil and exhausted. The Japanese sailors surrounded us and regarded us with cheerful curiosity. They took cotton waste and spirit and cleaned the oil off us, firmly but gently. It was – extraordinary to relate – a friendly welcome. I was given a green shirt, a pair of khaki shorts and a pair of gym shoes. Then we were escorted to a large space amidships and politely invited to sit down in comfortable cane chairs. We were served hot milk, bully beef and biscuits.

After a while the captain of the destroyer came down from the bridge, saluted us and addressed us in English: 'You have fought bravely. Now you are the honoured guests of the Imperial Japanese Navy. I respect the English navy, but your government is very foolish to make war on Japan.'

That fine officer searched for survivors all day, stopping to pick up even single man, until his small ship was overflowing. An awning was spread over the fo'c's'le to protect us from the sun; lavatories were rigged outboard; cigarettes were handed out; and by a biblical type of miracle, our hosts managed to give all 300 of us food and drink.

The only order we were given was not to smoke after dark lest 'English submarine' should see a lighted cigarette. The Japanese did not know, it seems, that there were no English submarines in the Java Sea. Yet they had continually stopped to rescue every survivor they could find.

Thanks to this destroyer and other Japanese ships, *Encounter* only lost seven men, and *Exeter* a surprisingly small number also. The survivors from *Pope* were rescued by the Japanese two days later.[7]

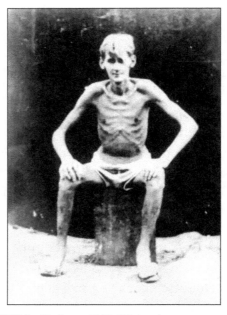

An unidentified Allied POW, freed in August 1945. (US Army)

But once imprisoned on land, the situation was grimmer. And towards the end of the war their presence in the face of the advancing Allies was illogical, according to the Japanese command's way of thinking.

In the summer of 1945, Marshal Terauchi issued a significant order: at the moment the Allies invaded the main islands, all prisoners were to be killed by the prison-camp commanders.[8] The order would have freed up all of those operating the POW camps to fight directly against the Allies. A typical progression of this order, recovered in Formosa, advised on their fate: 'Dispose of the prisoners as the situation dictates … it is the aim not to allow the escape of a single one, to annihilate them all, and not to leave any traces.'[9]

This order, according to James Bradley's *Flyboys*, may have come from Vice Minister of War Shitayama. Bradley quotes it in its entirety:

> When the battle situation becomes urgent, the POWs will be concentrated and confined in their location and kept under heavy guard until preparation for the final disposition will be made. Although the basic aim is to act under superior orders, individual disposition may be made in certain circumstances. Whether they are destroyed individually or in groups, and whether it is accomplished by means of mass bombing, poisonous smoke, poisons, drowning, or decapitation, dispose of them as the situation dictates. It is the aim not to allow the escape of a single one, to annihilate them all, and not to leave any traces.[10]

American pilot Louie Zamperini, imprisoned south of Tokyo, later wrote of two dates circulating in the POW camps in Japan. One was 15 September 1945, with all prisoners to be taken into the countryside, executed, and their bodies burned. The date, referred to as the 'kill-all order' by the POWs, was spoken of widely by sadistic guards. In some camps, large pits were prepared for body burial. In some camps, the date was said to be 22 August.[11]

Rohan Rivett, writing in the famous memoir *Behind Bamboo*, said of their POW camp commandant:

> Friendly Koreans had warned prisoners that Neguchi was preparing to massacre us all. At the time many were skeptical, but Japanese documents and other evidence discovered since the capitulation indicate that all camp commanders had received orders to kill prisoners in the event of paratroop landings or invasion by Allied forces. In the light of Allied plans, it seems certain that the attempt to massacre all prisoners in Siam would have begun within a few days. At Nakom Paton, the date 28 August was already specified.[12]

Leo Van Der Hoeven, an officer in the Netherlands Marine Corps, captured in 1942, later told members of his family of an incident towards the final days of the war. He had survived the Burma Railway and was in a camp near Ubon, in Thailand. One day working parties were commanded to begin digging long trenches, six feet wide, outside of the camp. One of the Australians commented that he 'didn't think the Japs were taking up gardening'. The war ended a few days later.[13]

In anticipation of the 'kill-all' order, some Japanese prisons began killing off captives in August 1945. All of the POWs on Ballale, Wake and Tarawa were executed, and at Palawan, all but 11 of the prisoners were dispatched. Such attitudes, as previously discussed, militated against a warning demonstration of the A-bombs. As Truman's Interim Committee noted, American POWs might be placed in the blast zone of any showcasing of the atom blasts.[14] [15] *Enola Gay* pilot Sweeney later wrote: 'Japan stalled. The killing went on. Every day hundreds of Americans continued to be killed and wounded in battles throughout the Pacific, in Southeast Asia, and in barbarous prisoner of war camps.'[16]

Aircrew then became the target for immediate execution rather than imprisonment. On the island of Kyushu, Toland records that eight American B-29 crewman were beheaded on 11 August 1945, and another 16 following the Emperor's surrender broadcast on the 15th.[17] After a firebomb raid of 23–24 May, which burnt Tokyo's military prison to the ground, all 62 American airmen imprisoned there 'died in the raid' – in reality executed, as 400 Japanese inmates all survived. The prison commandant was convicted of the war crime after the surrender.[18] [19]

Alistair Urquhart survived the invasion of Singapore and POW camps, and then being torpedoed by a US submarine while being transported across the South China Sea by his captors in 1943. He then lived through the bombing of Nagasaki. A historian researching his story suggested he was lucky to escape being dispatched at the hands of his captors:

Narrator: Many are convinced that the bomb also saved the lives of Alastair and his fellow prisoners.

Meg Parkes, FEPOW History researcher: We know that the orders had been given by the Japanese military that all prisoners of war were to be exterminated in early September 1945; that if the war hadn't ended when it did, I have no reason to doubt that that is exactly what would have happened.[20]

POWs arrive in Darwin, September 1945. (Australian Army)

Prisoners of war had already been massacred by the Japanese, so there was no precedent-setting to be overcome. On Wake atoll, fearing imminent invasion on 5 October 1943, 98 Americans were executed. On the island of Ballale, between 70–100 British POWs were executed for the same reason in spring 1943. On Tarawa, in late 1942, 22 Americans had been killed after a fight between American and Japanese naval ships off the island.[21] In 1945, James Fahey recorded on board USS *Montpelier*:

> When our invasion forces were on their way to land on Mindoro, the Japs thought we were going to make the landing here. The prisoners were forced to dig long trenches and then gasoline

was poured on them. A match was then set to the gasoline. The prisoners were human torches ... it is going to be a pleasure to bombard this island and blow the defenders to bits.[22]

The Japanese had form in this area. In what became known as the Rape of Nangking, an estimated 90,000 Chinese soldiers who had been captured were executed over a period of six weeks following the collapse of the city's defences in the invasion of December 1937:

> The elimination of the Chinese POWs began after they were transported by trucks to remote locations on the outskirts of Nanking. As soon as they were assembled, the savagery began, with young Japanese soldiers encouraged by their superiors to inflict maximum pain and suffering upon individual POWs as a way of toughening themselves up for future battles, and also to eradicate any civilised notions of mercy. Filmed footage and still photographs taken by the Japanese themselves document the brutality. Smiling soldiers can be seen conducting bayonet practice on live prisoners, decapitating them and displaying severed heads as souvenirs, and proudly standing among mutilated corpses. Some of the Chinese POWs were simply mowed down by machine-gunfire while others were tied-up, soaked with gasoline and burned alive. [23]

As the war became grimmer for the Japanese, it is more than likely that they would have seen their military resources being used in the camps as misdirected. Killing off their prisoners so to direct the expenditure of food and guard personnel to their own resistance would have been paramount. In this way the short sudden end to the war – brought about by the A-bombs – saved thousands of Allied military lives.

The destruction of civilians in those areas overrun by the Japanese also can't be left out of the moral, and even mathematical, decision behind using the A-bombs. Historian Robert Newman calculated that 17 million had died as a result of it. He further analysed that each month 'upwards of 250,000 people, mostly Asian, but some Westerners' would die.[24] Given that optimistic calculations of a conventional invasion would see the war continuing until at least November 1946, it is a fair prediction to say that the bombing of the two Japanese cities saved the lives of many millions of people outside of the combat forces of the Allies and Japanese.

POW Lester Tenney wrote of the actual end at length:

> In the late spring of 1945, I saw that the cruelty with which we prisoners of war were treated was only increasing. Our guards told us that Japanese units facing attack had received orders to kill all military and civilian POWs in their custody. They were to unburden themselves to focus on the fight. The executions were to begin 17 August. No Japanese soldier or civilian was preparing to surrender that August.
>
> Early on the morning of 9 August, from the POW camp where I was held some 30 miles across a bay, I saw the sky over Nagasaki change. It glowed red and the air turned warm against my skin. Until then, red was the color of my subjugation. My Japanese guards were certain that red had a uniquely Japanese meaning. It wasn't just the central color of their flag, it was viewed as emotionally representative of their pure spirit and sincerity. The red sky over Nagasaki ended those illusions.
>
> At that moment, I made a bet with a friend that soon we would all be set free. I was right.
>
> Japan's surrender saved us. The dropping of the bombs, as Emperor Hirohito himself acknowledged, was the only thing that made that surrender possible. As he explained to his subjects, 'Should we continue to fight, it would only result in the ultimate collapse and obliteration of the Japanese nation.' The bombs inflicted indiscriminate, total devastation, as no battle or bombing before, showing the consequences of trying to fight to the end. The bombings destroyed hope and glory, past and future.

It's also true that the bombings were acts of tragic and unprecedented violence. The bomb – this 'cruel weapon', as the stunned Emperor recorded in his surrender message on 15 August – ruined two cities, brought suffering and death to many tens of thousands of people and drastically altered landscapes and ecologies. Its use also transformed the nature of modern warfare and erased the last faint lines separating civilian and military, illegitimate and legitimate targets.

We POWs – men who were starved and tortured, who suffocated in the holds of hell ships, who were beaten at will, who died for lack of medical care, and who saw friends worked to death – have no doubt that the atomic bombs ended the war. The bombs took away all the justifications for Japan to continue to fight.[25]

Recovering POWs at Moratai with sailor, (l/r) Alex Hilliard, Arthur Deakin, Junior Edwards, Chips Crouch, Eddie Gilbert

George MacDonald Fraser, serving with the British Army, was of a more circumspect opinion. He wrote of his time at the end of the war:

It is now widely held (or at least it has been widely stated) that the dropping of atomic bombs was unnecessary because the Japanese were ready to give in. I shall say only that I wish those that hold that view had been present to explain the position to the little bastard who came howling out of the thicket near the Sittang, full of spite and fury, in that first week of August. He was half-starved and near naked, and his only weapon was a bamboo stake, but he was in no mood to surrender.

One of the best prison camp memoirs is Laurens Van der Post's *Night of the New Moon.* He said that once the news of the Hiroshima and Nagasaki bombings filtered through to the Japanese camp in which he was a POW, the brutalisation of the prisoners ceased. The Japanese knew it was over for them. The previously brutal guards and officers became deferential, one explaining to Van der Post: 'When we Japanese switch, we switch sincerely.'

It seems much of the POW situation, and their role in the A-bombings, has been forgotten years later. But not by all. Here is one letter to the editor of *The Australian*, that nation's national paper, on the 70th anniversary of the use of the bombs:

> I sense a certain rewriting of history taking place 70 years after the first, and hopefully the last, use of atomic weapons. The ABC in particular is casting Japan as a victim of the atomic explosions. Yes, hundreds of thousands died and this is regrettable. However, something seems to have been forgotten – Japan was the aggressor and started the war in the Asia-Pacific region. Japanese forces directly caused the deaths of more than ten million people. Many of these were civilians, especially millions of Chinese killed by the invading Japanese. Other atrocities included enforced prostitution of 'comfort' women, mistreatment, execution, starvation and forced labour of prisoners of war (including thousands of Australians), and 'medical research' conducted on civilians and prisoners.

The atomic weapons very much helped the war to end and caused the freedom of millions who had been oppressed by the Japanese. It also saved the lives of thousands of Allied troops who would have died if there had been a land invasion of Japan. It also saved my great uncle's life who was ill in Changi POW camp having suffered years of abuse. He was rescued and given medical treatment just in time. Lest we forget the carnage that was caused by Japanese imperialism.

Tim Gillespie, Kilsyth, Victoria.[26]

Conclusion

This book is largely a numerical accounting. To the number of lives *saved* by the use of the atomic weapons, we must add the approximately 300,000 saddest of them all – the POWs of the Japanese who stayed alive because of their use.

WHAT ALLIED CASUALTIES WOULD HAVE BEEN EXPERIENCED IF THE A-BOMBS HAD NOT BEEN USED?

Overview: In this chapter, we analyse how many deaths would have been incurred, looking at a two-stage invasion of Japan. Combat deaths would have resulted in approximately 767,000 lives lost, with four times that wounded: 3,070,400. Added to that would have been the execution of 300,000 POWs. In addition to this, given the loss of life in Japanese-held territories, the figure of around 4,567,000 dead is obtained. Operation Zipper – the Commonwealth assault of the Malayan Peninsula – is studied as an example of how an amphibious operation might have had problems.

The estimates of how many Allied military personnel would have died in a conventional invasion of Japan have been given in all sorts of ways over numerous years. However, it is sometimes coloured by political partisanship. And sometimes it is very low because the person wanted to justify their attacks on the A-bomb supporters. On the other hand, sometimes it is very high because the person wanted to justify the reverse: arguing the A-bombs should have been used.

On occasion too, the argument focuses only on the 'initial stage' of the Home Islands figure, as if the Japanese would have then given up. It is important then to remember that the assault would have been across beaches to positions ashore, and then it would have undergone a consolidation period while supplies were consolidated, which would have then been followed by a 'breakout' through Japanese resistance. This would have been no simple operation. For example, in very simplistic terms, Operation Cobra, the breakout from the French D-Day consolidation, occurred some seven weeks after the D-Day landings, and depended on another action – Operation Goodwood – to distract enough German forces to allow its success.

A Buffalo, loaded with Marines, churns through the sea bound for beaches of Tinian Island near Guam, July 1944. (USN)

Sometimes writers critical of the failure of the United States prefer the atom bomb over the amphibious assault have some sort of imagined universe in which the entire war halted, and then an invasion begins. They forget that huge collections of personnel and machines can't be suddenly put into stasis. They forget that military aviation in World War II killed more than actual combat itself, but that the training would have had to go on to keep aircrews at their peak. This would also be the case with the gunners, the infantrymen, the paratroopers, the sailors, the glider pilots, the tank crews – all of the complicated apparatus of millions of people.

At the end of this chapter, therefore, the numbers will be calculated from the information available. In the following chapter, the next part of this equation will be done for the Japanese defenders.

The totals are appalling.

A burial at sea of several servicemen who had died in combat. (Taken by a USS *Lexington* photographer. US Navy Photo)

The war was intensifying

Some of this is not surprising. General Sweeney, pilot of the second atomic aircraft *Bocks Car*, stated that '900 Americans were killed or wounded each day' at that period of the war, and therefore delay in forcing the Japanese surrender was a critical factor.[1] And time too was of the essence. A steadily mounting toll of deaths as the war intensified was having a terrible impact on many countries. For example, US deaths for the entire war are cited as 405,399, factoring in accidents and sickness and other factors.[2] A figure of 936,259 total casualties does not include figures for personnel hospitalised and returned to units.[3] The point is, however, that with a population of 140 million[4] in 1945, and nearly six million people[5] under arms – that is, one in 23, including babies, children, females and elderly, who were largely disengaged – the United States' population was being strongly impacted by the war. The steadily climbing toll was accelerating steeply too as the Allies commenced their final island assault phases: Sweeney again says that in the three months of Truman's presidency, 'The United States had sustained almost half of all Americans killed and wounded in the Pacific since Pearl Harbor.'[6]

Such alarming statistics are of primary interest to this work. The US Army fatality figures alone show a phenomenal rise through the three complete years of the war, but the Navy's also reflect the same inevitable rise:

Year	US Army fatalities[7] All ranks/ all theatres	Remarks	US Navy fatalities[8] All ranks/ all theatres	Remarks	Deaths per year	Deaths per week average
1941	810	n/a	2155	n/a	2965	57
1942	20,734	2549% increase from previous year	2809	30% increase from previous year	23,183	446
1943	41,638	101% increase from previous year	4524	61% increase from previous year	46,162	888
1944	149,822	260% increase from previous year	7685	69% increase from previous year	157,507	3028
1945	95,280	-36% decrease from previous year	11,446	49% increase from previous year	*See notes below*	

Year	US Army fatalities[7] All ranks/ all theatres	Remarks	US Navy fatalities[8] All ranks/ all theatres	Remarks	Deaths per year	Deaths per week average
			Projected figures if the war had continued			
1945	389,537	If 1945 had continued with the same 260% increase over 1944.	12,987	If 1945 had continued with the same 69% increase over 1944.	402,524	7740
1946	658,317	If 1946 had continued with the same 260% increase over 1945.	21,948	If 1946 had continued with the same 69% increase over 1945.	680,265	13,082

Notes:
- The inverse proportion of a higher fatality count for the Navy in 1941 versus the Army is a reflection of the Pearl Harbor strikes, which killed more Navy than Army personnel.
- The Allies stopped fighting in early May in Europe, and in early August in the Pacific, thus accounting for the dip in Army figures. The Navy's percentage increase in 1945 is a reflection of its increased tempo and force size, with more carriers, battleships, cruisers, destroyers and submarines committed every month.
- Size of the US Forces at the end of the war: Army: 8,267,958; Navy: 3,380,817; Marines: 474,680; Coastguard: 85,783; Total: 12,209,238.
- The table above does not include the US Marines. Although a total of 19,733 fatalities is a widely circulated figure[9] for World War II, a year by year progression has not been located. Their fatality figures would be most difficult to calculate in a hypothetical Home Islands assault, but it would have to be estimated as high, given their primary role of amphibious assault.

The table above is a limited attempt but quite a realistic one in trying to achieve a fatality count – per week – for US forces. If the war had continued through 1945, it would have meant around 8000 fatalities a week, given the addition of the Marines in a rough estimate. If the war had continued through 1946, an average of around 13,500 a week would have been incurred. Given the presence of other Allied forces – the British Empire and its Dominions, and other countries, why should we not say a realistic estimate of deaths of around 15,000 a week?

Saving lives was an imperative in most minds. In an edition of *Harper's* magazine, US Secretary of War Stimson wrote: 'My chief purpose was to end the war in victory with the least cost in the lives of the men in the armies which I had helped to raise.' In his following paragraph, he noted the use of the weapons ended the firebombing of Japanese cities and the blockading of their ports, thus saving their citizens' lives too.[10]

A Hellcat fighter takes off from the flight deck of the USS *Lexington*. (Photographed by Captain Edward Steichen US Navy)

For some revisionists it doesn't matter. Collie, for example, criticises the haste in which the second bomb was deployed, saying that 'the invasion of the Japanese Home Islands wasn't scheduled till November'.[11] So what? As Sweeney points out: 'During the three short months since Harry S Truman had been president, the United States had sustained almost half of all Americans killed or wounded in the Pacific since Pearl Harbor.'[12] Anyone reading the first-hand accounts of those times is drawn into realising that as the war neared Japan, everyone was living on borrowed time. EB Sledge's First Marine Division was to make a landing close to the Yokosuka Naval Base, 'one of the most heavily defended sectors of the island'. The Marines were told, he recalls, that:

> ... due to the strong beach defences, caves, tunnels, and numerous Jap suicide torpedo boats and manned mines, few Marines in the first five assault waves would get ashore alive – my company was scheduled to be in the first and second waves. The veterans in the outfit felt we had already run out of luck anyway .... We viewed the invasion with complete resignation that we would be killed – either on the beach or inland. [13]

Fussell points out that 'John Kenneth Galbraith is persuaded that the Japanese would have surrendered surely by November without an invasion.' Galbraith thought the A-bombs unnecessary and unjustified because the war was ending anyway. The A-bombs saw, 'a difference, at most, of two or three weeks'. But at the time, with no indication that surrender was on the way, the kamikazes were sinking American vessels; the *Indianapolis* was sunk (880 men killed), and Allied casualties were running to over 7000 per week. 'Two or three weeks,' says Galbraith. That is 21,000 of your own people who you are sacrificing dead and seriously wounded.[14] And with no indication from the Japanese militarists they would surrender.

Gailbraith's argument loses much credibility anyway if it posits that an invasion could have taken place within weeks. The ability to carry out a massive amphibious assault was not something that was kept in a box to be take out and used as necessary. It was made up of skill sets, which had been painfully acquired and used across the Pacific. They included: landing on beaches; landing under fire; attacking defence positions, calling down artillery/air support; storming enemy positions; consolidating against ground counter-attack; establishing a beachhead for supplies; establishing defence against air attack; positioning and ranging artillery for defensive usage; bringing in reinforcements; reconnaissance prior to further advance; and more.

Aircrewman wounded in a strike on Rabaul is removed from his aircraft on the carrier USS *Saratoga*, November 5, 1943. (Lieutenant Wayne Miller, USNR, US Navy Photo)

All of these skills needed to be practised prior to use. Many were complicated operations involving personnel and equipment from different services and units. For example, naval ships attacking positions ahead of advancing infantry needed careful establishment and to practise the fire mission orders that would produce a bombardment. Troops needed to practise it in simulation, and then use real explosives. Such rehearsals took enormous amounts of time and space to set up.

Both sides realised that the conventional assault would produce high casualty levels. General Le May:

> Even given that strategic bombing could have ended the war without the atomic bomb, I think it was a wise decision to drop the bomb because this action did hasten the surrender process already underway .... What guided me in all my thinking, and guided all our efforts – the reason the Twenty-First Bomber Command worked like no other command during the war and the thing that kept us going – was the million men we were going to lose if we had to invade Japan .... The atomic bomb probably saved ... perhaps a million American casualties.[15]

American troops chat near a dead Japanese soldier on Iwo Jima. (USMC)

Professor Saburo Ienaga, who waged a campaign post-war to obliterate censorship of Japanese crimes in the war, suggested that the main reason for the use of the A-weapons was for the Americans to avoid the 'huge casualties expected in a landing on the Home Islands'. He does not discuss how many Japanese would have died specifically, but throughout his work *The Pacific War* there is a theme of total obliteration of the nation if a conventional assault had gone ahead.[16]

General Le May again:

> You're going to kill an awful lot of civilians. Thousands and thousands. But, if you don't destroy the Japanese industry, we're

going to have to invade Japan. And how many Americans will be killed in an invasion of Japan? Five hundred thousand seems to be the lowest estimate. Some say a million.[17]

At Potsdam, Army Chief of Staff General George Marshall had warned President Truman that an invasion would cost more than 250,000 American lives.[18] The feasibility of this has been much debated. Various other interpretations put it at half a million, and another in which General Marshall at Potsdam was talking of a figure of up to a million American invasion casualties. One of Stimson's aides had commissioned a report by scientist WB Shockley, and this contained a figure of 1.74 million casualties, out of which between 400-800,000 would be fatalities.[19]

Henry L Stimson, who was US Secretary of War in 1945, 'later claimed that half a million American lives would have been lost in an invasion'.[20] Frank has suggested American deaths of between 32,700 and 147,500.[21] Historian Barton J Bernstein disagrees, suggesting: 'about 25,000 Americans would probably die in the first invasion of Kyushu, and 21,000 in the follow-up invasion of Honshu'.[22]

There seems to be little consensus. 'Some authorities claimed that the dropping of the bomb was justified because an invasion would have cost the United States half a million casualties – though others disagreed and put the figure as low as 40,000.'[23] A figure used in one of the latest comprehensive documentaries on the Hiroshima raid suggests 'one million Allied and one million Japanese' would die in a conventional assault on Japan.[24] The rationale for the figure is unknown. But it is possible to give some sort of assessment from the conventional calculation of assaults against fortified and prepared positions across the ages.[25]

In general, the advantage is with the defender, and a four to one advantage in numbers is necessary for the attack to be successful. This was of course not going to be the situation in the Home Islands: the attack force would be in the hundreds of thousands against millions of defenders. But also obvious is that such a calculation is fraught with other variables; for example, due to the fact that the quality of the attack force would be far higher than any local militia they might encounter. Other aspects would include:

- *Training.* Some Western forces had over a year of high quality training given to them before they deployed overseas. For example, the famous *Band of Brothers* television series, based on the actual experiences of Easy Company of the US Army's 101st Airborne Division, depicts them being forced through actual explosions and literally bloody situations, where animal offal was used to bring home to the trainees what they might encounter. Then again, this could be measured against the training given to Japanese teenagers who might never be given a firearm.

- *Ground.* The planned situation for the Japanese would be one where they could force the incoming invaders to fight them on the ground of the defenders' choosing, where they would have the advantage of slope, height, terrain and more. The Duke of Wellington is said to have told his commanders that he had the ground of Waterloo 'in his pocket' for some time as being an ideal place to fight. The choice of ground in the Home Islands would have been in the Japanese pocket: the choice of where to fight lay almost entirely with the Japanese, and instead of one battle there would have been thousands.

- *Equipment.* Here the advantage of technology would lie with the Allies, whose airpower by now was developed ahead of the Japanese; whose tanks were superior, and whose artillery was just as good. But the Japanese artillery would be sited more carefully and situated to take advantage of depressions, caves, slope and so on.

- *Morale.* This was known to be, both before Napoleon's famous dictum, worth an enormous amount in combat power. The morale of the attackers, as we have seen, would have been likely to be low, at least at first, knowing of the difficulty of their situation, but it may well have risen with anger. The morale of the defenders may also have been low, given their foreknowledge of their situation, but then it would have been likely bolstered by the same tenacity the Japanese armies had always exhibited.

Anti-aircraft gun crews of a US Navy cruiser strain to spot the status of an unidentified plane overhead. (US Navy Photo)

In essence, there was a fair understanding of the difficulty of the mission, but the above factors are so variable it would be difficult to calculate the cost. There was a fair degree of practical realisation going in through 1945, however, as to how many dead and wounded there would be. One of the stories that illustrates this is that of the Purple Heart, the US medal given to dead and wounded personnel. There were not going to be enough:

> The Navy had believed that its initial 1942 order for 135,000 Purple Hearts would be sufficient for all wartime needs but found that it had to order 25,000 more in October 1944 – and, alas, 50,000 more in the spring of 1945. These orders could not be fulfilled until as late as the next year – months after soldiers and Marines were expected to fight their way ashore while sailors battled fresh waves of Kamikazes.[26]

Back in the United States, the director of the mint responsible reprimanded her Philadelphia facility, which was responsible for producing the medal's central components: 'Think of the 20,000 heroes at Iwo Jima, due to receive the Purple Hearts which we are unable to supply!' The Navy made arrangements with the Army to 'borrow' 60,000 decorations. Further analysis caused an order for 1,506,000 Purple Hearts to be made for the war effort – the stock was used throughout the Vietnam War and is still being used today. This may be as good as we can get to the understanding of how much the US forces thought the invasion would cost them.

Operation Zipper

As noted above, vigorous practice was going to be needed to sharpen skill sets. Harper notes in *Miracle of Deliverance* that no good knowledge of the invasion beaches could be compiled because of the need to keep the Japanese defenders guessing as to where the landings would take place.[27] The Normandy D-Day planners were aided by the Allied knowledge of what were summer holiday beaches in the landing areas. Indeed, planning as to the gradient, surface and sub-surface composition had been gained there by the gathering of holiday picture postcards beforehand. No such foreknowledge would have been available for Japan, with the country rarely visited by people from the Allied nation populations prior to the outbreak of the war.

Operation Zipper, which took place after the A-bombings, was an illustration of what may well have been the scenario landings for the Coronet and Olympic beaches. Even though it was being held without Japanese troops opposing the landing, it was a disaster. Zipper was the code name for the part of the invasion force that landed in the Port Swettenham area to help in the re-taking of Malaya. The first landing took place on Sunday 9 September 1945:[28]

> Even though the beach looked firm and had been assessed as such in the intelligence preparation for Zipper, the sand surface was not stable enough for vehicles. Approximately 800 sank into the sand and were written off. One officer commented: 'It ended in such chaos that it would have been catastrophic if the atomic bombs had not been dropped and we had, therefore, faced an opposed landing. The result is really unimaginable. So far as I can see there would have been wholesale slaughter.'[29]

It was common to hear remarks like, 'My God, one sniper would have done for the lot of us.'[30] Ships were stranded on sandbars; vehicles disappeared without trace into the water, soldiers drowned and dead bodies were common, and confusion reigned ashore.[31] Operation Zipper aimed to put a substantial force across the beachhead, and in actuality delivered far less than that.

Potential[32]	Personnel target	Vehicle target	Stores target
Aim	97,506 troops	9157 vehicles	81,910 tons
Achieved	19,364 troops	3032 vehicles	14,000 tons
Percentage of the aim	19.8%	33%	17%

One reaction from a US combat veteran was:

> Thousands of British assault troops would have been destroyed too, the anticipated casualties from the almost 200,000 men in

the six divisions (the same number used to invade Normandy) assigned to invade the Malay Peninsula on 9 September. Aimed at the reconquest of Singapore, this operation was expected to last until about March 1946 – that is, seven more months of infantry fighting. 'But for the atomic bombs,' a British observer intimate with the Japanese defences notes, 'I don't think we would have stood a cat in hell's chance. We would have been murdered in the biggest massacre of the war. They would have annihilated the lot of us.'

Escort carrier USS *Gambier Bay* was sunk by Japanese gunfire during the Leyte Gulf engagement (US Navy)

Most of those who took part in Operation Zipper felt at the time that the atomic bombs were the only factor that saved them from being embroiled in a bloodbath. To them Churchill expressed the Allied development of the atomic bomb exactly right – for them it was a miracle of deliverance. [33]

It does not matter. No politician would have agreed to the scenario, certainly not then and not now either, of having a weapon of such immense power as 'one plane [bomb], one city' and not use it. The leader of a country at war can't and will not say, 'We're sorry soldiers – but 40,000 of you are going to have to die rather than have us kill too many of the enemy with our new weapon.' As far as can be determined, this aspect of the situation was first revealed by Robert James Maddox in his essay 'The Biggest Decision: Why We Had to Drop the Atomic Bomb' in 1995. He wrote:

> One can only imagine what would have happened if tens of thousands of American boys had died or been wounded on Japanese soil and then it had become known that Truman had chosen not to use weapons that might have ended the war months sooner.[34]

Labelled originally "Scratch another Meatball – Saipan Operations." Photo by a USS *Kitkun Bay* photographer. (US Navy Photo)

This political angle must be explored more fully. The chances of Truman and any supporters of using the A-weapons suppressing the news of it were non-existent. If we posit the possibility of such people deciding, on the basis that too many Japanese were to be killed in such an attack, or alternatively, that A-weapons were simply non-usable for ethical means, how would the situation have unfolded?

First, there would doubtless have been many people who knew about the atomic work who would not have supported the decision. The Manhattan Project had been underway for years by the time decisions were being made in mid-1945.[35] There were thousands of people working on the technology developments: machinists for the bomb-casings; B-29 mechanics who were modifying the bomb-bays; people building the test towers for the original explosions; people working on the technical development of the bombs themselves, aircrews developing flight test equipment from[36] September 1944; and of course all of the original scientists themselves. Some personnel had been engaged for six years, with the appointment of the Advisory Committee on Uranium, which met for the first time on 21 October 1939.[37] By mid-1943, at Oak Ridge, the number of personnel working directly on the atomic bomb development had reached 15,000, and by late 1944 around 50,000 were involved.[38]

Therefore the chances of the atomic weapon possibilities being extinguished without public knowledge were zero. If the Project had been disbanded and the idea dropped because of the potential for excessive enemy destruction, the concepts would have quickly become widespread public knowledge anyway. In fact, there were copious leaks, some of them resulting in newspaper stories, even before the Trinity test, let alone after it.[39]

Furthermore, once the test explosion of the Trinity test bomb had taken place, the military aspects relating to the destructive power available were obvious:

... the device exploded over the New Mexico desert, vaporising the tower and turning asphalt around the base of the tower to green sand. The bomb released approximately 18.6 kilotons of power, and the New Mexico sky was suddenly brighter than many suns. Some observers suffered temporary blindness even though they looked at the brilliant light through smoked glass. Seconds after the explosion came a huge blast, sending searing heat across the desert and knocking some observers to the ground. A steel container weighing over 200 tons, standing a half-mile from ground zero, was knocked ajar. (Nicknamed Jumbo, the huge container had been ordered for the plutonium test and transported to the test site but eliminated during final planning.)[40]

A later report was more prescriptive:

Los Alamos scientists now agreed that the blast had been the equivalent of between 15,000 and 20,000 tons of TNT, higher than anyone had predicted. Groves reported that glass shattered 125 miles away, that the fireball was brighter than several suns at midday, and that the steel tower had been vaporised.[41]

Marine Pfc Douglas Lightheart (right) cradles his 30-cal. machine gun in his lap, while he and his buddy take time out for a cigarette, while mopping up the enemy on Peleliu Is. (Cpl HH Clements, September 14, 1944. USMC)

The capability of the weapon was easily seen: there was enormous destructive power available from just one bomb, which would therefore require just one aircraft to deliver it, and with Allied air supremacy over the target, the bombing mission's success would have been assured. The new weapon was likely going to be far more powerful in terms of being able to destroy the enemy than the multi-bomber missions, which had previously been required. It would not have taken too much analysis to see that Japan could be destroyed city by city at almost no resultant loss for the Allies: there may have been some technical mission failure resulting in aircraft and lives lost, but that was an acceptable risk, lessened even more by growing Allied air superiority over the Home Islands and the suppression of enemy fighter and anti-air gunnery.

Any decision to not use such attack methods could and most certainly would have been leaked to the media. Although not as pervasive as today's constant world of communication, the newspapers of the time were following the war day by day. The tone of the war was fiercely aggressive in America, and had been so since the surprise attack on Pearl Harbor, which enraged most of its citizenry, including the armed forces when it broke out:

> In a US movie theatre in North Carolina, when the commencement of the war was announced, all of the Marines present burst into their anthem 'From the Halls of Montezuma'; threw their hats in the air, and then 'snake danced in the aisles', according to one of their officers, who pondered: 'Do the Japs know what they have started – if they could see the reactions of the Marines?'[42]

It was not important in the public's minds as to how many Americans would have died in a conventional assault – they just wanted it finished at the lowest cost possible. The country had been witness to the enormous expense, effort required, and lives lost in the D-Day assaults of almost exactly year previously, in the D-Day landings. They had heard of the cost involved in the five beach landings, particularly at Omaha, where the American assault (their second beach out of the total of five attacked by the Allies) had seen many US lives lost. The Battle of Normandy, summing up the amphibious attacks and the fighting afterwards, incurred approximately 425,000 casualties.[43]

The home audiences had watched as famous generals such Patton and Montgomery had smashed their way across Europe, and had seen how fiercely the Germans had fought. The tenacity of the Japanese had already been seen in campaigns such as Saipan and Okinawa – the Japanese were just as tenacious, perhaps even more so, if not as well equipped as their Axis cousins. The Americans by now knew precisely what they were up against:

> On Okinawa where the US Marines took extremely heavy casualties to take the island, one platoon leader told new green replacements in no uncertain manner about the calibre of the enemy they faced:

> Pointing his pistol at these bewildered lambs, he concluded, 'And if I hear any bullshit about the Japs being lousy fighters, I'll shoot you. If one of you motherfuckers says they can't shoot straight, I'll put a bullet between your fuckin' eyes before they do.'[44]

Bob Neiman, the Executive Officer of the 1st Tank Battalion of the US Marine Corps, thought of the Japanese as 'tenacious, among the finest fighters in the world, next to the Marine Corps ... well trained, well disciplined, with little regard for their own lives'.[45] The cost became known almost immediately for any unit going into combat. One GI battalion, the 1st of the 307th Infantry Regiment, lost more than half its men in eight days, including eight company commanders in a thirty-six-hour period.[46]

Japanese resolve was often extremely strong, with the infantry holding their positions in the face of odds that would have broken the hearts of many Westerners. One account from a Japanese soldier describes advancing to the Allied positions at night in an effort not to take the ground – the Japanese unit was not strong enough for that – but to get the enemy to retreat enough so that the ammunition, food and equipment they left behind could be taken by the Japanese for their own use. Then they would go back to their own positions, to fight and die for another day. Those wounded who could not contribute were apologetic:

> If he were heavily injured he would regret overtaxing his mates. Those men passed away saying, 'Excuse me. I regret dying.' They died apologising and weeping. The battlefield takes the life of such brave men, and there is no way of helping them. We were short of food, but most distressing was that we did not have bullets. Still, we did not give up …. [47]

Marines smoke out Japanese from a cave at Naha, Okinawa. (USMC)

The reaction of the Allies was ferocity. US Navy Admiral William F Halsey exhibited in his characteristically blunt way the overall aggression developed, even at the strategic level, to any Navy personnel landing at Tulagi. A large sign proclaimed: 'KILL JAPS. KILL JAPS. KILL MORE JAPS. You will help to kill the yellow bastards if you do your job well.'[48] In summary, Allied anger was at a fever pitch.

The reaction of Americans to a decision to not use a new super-weapon would have been incredulous, furious and aggressive. Newspapers would have thundered with headlines proclaiming that not one American life should be lost if there was an alternative. Truman's Democratic Party, and indeed every Congressman and Senator, would have been savagely attacked. The fact that America was founded on revolution would have been quickly on people's minds, and this was a country where firearms were easily at hand. An armed insurrection would have been a very real possibility. As the immense machinery of the proposed conventional attack would have moved into motion, the fury would have only grown stronger.

To countenance the idea that with the knowledge of the atomic weapon's possible capabilities becoming publicly known, and a conventional assault gathering pace, against the idea that Truman could have refused to use the new weapons is fantasy. If he had done so he would have been deposed from office, by public revolt or military coup, and a more co-operative leader installed.

This is not to say that this would have been a peculiarly American attitude. No country in this situation would have endured it – certainly not in 1945, and most likely not today. The number of the country's own war dead is almost immaterial. Be it 40,000 or 250,000, any country in the situation of killing thousands of its own people – or none at all – just because the enemy death count is going to be 'too high', is fantasy. Imagine yourself as a mother of a soldier in the United States at that time hearing such an argument. As General Sweeney noted of the revisionist arguments 'making the rounds' in 1995, which suggested 'only 46,000' Americans would have died in an invasion. He asked:

Which 46,000 were to die?

Whose father?

Whose brother?

Whose husband? [49]

Marines swarm over a pillbox on Tarawa, braving fire to silence the defenders. Photo by Warrant Officer Obie Newcomb, Jr., USMCR. (US Marine Corps)

J Samuel Walker cites a figure in the US Army alone of 3233 deaths for the month of July 1945, and notes that if that had continued without the use of the bombs and the invasion plans had been running to plan, then another approximate 9700 deaths would have occurred by November. That is before any invasion would have started.[50] Stimson thought:

> We estimated that if we should be forced to carry this plan [the invasion] to its conclusion, the major fighting would not end

until the latter part of 1946, at the earliest. I was informed that such operations might be expected to cost over a million casualties to American forces alone. Additional large losses might be expected among our allies, and of course, if our campaign were successful and if we could judge by previous experience, enemy casualties would be much larger than our own.[51]

Frontline casualties would have been enormous, even if the assault had been characterised by artillery and air strikes first. This was the situation at Okinawa, and yet (for example) EB Sledge's Marine company experienced a 153 percent casualty rate: that is, they took dead and wounded to a level that exceeded their original number of personnel completely, plus another 53 percent.[52]

Total of predicted Allied fatalities resulting from a conventional invasion of Japan, starting in November 1945 and terminating at the end of 1946

These calculations start with a caveat: the fatality counts here could be raised or lowered by a number of factors. For example, kamikaze operations could have been more effective, given the close range they would be flying to. A Japanese surrender after Phase 1 of the invasion could lessen the number of Allied military dying massively. People in Japanese-held territories could have risen in revolt, perhaps lessening their death count, but then again perhaps raising it through combat. However, each section of the table should be considered as a realistic scenario.

Type of person dead	Cause of death	Number dead	Notes
Military aviators	Through combat in the entire operation.	17,000[53]	Taking D-Day as an equivalent.
Military aviators	Through accident in the entire operation.	40,000[54]	See note below. Also that 'in the preparation period and run-up to D-Day, Allied air forces lost nearly 12,000 men in over 2000 aircraft'.[55]

Type of person dead	Cause of death	Number dead	Notes
Naval personnel	Through combat against kamikaze air strikes in the landing phase of Kyushu.	100,000	Using the Okinawa figure of 200 aircraft killing 12,300 servicemen, with 1500 aircraft kamikaze strikes predicted for the Kyushu invasion.[56]
Naval personnel	Through combat against suicide boats, submarines and divers.	3200	Suicide boats (9200 total) estimated at 1% success rate; submarines and divers at nil. See explanatory note below.
Army/ Marines	Through combat in the landing phase of Kyushu.	50,000	Taking D-Day's 37,000[57] as an equivalent[58] for the first figure, and taking Truman's advisors (see note below) for the second of 79,000, a middle figure is arrived at.
Army/ Marines	Through combat in the invasion phase of Kyushu.	316,000[59]	Using the Truman advisor figure.
Naval personnel	Through combat in the landing phase of Honshu.	41,150	Calculated as 50% of the Kyushu figure, given the intensity of Allied air operations against manufacturing and airfields, and with air superiority, meaning less kamikaze aircraft.
Army/ Marines	Through combat in the landing phase of Honshu.	50,000	Using the same figure as Kyushu, rationalising this as being where Japan would concentrate more strongly, with Tokyo (and Nagano cave complex) being the centre of gravity.
Army/ Marines	Through combat in the invasion phase of Honshu.	158,000	50% of the Kyushu figure, arguing a) that Japan's capacity is waning, b) Allied air superiority would become supremacy, and c) it would have brought in enormous amounts of heavy artillery and armour since taking Kyushu.

Type of person dead	Cause of death	Number dead	Notes
Sub-total – total combat deaths		775,350	
Prisoner of war	Execution	300,000[60]	Figured to take place from the moment it became apparent an invasion of the Home Islands was starting, at the orders of Field Marshall Terauchi.
People dying in Japanese-held lands	250,000 people a month over a 14-month period.	3,500,000	Argued by Robert Newman from starvation, disease, executions, and battle deaths, in all of the areas held by the Japanese across their conquered territories, especially China.[61]
Total deaths		4,575,350	
Total wounded		3,660,280	Using 4/5ths of the total casualty count.

Explanatory notes

Military aviation

The figure of 16,714 is the D-Day fatality total. Comparing D-Day to a Kyushu attack seems a logical start. It would require a book to describe the operations of the 3000 carrier aircraft envisaged for the initial Home Islands assault. These would be backed up by B-29 operations from Tinian and Okinawa. Given the USAAF lost 35,946 killed in accidents in the entire war, from December 1942 to August 1945, but that their operations became slowly but steadily more intense, this seems reasonable for a 14–15 month period of absolute intensity. Note that the Kyushu operations would include USAAF, USN, RAF, RN as the major forces, but there would be thousands more aviators from other Allied countries.

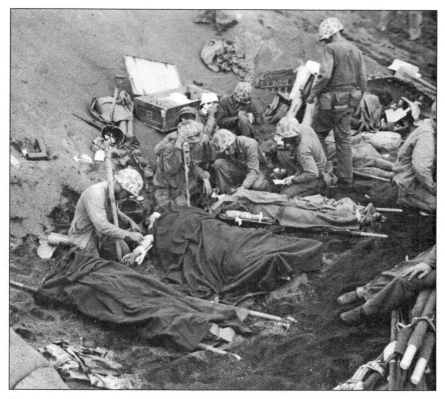

Navy doctors and corpsmen treat Marines on Iwo Jima. (US Marine Corps)

Army/Marine combat in Kyushu

Historian Barton J Bernstein suggests: 'about 25,000 Americans would probably die in the first invasion of Kyushu, and 21,000 in the follow-up invasion of Honshu.' US forces were 2/5ths of those across the five beaches at D-Day; the others being Canadians (1/5th) and British. In the Pacific, there would have been substantial numbers of Australians, New Zealanders, and units from other countries. Truman's military advisers, in a White House meeting on 18 June 1945, predicted that 30–35 percent of the 770,000-man invasion force could reasonably be expected to be killed or wounded during just the first 30 days of the invasion of Kyushu. Translation: 231,000 to 269,000 dead or wounded Americans in the first 30 days of combat. It was estimated that it would take 120 days to secure and occupy the entire island.

By the end of that four-month period, American casualties could realistically reach around 395,000.

Suicide boats

One estimate is that 2000 of these boats would have been ready for the defence of Kyushu. Another source suggests: 'These suicide boats were produced in great number, 6200 for the Navy and 3000 for the Army.'[62] One account suggests that during the 88-day Okinawa campaign, almost 700 suicide boats, supported by about 7000 troops, sank two American ships and damaged five and probably damaged another. [63]

This means at hitting only eight out of 700, that is 1 percent of their targets. Of those struck, only 25 percent sink, the rest of the vessels would be damaged. For Kyushu, if the Japanese had 2000 boats available, they would hit 20 targets, of which five would sink. For Honshu, if they have 7200 left, they would strike 60 vessels, of which 15 would sink.

Their pilots' training would have told them to aim for the largest ships. However, conventional naval tactics meant that such ships were screened by destroyers and frigates. An explosive strike on one of these would probably kill 2/3rds of the crew, thus estimating 100 persons per ship @20 ships, being 2000 personnel KIA. For the damaged ships (15 at Kyushu, and 45 at Honshu), we might estimate 20 personnel KIA, thus 1200, for a 3200 total.

Their 'swarm' tactics, to use a modern naval term, would have been reasonably successful. One argument for seeing some positive results would have been that the concept of your naval vessel being attacked by numerous small surface boats, moving fast on erratic courses, was quite new to the Pacific War. Allied naval vessel commanders had learnt through bitter experience how to come with attacks from the air from numerous aircraft at once. One look at a 1945 Allied warship proves that: the AA systems crammed into every possible part of the ship were indicative of how necessary such weapons were to cope in the environment of high-speed aircraft, some of which were kamikaze, but others of which used bombs, guns and rockets. The AA systems could have been used, often with adaptation, against small boat targets. But the 'leakage' – another modern term – would have seen some boats get through. (The swarm concept is still in use today, and in particular was thought of as feasible for USSR, Iraqi, and Iranian forces up to the present.)

Suicide submarines and divers

These are rated as totally ineffective. Naval tactics would have called for extensive lengthy depth-charging ahead of any landings. Ships standing off and waiting for the start of the assault would likely have been protected by minefields, and certainly by picket ships, depth-charging routinely even without gaining contacts. Landing boats would have seen explosive charges hurled ahead of them if the presence of divers was suspected.

The midget submarines of the Japanese were useful in general only if used as a surprise weapon. And they were not very effective even then. For example, the three-boat attack on Sydney Harbour in Australia, in May 1942, saw three submarines used, and all lost, for a total of 21 Allied naval personnel killed. The Japanese had the advantage of surprise, and a leisurely reconnaissance: they even overflew the city the previous day without the plane being recognised as Japanese and fired at. The boom net protecting the harbour was unfinished, and the three boats simply went around one end. Even with all of these advantages, they missed their primary target – the cruiser USS *Chicago* – and sank a ferry accommodation vessel instead. All three submarines were then engaged and lost. In a major assault on the Home Islands, their advantages would have been negated, and the slow, clumsy, and usually single-shot weapon concept of the tiny boats would have amounted to nothing.

Conclusion

The Allies would have taken every feasible precaution to prevent their own losses in a conventional invasion. Even so, they would have lost nearly 800,000 dead in combat operations alone. Their own prisoners in the hands of the Japanese – another 300,000 – would have also died. Meanwhile, the impact of the war on the lands held by the Empire would have been in the millions. All of these people had their lives saved by the deaths of the approximately 200,000 who died at Hiroshima and Nagasaki.

Transfer of wounded from the USS *Bunker Hill* to the USS *Wilkes Barre*. (US Navy Photo)

WHAT CASUALTIES WOULD JAPAN HAVE LIKELY EXPERIENCED IF THE A-BOMBS HAD NOT BEEN USED?

Overview: In this chapter, we analyse the loss rates of the Army and Navy, militias and 'armed civilians', and of the effects of Operation Starvation upon the population of the Home Islands. Taking a figure of 72,147,000 for the overall population, the study concludes that approximately 27,879,000 Japanese would have lost their lives by the end of a 14-month long conventional invasion, which would have ended in December 1946. Caveats around this figure are explained.

Military casualties

The Japanese fought like no other armed force. For them, aggression continued until you could no longer fight. If wounded, you fought on as best you could. Death was far more preferable to capture. The *Pacific War Encyclopedia* notes that until the collapse of the Japanese resistance, only 11,600 Japanese military were taken.[1]

In one South-East Asian attack, the commander of the Japanese 33rd division noted that two battalions lost 953 out of the 1200 men they started with.[2] This defies the conventional military wisdom that states that a force will not take more than 30 percent of its personnel as casualties before they break.

The strength of the Japanese Army lay 'in the spirit of the individual Japanese soldier. He fought and marched till he died. If 500 Japanese were ordered to hold a position, we had to kill 495 before it was ours – and then the last five killed themselves'.[3] General Slim noted that in the last stages of the war: 'We were killing Japanese at a rate of over a hundred to one.'[4]

Thirty-five percent of the Allied troops engaged at Okinawa became casualties.[5] Twenty-nine Allied ships were sunk, around 12,000 Americans died and 40,000 were wounded.[6] If that was the price exacted for taking one island, what would be the price of taking Japan itself?

The final use of the super-battleship *Yamato* is a good example of how wasteful the Japanese military was prepared to be with its own people. She and her sister *Musashi* – lost in the Battle of Leyte Gulf – were the largest battleships ever built.

There was little use for *Yamato* in the dying days of the Imperial Japanese Navy: the Home Islands were being steadily hemmed in by submarines and aircraft carrier battle groups. Yet she was sent on a suicide mission. *Yamato* was sunk with the loss of 3000.

Year Completed	*Yamato*: 1941 [7] *Musashi*: 1942
Displacement	71,659 tons
Dimensions	862'10' x 121'1' x 32'11'
Speed	27 knots
Armament	• 9 x 18.1'/45 • 12 (later 6) x 6.1'/60 • 12 (later 24) x 5'/40 DP • Up to 150 x 25 mm AA • 4 x 13 mm AA
Armour	• 16.1' belt (inclined) • 11.8' bulkheads • 9.1' deck • 25.6' turret face • 19.7' conning tower
Crew	2800

The excellent Combined Fleet research project takes up the story:

With the battle for Okinawa raging full force, it was decided to send super battleship *Yamato* on a suicide mission to the island. Ostensibly, her sortie was designed to draw off American airpower in order to allow a massive suicide strike by land-based aircraft from Japan to hit the American invasion forces ringing the island. Accordingly, *Yamato* was fueled for a one-way trip and sent out with nine escorts led by the light-cruiser *Yahagi* …. In the event *Yamato* made it to the island, her orders were to beach herself and make use of her 18.1' guns in support of the land fighting there.

She was met by aircraft of Task Force 58 shortly after noon on 7 April. Attacked in waves, *Yamato* could do little but absorb the punishment inflicted by at least five 1000 lb bombs and ten torpedoes. By approximately 1420 hours it was all over; *Yamato* had capsised to port and exploded. Five of her escorts had been sunk as well. A total of 2498 men had been lost aboard *Yamato*, 446 from *Yahagi*, and a further 721 from the destroyers.

The US forces lost 12 aircraft and their crews.

It was a ridiculous sortie. The Japanese knew full well the devastating power of aircraft against surface vessels – they had sunk the Royal Navy ships *Repulse* and *Prince of Wales* themselves years earlier, and they had seen the full power of the American carriers at the Battle of Midway. The three following years had further consolidated and strengthened carrier airpower, and the Japanese had all but been wiped out in the Battle of Leyte Gulf months earlier, where they had lost three battleships, four carriers, 10 cruisers and nine destroyers for a much lesser cost to the Americans, who had the capacity to absorb punishment where the IJN did not.[8]

The possible gains for the Japanese did not warrant the risk. There would not have been one naval officer in their command who would have rated their chances of success at more than 5–10 percent. The concept of using *Yamato* as a beached gun base was not an established tactic, and moreover it would have lost her the advantages of manoeuverability and tactical retreat. She would have provided a stationery target to be blasted apart by long-range naval gunnery and air strikes. Yet she was sent on her suicide mission, with the loss of 3000 trained sailors. Can there be a better example of how Japan would have spent the lives of all of her military forces?

A page from a WWII US forces publication describing how to search Japanese prisoners.

A page from a WWII US forces publication describing how to search Japanese prisoners.

Leyte Gulf as an example of attrition to come

The Battle of Leyte Gulf shows further how the Imperial Japanese Navy fought to the end. Leyte Gulf, fought over 23–26 October 1944, was the last gasp of the Navy. Despite enormous bushido fighting spirit, it was evidence of dismal strategic planning, failure to concentrate forces, and failure to consolidate possible success. But, critically as an example of how the fighting on the Home Islands would have gone, none of this seemed to matter. An enormous amount of Japanese lives were, by Western thinking, wasted. But that was not how the Japanese saw their mission.

Nearly three years after Pearl Harbor, the Japanese were critically short of aircraft pilots. They therefore devised using the actual ships – the aircraft carriers, *sans* pilots – as a lure, in an effort to prevent Allied amphibious landings in the eastern Philippines. With carriers deploying from Japan, three flotillas would converge from the south and west and annihilate the enemy landing forces.

Two cruisers of Strike Group A, *Maya* and the flagship *Atago*, were sunk at dawn on 23 October by the submarines *Darter* and *Dace* – the Japanese admiral Kurita was forced to swim for safety. The following day, land-based aircraft took the initiative and attacked the US 3rd Fleet. The light carrier *Princeton* was set on fire and eventually lost. In reply, American planes sank the super-battleship *Musashi*.

Force C, under Admiral Nishimura, was now the target, emerging into Surigao Strait on the 24th with two battleships, a cruiser and four destroyers. They were met by Allied battleships, cruisers, destroyers and PT boats. Only one of the Japanese ships survived.

To the north, Admiral Halsey's force had sighted the aircraft carrier decoy and turned away. This mistake allowed Kurita to emerge. The Japanese now nearly turned the tide of the battle: Rear Admiral Sprague's force of six light carriers was caught by surprise, with battleship gunfire erupting around them. The US force fled, deploying aircraft and its destroyer screen in desperation. Kurita was nearing victory, having sunk the carrier *Gambier Bay*, when he called off his ships, believing he was about to be trapped by a returning Halsey.

The Americans were soon under assault by a new tactic – Zero fighters as kamikazes. Carrier USS *St. Lo* was lost and others damaged. But the Japanese carriers were found and destroyed by massive air strikes. Some ships escaped, but the loss of three battleships, four carriers, ten cruisers and nine destroyers was a terminal blow, and the deaths of 12,500 skilled naval men was a further hammerblow. Any other future Japanese naval forces would have been committed, even piecemeal, to the battle that would simply have resulted in their annihilation.

A rare US Navy photo of action in the Battle of Leyte Gulf. (US Navy picture)

Civilian casualties

Massive civilian casualties would have been experienced in a conventional mainland assault, particularly because of the difficulty for Allied soldiers to identify who were military combatants, and who were harmless civilians. This was a common problem in Vietnam decades later, where the Allies there were fighting two forces: the uniformed North Vietnamese Army, and the non-uniformed Vietcong.

Lieutenant Calley, of the infamous My Lai massacre, was charged for his command of soldiers who shot down civilians, but as was found, this was not unusual in combat then, or combat in 1944–45.

It was a common problem in World War II already. Twelve thousand Belgian and French civilians died when they were mistakenly targeted after the D-Day landings because their geographic position was confused.[9] But in the Pacific, it was even more confusing. For example, in some locations Japan civilians were not allowed to surrender. Veteran Rick Spooner remembered:

> I can recall vividly lines of civilians coming across the dykes in the rice paddies, and ... the Japanese mowed them down ... I'm talking about groups of 40, 50, 60 in line being fired at by their own troops ... they must have firmly believed their own propaganda about how we would brutalise them.[10]

Japan routinely would use disguised soldiers for advantage. In one incident on Okinawa, Japanese soldiers disguised as civilians were coming through the American lines, and as Rifleman Herman Buffington says, 'we were ordered to shoot some of these people'.[11]

When the island of Saipan was captured, thousands of civilians killed themselves, most by leaping from cliffs, rather than submit to the American conquerors. The Japanese command, it seems, were confident the entire population would fight and – if necessary – die:

> The simple mathematics of scale and distance that would surely come into play as the fighting drew nearer to Japan, and eventually on the Home Islands themselves. General Jonathan Wainwright, held by the Japanese since the US defeat in the Philippines, was told by a confident Japanese colonel that there are 100 million people in the Japanese Empire, and it will take ten times 100 million to defeat Japan. To move such a force against Japan, even if you have that many warriors, would be impossible ....[12]

This was to be regretted, but it was seen as duty. Vice-Admiral Matome Ugaki wrote in his diary: 'It's only to be expected that fighting men should be killed, but for women, children and old men in such large numbers on a helpless, lonely island to prefer death to captivity – what a tragedy!'[13]

Yamashita notes that despite isolated acts of resistance, they did not prevent most Japanese from conforming to the demands of the state that they prepare for the 'Grand Suicide of the One Hundred Million'.[14] The historian Max Hastings summed that up: 'None but the people of the *Yamato* nation could do such a thing. If 100 million Japanese could display the same resolution, it wouldn't be difficult to find a way to victory.'[15]

James Bradley in *Flyboys* argues that the example of Saipan and other islands meant that all of Japan's population would die in the defence of the Home Islands. It would be the 'Gyokusai [Honourable death] of the One Hundred Million', referring to the often cited but exaggerated population figure.[16] Bradley gives numbers similar to the previously cited 'Saipan ratio' – the same but with Attu added and Saipan listed as 98.3 rather than 97 percent.

Location name	Defenders	Survivors	Percentage dying of the initial total
Attu[17]	2350	29	98.8%
Tarawa	2571	8	99.7%
Makin	300	1	99.6%
Roi-Namur	3472	51	98.5%
Kwajalein	5017	79	98.4%
Saipan[18]	29,000	500[19]	98.3%

Bradley outlines how the story of the civilian deaths 'shocked even battle hardened Marines'. It was not only the civilians committing suicide, but the Japanese soldiers killing their own countrymen. One 'observed a Japanese sniper who drilled the man from behind, dropping him into the sea. The second bullet hit the woman. The sniper would have shot the children, but a Japanese woman ran across and carried them out of range'.[20]

In the European theatre, any civilian in such a situation, and observing how troops react against fire, was sensibly advised to take precautions. Often white sheets or towels signaled civilian acceptance, as well as a rejection of aiding retreating troops or 'left-behind' units such as the Werwolf teams formed by the Germans in the last months of the war.

As HR Trevor-Roper points out, the nature of these teams is often misunderstood, and in fact they did little damage and formed no credible resistance, in part because they had expected to fight in uniform and did not.[21] They were primarily supposed to fight behind enemy lines as an arm of the German forces. But considerable resistance was expected, and so the oncoming Allied armies of World War II took village after village, and town after town, with fierce determination, as James Lucas puts it:

> God help any village if a shot was fired at the US troops, or if a rocket flare indicated a Panzerfaust team in action. In such cases, the American commander on the ground called down an air strike and anything that survived the fury of the aircraft was smashed in the systematic and prolonged bombardment of tank guns.[22]

Given that this was the occasional German reaction, but this would have been the norm in Japan, what would Allied attitudes have been towards each village and town? What is a force to do when civilians may be unwillingly used as combatants, or when a side suspects that civilians are disguised combatants? Most military historians admit that this would have been the scenario. Terry Charman, Senior Historian Imperial War Museum, is of the opinion that the atomic attacks:

> … saved Japanese lives as well because had there been an invasion of the Japanese islands the entire population was going to be mobilised to fight the American – (also) British and Australian components – but principally American invaders, and it would have been a massacre.[23]

Japanese battleship *Yamato* pictured fitting out, with light carrier *Hosho* on right. Although the mightiest such combat vessel ever built, by the time of a conventional assault much of Japan's Navy was destroyed. (US Navy picture)

This was precisely the situation the Americans in Vietnam were drawn into decades later in the 1960s and 70s. The infamous Lieutenant William Calley was court-martialed for destroying a village from which his troops had taken fire, and where civilians were perceived as actually being 'VC' – that is Viet Cong, non-uniformed guerilla fighters for the North Vietnamese cause. In *His Own Story*, Calley recounted that he had received around '5000' letters during the period of his trial. He listed some of the statements in which some recounted events similar to the massacre. Comparisons with the earlier Korean and World War II conflicts were often made:

I served in Korea from June 1953 to August 1954. I heard of many similar incidents.

I'm a retired marine. I spent 20 years in the service of God and Country. I was in two operations in Korea where women and children were killed.

In 1943, 1944, 1945 and 1946, I was a first lieutenant with 45th Infantry Division. I was witness to many incidents similar to the one you're being held for.

I served in combat in the German war. My fellow soldiers and I did on occasion kill enemy soldiers, civilians and children. Marquess of Queensbury rules do not prevail in war.

During my duty in Africa, we were under orders to shoot the Arabs to keep them from taking our clothes.

I was given the order to seal a cave where a mother and her eleven or twelve children were holed up. This took place in 1944 on the island of Ie Shima.

On Okinawa, I saw men throw grenades on old men and women, figuring what the hell – they're the enemy ....

Many years ago I had a platoon, and we went through the villages as you and your people had to.[24]

July 1944 US Marines walk away from a Japanese foxhole after bombing it. (USMC)

One variant on the situation, however, was that it would have indeed been the case that most civilians would have been combatants. In Vietnam, it was not that usual but such incidents were plentiful enough. Calley recounted that he was amazed that he had been charged when it was common practice to target civilians:

> I couldn't understand it. An investigation of Mylai. Why not Operation Golden Fleece? Or Operation Norfolk? Or Operation Dragon Valley? Or why not Saigon itself? We had killed hundreds of men, women and children there in February and March, 1968: in Tet ... simply read it in *Stars and Stripes*. Or the *New York Times*.[25]

Okinawa as a warning of what was to come

It was not just on Saipan that the Japanese military showed willingness to expend their own civilians' lives, either as combatants, or to deter the attack. In Okinawa, the Japanese military drove civilians, including children, towards the front lines of American Marines. Supposing them to be troops, the US soldiers opened fire.[26]

One of the US soldiers involved thought the Japanese took this action for two reasons: to get the Americans to expend ammunition, and to lower US morale when they found out what they had done. In the latter case, it apparently indeed had a devastating effect when the reality of the situation became clear to the men, as they saw the results of their actions.[27]

In the final days of taking Okinawa, the American forces used loudhailers broadcasting calls for surrender in Japanese, and they leafleted the areas where the enemy was still holed up. Some of the civilians on the island began to surrender, but unfortunately this meant they were targeted by Japanese soldiers, presumably, one American commented wryly, 'To save them from a fate worse than death' – surrendering to the enemy. Suggestions as to how many civilians died on Okinawa range from 75–140,000 in one estimate, to nearly two hundred thousand:[28]

On 2 July, the Okinawan campaign was officially declared ended.

In almost exactly three months Americans had lost 12,520 GI's, Marines and sailors, dead and missing. The Japanese lost 110,000 troops. In addition, civilian casualties reached unprecedented proportions. Caught between two armies, approximately 75,000 innocent men, women and children died.[29]

A widely circulated film gives a fearsome body count for one three-day battle: 'On Okinawa, in the major counter-attack, where 'over three days, the Americans killed over 7000 Japanese'.[30] The fighting was extremely fierce with no quarter given. Sugarloaf Hill, a major vantage point on the main island, changed hands 14 times as the Japanese and Americans counter-attacked each other every time the other side won it.[31] One Marine later remembered: 'You did not think of taking prisoners, it just didn't happen. If they looked dead, then two in the head to make sure.' [32]

Manchester, who fought on Okinawa as a Marine and visited more than 30 years later, says that 207,283 people died there, more than 77,000 of them being civilians.[33] He said that when the Marines entered Naha, the capital city, 'Okinawan bodies were everywhere – in shops, in gutters, hanging from windows. Once a city of 65 thousand, Naha now teemed with Jap mortars and machine guns.' [34] In essence, Okinawa killed around 200,000 Japanese people for the defence of an island that was roughly 640 kilometres/400 miles from Japan. President Truman used it as an example of what would happen in a conventional assault: 'I do not want another Okinawa from one end of Japan to another.' [35]

The predicted extent of civilian casualties in the Home Islands invasion

Sometimes civilians are targeted for military necessity to cause panic, and the general breakdown of civilian infrastructure can aid the enemy. During the retreat in France in 1940, British gunner William Harding saw German aircraft diving and strafing civilians on the packed roads.[36] Cam Bennett was part of the Australian force landing in Greece in World War II. He witnessed the Greek civilians – old men and women, and children – being low-level bombed by the German air force, in an attempt 'to inflict casualties, to create panic, to do as much harm as possible against those who could not hit back, so that the will to resist would be shattered'.[37] Australian infantryman Roland Griffiths-Marsh was also there, and indeed took prisoner a downed Stuka pilot who discussed the practice with him. The Germans, he was told, justified it on the grounds it led to panic and a rapid disintegration of the will to fight on the other side, thus shortening the war.[38]

The town of Caen's civilian infrastructure was targeted after D-Day to prevent it being used by the Germans. Leaflets were dropped by aircraft, warning that the railway station, electrical depot and other centres would be attacked. The buildings would be blown into the streets to delay German tank movements. But many civilians had nowhere to go and were killed as a result. Fighting between the opposing sides saw the escaped residents of a local lunatic asylum wandering between the soldiers. The retreating German tanks were targeted on the roads by RAF Spitfires, and inevitably the civilians also on the roads were hit. [39] In another incident when the German forces in World War II called on the Dutch to surrender Rotterdam in World War II, and no surrender was forthcoming, the German air force attacked the city, bringing condemnation that 30,000 civilians had been killed. In fact, the number was under 1000, but despite care being taken to avoid unnecessary bloodshed, civilian loss of life was inevitable.[40] What became known as 'collateral damage' in later years is simply a spillover effect: unfortunate but inevitable.

Civilian actions are of extreme significance. Peter Young, fighting in a Commando unit in World War II, was present when 'a farmer fired his shotgun at 6 Troop. This act proved fatal to him ....'[41] And so picking up a weapon turned a civilian into a combatant. In 1940, the retreating British fired at what looked like civilians on their retreat in France. When Gunner William Harding questioned the shooting of an old woman among the forces in front of them, he was told: 'Orders mate, we are to shoot anyone dressed in cloaks, etc., looking like priests, as many are infiltrating fifth columnists carrying tommy-guns and some of our blokes have been killed.'[42]

On another occasion, Harding was present when the rifleman next to him shot a woman running out of a house, and when Harding protested, the soldier said that 'five of my company have been shot by Germans dressed as nuns'.[43] Lieutenant-Commander Alexander Stanier, commanding the 1st Battalion of the Welsh Guards, was presented with a priest whose Bible had suspicious notes in it, according to Stanier's Intelligence Officer. The priest was thrown into a river and presumably drowned.[44]

Scenes like this would not have eventuated. Watched by a group of locals, German prisoners of war in the French town of Solesmes, 1 November, 1918, near the end of World War I. (Henry Armytage Sanders/ National Library of New Zealand)

Jacques Raboud saw German aircraft in 1940 strafing a civilian train full of retreating civilians, and three days later Italian aircraft shooting up civilians on the road.[45] But not all civilians killed were the result of deliberate targeting of non-combatants. In the last months of the war, with the Luftwaffe largely banished from the skies, Allied fighters roamed above the roads of Europe, looking for targets. Anything that moved could be shot, noted pilot Typhoon pilot Richard Hough, as only the military had petrol, but sometimes there were military units deliberately placed within ox-drawn civilian columns, so 'of course we killed civilians – we couldn't help it', noted Hough.[46] Is there any reason to suppose that the war in the Home Islands would have seen any different action?

How many Japanese would have been taken prisoner?

It is worth restating, to underline the vehemence of the defenders. The Japanese Army fighting in the Pacific in World War II presents a perhaps unique example of refusal to become prisoners. It would seem to be the case that historically armies both give and take surrender. It is logical to take it from a command perspective, because it achieves the aim of defeating the enemy – the more surrendered soldiers they have, the less they can fight.

But the Japanese were different. The Japanese Army would, on the whole, refuse to surrender. Major General J. Lawton Collins noted:

> The Japanese on both offensive and defence die determinedly rather than give up. Many cases are recorded of men so weak with hunger and disease that they could not stand who stayed by their weapons, pulling the trigger as long as there was life. Surrenders by able-bodied, well Japanese were negligible ....[47]

A significant pair of photographs in Eric Bergerud's comprehensive account of the theatre – *Touched with fire: the land warfare in the South Pacific* – shows a Japanese soldier in the sea.[48] The caption explains that he was one of four who would not surrender to some Australian troops, and the soldiers therefore shot them. The Japanese holds a grenade to his head, and then, the caption explains, he set it off.

There was a lot of this sort of suicide. British Commando Peter Young was leading some men while trying to take a prisoner when they came across a wounded Japanese who simply blew himself up with a grenade rather than be taken.[49] General William Slim tells of a Japanese Army unit trying to withdraw over a river, while they were being pressed hard by Allied troops. Eventually, with most of their force cut down, the remaining Japanese formed up in ranks, and rather than come forward and surrender, they instead 'marched steadily into the river and drowned'.[50]

An account from a Japanese soldier describes how those too badly wounded to fight were treated: 'It became a routine that a soldier who was emaciated and crippled, with no hope of recovery, was given a grenade and persuaded, without words, to sort himself out.'[51]

Engineer officer Bob MacArthur watched Japanese kill themselves. 'It was the damnedest thing. I watched them up on a ridge, taking their grenades – they had a button that detonated them – bang them on their helmets and hold them to their chest while they went off. I couldn't fathom it.'[52] Corporal James Day said in his entire Pacific War, his platoon took only one prisoner: '… they just wouldn't surrender'.[53]

On Okinawa, the Japanese commander made a decision after some days of fierce fighting. He withdrew his force to an escarpment where they would fight to the death. A Japanese soldier observed around 3–400 wounded attempt to come along with the main body of the troops, some of them double amputees, 'pleading to be taken along'. Many of those too seriously wounded to be moved stayed behind, equipped with cyanide or grenades, so they could take their own lives but also take some of the enemy with them.[54]

The savagery of the fighting on that island is illustrated by the fact that no American soldier was taken prisoner there, and the US forces showed a similar inclination, one soldier saying after the end of the fighting that they didn't take any captives until after 18 June 1945, when Japanese started to surrender. One account says that 7401 were captured, but 110,071 died, although these numbers are much varied owing to the destruction and paucity of records.[55]

The civilian forces often showed equal stubbornness. On Okinawa today, a popular tourist destination sees visitors from Japan paying their respects at the Cave of Virgins. This was the death site of:

> … eighty-five student nurses. Terrified, they had retreated into a cave. Marines reaching the mouth of the cave heard Japanese voices within. They didn't recognise the tones as feminine, and neither did their interpreter, who demanded that those inside emerge at once. When they didn't, flamethrowers, moving in, killed them all.[56]

Australian Army Colonel Cummings was in New Guinea when two wounded prisoners who had been captured for intelligence purposes were being rowed in a small boat out to a lugger. Suddenly, the two attacked their captors and then capsized the boat, drowning themselves in the process.[57] In the actions around Milne Bay in September 1942, Japanese positions were called upon to surrender; the result was, according to Warrant Officer David Marsh, that 'they immediately opened fire on us'. In another case, native police, who had joined the Australian forces, received the same greeting when trying to capture three downed pilots. Observing the enemy was armed by this time only with revolvers, they waited until they had counted six shots from each, and then closed in for the kill.[58]

Smashed by Japanese mortar and shellfire, trapped by Iwo Jima's treacherous black-ash sands, Amtracs and other vehicles of war lie knocked out on the black sands of the volcanic fortress. (US Army)

The Imperial Japanese Army had a bad reputation for treachery and cruelty. Australian servicemen found early in the New Guinea campaigns that the Japanese treated prisoners badly: Signalman George Barker said of two comrades that they had been 'tied and bayoneted'.[59] Captain Charles Bicks found several men, including some of his own battalion, who had been captured, and then executed, their hands tied behind their backs.[60]

A later report by Sir William Webb, the Chief Justice of the Supreme Court of Queensland, found that between 26 August and 6 September 1942 at least 24 Australian soldiers were executed.[61] The Americans encountered the same sort of actions. Nine American Marines left behind after a submarine-borne raid on the Gilbert Island were executed soon after their capture.[62] An American patrol on Saipan found five of their comrades dead, their legs bound with wire, and bullet holes in the back of their heads.[63]

The incoming forces fighting the Japanese in World War II quickly adopted to new tactics in the face of the level of resistance. Japanese in a hospital were given no chance to surrender, because some held grenades under their blankets.[64] On Tinian Island, where it was thought that there were Japanese soldiers in caves, they were, in some areas, targeted with loudspeaker broadcasts urging them to surrender. Individual caves were given a call from outside by Marines, and if there was no response, the cave was sealed.[65] In New Guinea in January 1943, despite being in hopeless positions, they 'actually charged forward to a defiant, faster finish'.[66]

American soldier Louis Maravelas said of the Japanese he fought:

> ... they were simply stupid. They sacrificed their own men needlessly, for no purpose at all. During a battle along the Matanikau, three or four were straggling towards us as though they were going to surrender. There must have been a dozen of us with a bead on them. Sure enough, one bent over and there was a carbine or submachine gun slung on his back that a comrade tried to grab. We shot them down instantly .... They did this type of thing so many times. It got to the point where we took no prisoners. It wasn't a written order, but a way to survive. No one should take a chance to take a guy prisoner who might kill him.[67]

The folly of the general feeling of the Japanese on surrender was further illustrated by the actions of the soldiers defending an atoll 75 miles south east of Tarawa. Their commander, addressing them with sword in one hand and pistol in another, accidentally shot himself in the head. And so, as Derrick Wright tells us, 'The distraught troops, unable to make any decisions without their commander, had dug their own graves and killed themselves ....'[68]

On Iwo Jima, the Japanese General Kuribayashi was sent a message, carried by two Japanese prisoners, advising that 'his position was now hopeless and he could surrender with honour'.[69] The note reached him, as had another previously, and Radio Tokyo by then was broadcasting that the island was fully penetrated by US Marines. Nevertheless, he refused to surrender.

Wearing a parade uniform and carrying a sword, a Japanese officer in New Guinea, with his position overrun, challenged the advancing Australian troops. He '... went whoosh with his sword, and he carved all the bits of the side of the palm fronds,' inviting the soldiers to take him, one presumes, with their bayonets. He was given a count of ten to surrender and then shot.[70]

Soldiers in the same tactical situation showed the same spirit as elsewhere: Lieutenant Doug McClean observed: 'They seemed to want to die and we were delighted to oblige them. They didn't give in, they didn't surrender and therefore there is no point in saying we showed them mercy'.[71] LM Opie thought 'they were ready to die; when we overran their positions, their personal papers had been laid on the edge of their weapon pits'.[72] Towards the end of the war, Cam Bennett, leading a company of the Australian Army, noted that in the rare event of taking a prisoner it was difficult to get them taken to the rear alive. 'It was essential to send some of them back with a good reliable NCO or they would be shot by their guards while attempting to escape (so the guards said).'[73]

A Japanese assault was repulsed in late 1942 in New Guinea by an Australian force that had been underestimated in numbers. The Japanese retreated, and the Australians followed. While a sizeable portion got away, a large number were run to earth near the village of Gorari. The Australian forces surrounded the area, and after some exchanges of fire and a few intermittent night incidents, the two sides settled down to an uneasy calm. At dawn, the Australians went in at the charge, surprising many Japanese having breakfast. All of them were killed, with many Japanese fighting hard. Five hundred and eighty bodies of the enemy were later counted.[74] Later, at Gona, Japanese troops whose positions were taken after artillery fire were shot down 'as they fled along the beach or swam wildly out to sea'.[75] Every Japanese defending there died – around 1000 of them.[76]

The scale of the deaths was truly shocking. The island of Tarawa, two and a half miles long by a half-mile wide, saw over 1000 American lives lost,[77] and only 17 Japanese out of a garrison of 4836 captured.[78] During the assaults on Kwajalein Atoll in 1944, only 35 members of the 5000-strong Japanese garrison surrendered – the rest fought to their deaths.[79] Robert Leckie went in with the First Marines at the island of Peleliu, with 1500 men in his battalion; they were down to 28 effective soldiers when the final assault was made.[80] Perhaps the most well-known defence took place at Saipan, where around 28,500 Japanese died, with the Americans taking 16,631 casualties, out of which 3471 perished.[81] In New Guinea, 95 percent of the 200,000 troops sent there died.[82] And many Japanese held on in individual islands until well after the war ended, with surrenders being recorded through the 1940s, 50s, 60s and in 1972, when on 24 January, Sergeant Shoichi Yokoi was captured by two fishermen, 27 years after hostilities ended.[83]

This is not to say the Japanese were routinely dispatched if killing them could be avoided. The Pacific War was ruthless on both sides. Officer Dick Thom recalls his regiment only taking one prisoner, and US soldier Tom Walker had the same total for his unit.[84] But Eric Bergerud notes: 'If the circumstances were right, military honour and basic humanity on the part of many American and Australian infantry prevented the war from descending into the realm of simple slaughter.'[85] The Australian official history notes an example on 21 October 1943, when a Japanese sergeant who spoke English surrendered to 24 Battalion. He encouraged four more Japanese soldiers, who quickly surrendered. Of interest was the sergeant's story: his command's weaker members had been allowed to discard their ancillary equipment but had been made to retain one grenade to take their own lives rather than be captured by the Australians, who – they had been told – would torture them.[86]

In a later comment, Bergerud states that the 'Allies collected over 80,000 prisoners in the Pacific War.'[87] (This is in contrast to Bourke's claim[88] that by July 1944 only 1990 Japanese prisoners had been captured *in total* – her emphasis. The *Pacific War Encyclopedia* notes that until the collapse of the Japanese resistance, only 11,600 Japanese military were taken.[89]) And while surrender was mostly not an option for the Japanese, there were occasions when they broke and ran – at least, in the case of the Army, in one Marine's opinion, but he also held that their Marine Corps was as tough as America's own: 'Their Marines were well equipped and would fight to the bitter end. The Japanese Army broke under pressure, but not their Marines – when we met head on it became like running into a brick wall, neither side gave an inch.'[90] They were indeed tough troops. The US Marines who Robert Leckie fought with in the final year of the war took on the Japanese when they were probably at their most determined. Even when it was obvious that a unit was broken, its soldiers would still not surrender, and the Americans exterminated them. Robert Leckie's Marine comrades found that 'they all resisted, and they were all destroyed, bayoneted for the most part ...'.[91]

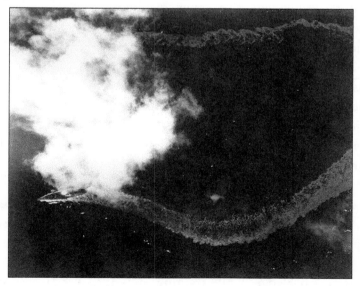

The *Yamato* manoeuvering to avoid being hit by torpedoes dropped by American planes north of Okinawa on 7 April, 1945 during her final mission. (US Navy)

It is illogical, given the evidence cited above, to presume there would have been any change in attitude, tactics, and normal practice in a conventional invasion of Japan. Hatred of the Japanese forces, firmly imbued in the Allies by mid-1945, would have continued in any invasion of the Home Islands. One Marine noted that very early on in the war, killing prisoners began when a Japanese bivouac was taken and pictures of mutilated Marines were found. The Marines began taking ears off dead Japanese in retaliation.[92] Bergerud commented: 'The hatred of the ground soldier toward the Japanese was on a completely different level from that found among sailors on warships or airmen … a sense of restraint existed in Europe that was absent in the Pacific.'[93] Not all of this was due to every soldier seeing atrocities. In fact, the psychologists surveying three divisions of US troops in the Pacific found that only 13 percent personally reported sighting such actions – the same rate as in the European theatre – but 45 percent said they had heard stories of them, as opposed to 24 percent in Europe.[94]

The attacking armies reacted by becoming more ferocious in their assaults. Australian Imperial Force infantryman Ben Love passed through a Japanese encampment the US forces had taken at night 'twenty-three days ago. They caught the Nips asleep – killed over 100 of them'.[95] It is worth noting in passing here that infantry combat did not then, and does not now, give the enemy a 'sporting chance', so enemy found asleep were routinely dispatched unless they could be easily taken prisoner. As soldiers in combat zones slept with their weapons, there was only a very slim chance of being taken – so why take it, would have been the argument.[96]

Captain 'Chips' Heron MC was leading a patrol of British Commandos at Pauktaw against the Japanese when they came across ten of them, six of whom he killed, including one officer, saying afterwards: 'The fellow had his back to us, sir! Thought I ought to shout "Oi", or something.'[97] Similarly, Private Bill McGee of the Australian Army commented in a matter of fact way on finding a Japanese asleep in a hut: 'he didn't last long'.[98]

Marine EB Sledge, while training in World War II, was told by his hand-to-hand combat instructor: 'Don't hesitate to fight the Japs dirty. Most Americans, from the time they are kids, are taught not to hit below the belt. It's not sportsmanlike. Well, nobody had taught the Japs that, and war ain't sport. Kick him in the balls before he kicks you in yours.'[99]

Confusion in the fog of war leads to accidents. Peter Young, fighting in a World War II Commando unit, was in command of troops who took surrender from around ten Italians one night. Then one of the British troops thought the Italians were attacking him and fired, which led to more shots: whether the Italians were killed is not clear.[100]

Around 60 German captives were killed in an action after D-Day by the US 11th Armored Division because the American soldiers, who were new to combat, mistakenly believed they were not to take prisoners.[101] Some of the advancing Canadians, following the D-Day landings, noted how difficult it was to take captives:

> First, they had to brave their own troops, then to face the opposing force, not always clear on their intentions. They come forward, aligned down the muzzles of enemy guns, and a single shot fired by one man can cause thousands of others to follow suit. This was not yet 'savagery' or 'revenge', it was 'SNAFU', or organised confusion. Nevertheless, men going forward to surrender were shot down.[102]

So for example, accidents happen routinely. An advancing tank saw four Germans coming out of a wood, and the tank's gunner opened up with a machine gun and shot two. Unfortunately, they were being escorted at gunpoint by an infantryman behind them, who had been wounded in the arm by the fire and was now loudly complaining about his prisoners being shot at. Major H. Wake, who recorded the incident, noted that it was a good idea therefore to remove prisoners' helmets and also to get them to keep their hands up all the time when being escorted.[103]

Eight German infantry were surrendering to a US corporal in 1945 when 'I saw the leader suddenly realise he still had a pistol in his shoulder holster. He reached into his jacket with two fingers to pull it out and throw it away. One of our guys yelled, "Watch it! He's got a gun!" and came running up shooting and there were eight Krauts on the ground shot up ....'[104] Similarly, three Germans surrendered to some Americans in late 1944, when one of their sergeants reached his hand into his coat, as did another, and one of their captors cut down all three with a burst from his submachine gun.[105]

After the Great War, the field of battle spread to include what the German General von Ludendorff called 'total war'. This meant that while von Clausewitz saw war as an extension of politics, Ludendorff argued for war to be total: the political had to be subordinated to the military. War was to be waged politically, economically, culturally, with propaganda, and all society should become a war machine.

This meant that war spread to include strikes against identified civilian targets, including strategic bombing, and in the ultimate efficiency of that, with atomic weapons against civilian cities. In such a war as this, civilians have become caught up in the desperate struggle of one society against another, both struggling to survive. In such combat, general strikes against civilians are the norm. And so the Zeppelin raids against London in World War I morphed into the attacks of V1 and V2 rockets in World War II; strategic bombing raids by thousands of aircraft Germany, and as mentioned, the atomic strikes of 1945. Pertinent to this work's overall themes is that as this sort of reality sinks home, the perpetrators of war become more savage. As previously discussed, Bomber Harris becomes a national hero, and people like Curtis Le May, who planned the air attacks on Japan, ponder the oddities of such lethality:

> Killing Japanese didn't bother me very much at the time .... I suppose if I had lost the war, I would have been tried as a war criminal ... every soldier thinks something of the moral aspects of what he is doing. But all war is immoral and if you let that bother you, you're not a good soldier.[106]

What Japan would have looked like. Saint-Lô town with Allied vehicles passing through, after it had been attacked from the air by Allied forces, to drive out the Germans. (US Army)

The nature of much of the weaponry used does not allow too much discrimination in targeting. As one World War II soldier put it: 'When you're an artillery man and you help to fire shells – at that time I guess at nine or ten miles away – you're not really conscious of what destruction you're creating.' Another thought that warfare was perhaps more civilised in older times when the firepower wasn't available to kill so indiscriminately: 'Many soldiers, particularly artillerymen and fliers, had to kill innocent women and children – non-combatants. Seems to me in a moral sense there's been a great deterioration in modern war.'[107]

Civilians can be targeted for information. Incoming Japanese forces landing to strengthen their presence on Guadalcanal found the Chief of Police, Jacob Vouza, and demanded information about where the American forces' strong points were. He refused to tell them so they tied him to a tree where he was bayoneted until they thought he was dead. Vouza later was able to release himself and crawl three miles to the American positions – he later quite understandably joined the Marines.[108]

And so the Japanese would have died by the millions. The British Admiral Mountbatten, said of a conventional invasion: 'Millions would have been killed, civilians and soldiers.' [109] Dr Taro Takemi, a past president of the Japanese Medical Association, said in 1963: 'When one considers the possibility that the Japanese military would have sacrificed the entire nation if it were not for the atomic bomb attack, then this bomb might be described as having saved Japan.' [110]

A question of numbers – how many would have died on the Home Islands?

In May 1945, the firebombing of Tokyo – by conventional means – killed more people than either of the two A-weapons' individual impact. Frank cites the Tokyo raid death figures: Daniels, which he calls 'the best single study', uses a figure of over 90,000 in 'Great Tokyo Air Raid'; Edoin in *The Night Tokyo Burned* prefers 100,000, as does Kato in *The Lost War*, and Tillitse in 'When Bombs Rained Down on Tokyo'. [111] Japan's population in 1945 was 71,998,104. [112]

It follows that if the war had followed conventional direction, such raids by massed flights of Allied aircraft would have been the norm. There would have been no other type of assault given the reluctance by the commanders of the various units to risk the deaths of their infantry until they were sure that all armed resistance had ceased. Aircraft raids minimised Allied casualties. There were other means of assaulting Japanese resistance: naval bombardment, artillery attack and close-range aircraft attack, for example. But all of these had more risks than using massed bomber raids.

Naval bombardment would have meant getting ships close to the Japanese coast. The range of naval guns of the time varied depending on the calibre, size of the charge, and so on, but a 9.2-inch gun had a range of around 25 kilometres/16 miles, depending on associated factors such as humidity, air pressure, temperature and so on. This distance was easily within range of Japanese kamikaze vessels, submarines and aircraft. The gun ships would have closed the coast to minimise the time spent in range of the enemy, but it still meant that they were placed in substantial danger. They would have been protected by the aircraft carriers of the massed Allied fleet, flying interception missions against kamikaze aerial attack. However, there was much less air expertise in intercepting surface vessels and submarines, and these engagements would have been largely left to the Allied fleet ships anyway. It is worth noting that the Allies had far less experience in taking on Japanese waterborne kamikazes, and the learning curve of gaining experience would have meant Allied failures resulting in death and injury for those engaged in taking out these attackers.

Artillery attack by Allied ground forces was not an option without landing on the Japanese mainland. Faced with determined resistance, we can surmise it would have taken quite some time to get ashore and become established in a beachhead, and then begin to push inland and take ground. The D-Day experience the previous year is instructive. The Allies off Normandy had almost air supremacy rather than air superiority: very few German aircraft were flying against the attackers' ships and covering fighters. They had immense fire support from the naval guns of ships lying off the coast and pounding the embedded German gun defences. Yet although the Allies had a good amount of time in which to assault the coast – weather was a prohibiting factor, and so too were the infantry formations' abilities to simply endure onboard life waiting to go in – when the decision was taken to hit the beaches, the Allies took substantial numbers of casualties.

The Allies off Japan, using conventional assault means, could have used aircraft carrier embarked squadrons to attack the embedded defenders. But again here a disproportionate number of aircraft would have been lost: disproportionate in that compared with conventional bombing, more lives would have been lost for the amount of bombs delivered. The aircraft carriers did not carry heavy bombers either.

Carrier aircraft using rockets and gunfire against land defences were in even more of a perilous situation. They necessarily got closer to use these short-range measures, and therefore a proportionate number of them took fire, either with death or wounds inflicted on their crew, or total loss of the aircraft, meaning a crash into the sea on the return track to the carrier, again with proportionate personal impact on the crew.

Although the Allied search and rescue service was by this time extremely well developed, ditching into the sea, or parachuting out of a burning or damaged aircraft was by no means a normal or safe experience, and losses imparted in such situations meant further injuries or loss of life. It would of course have been the situation for any aircrew shot down on the Japanese landmass that even if they survived they could expect little mercy from any soldier and militia/civilian catching them.

Given this analysis, it is feasible to posit that the Allied assault would have been characterised by conventional bombing, varying between a mix of high explosive – designed to wreck the defenders' capabilities for both offence and defence – and firebombing, designed to achieve not only just the general aspects of such destruction, but also to burn the population's homes, largely constructed out of wood, as well as kill the residents.

WWII-era Japanese propaganda poster produced for the Greater Japan National Defense Women's Association. Artist unknown.

The numbers of cities and towns left for such attacks were quite high. Some cities such as Kyoto had been spared attack altogether; others such as Hiroshima and Nagasaki were spared so that when atomic weapons were deployed their effectiveness could be calculated. This was an understandable precaution: there was no certain way to discover whether an A-bomb attack would be worth the time, money, risk and outcome other than by using it against such an undamaged target. But if the new weapons were off the possibility list of measures, then standard bombing would start against such undamaged population and resource centres.

From around mid-1945, these smaller population centres would have become available targets. The Allied intelligence apparatus would have carried out the necessary calculations, and therefore the outcomes would have been expected per mass raid. The efficiency curve as the raids continued would have been disproportional. In other words, as the raids continued it could be expected the toll on the Japanese would increase, and the Allied expenses lessened, for the Japanese defences and ability to repair their damage would lessen, and the Allies' expertise increase.

There is nothing to suggest that this strategy would not have been pursued. Phrases such as 'area bombing', 'intimidating civilian populations' and 'total warfare' had been in military usage for years by 1945. Attacks on civilian populations by the Germans in 1940 had cost 40,000 British lives, and unrestricted submarines were quickly the norm in the Atlantic, with many thousands of civilian vessels sunk.

The retaliation was massive, as the United States joined the war in Europe the Allies penetrated deep into German airspace, and cities such as Dresden and Cologne had been almost destroyed, along with their populations, later in the war. And still the Germans had fought on, enduring incredible losses. What reason was there to think the same measures would not be taken against Japan, and that the country's population would not perish in the same way? Indeed, evidence can be found that civilians would have been targeted indiscriminately in any invasion. The Intelligence commander of the Fifth Air Force in China, Colonel Harry Cunningham, noted on 21 July 1945: 'The entire population of Japan is [now] a proper military target ... there are no civilians in Japan ... we intend to seek out the enemy wherever he or *she* is, in the greatest possible numbers, in the shortest possible time.' (Emphasis added.)[113]

This work is concerned with two main numbers: how many would have died and secondly how many lives were saved by the sacrifice of those who died in the A-bomb blasts. It admits that the death count for the two A-bomb assaults is extremely difficult to calculate: for example, over what time period do we examine a death being due to it having been in the proximity of the blast range? A person may well have caught enough radiation in 1945 for it to be a primary cause of an extremely slow-reacting deleterious effect. For that reason the safest course of accounting is to take the highest figure: 200,000 deaths were caused by both Hiroshima and Nagasaki.

But here to posit the number of people who *may* have died in a conventional assault is doubly difficult. That is simply because any logical assessment may be critiqued by simply arguing that this or that might not have been the case. Nevertheless, it must be attempted, for this argument – that the Japanese were better off being A-bombed than invaded – has to start somewhere. And so the addition of the many sections of fatalities has not been done before.

One of the few estimates on the high side of the Japanese count was WB Shockley, a consultant in Stimpson's office. He proposed in a report of 21 July 1945: 'we shall probably have to kill at least five to ten million Japanese. This might cost us between 1.7 and 4 million casualties, including 400,000 to 800,000 killed.'[114]

Interestingly though, his 'report' was rather a letter of discussion, or proposal, rather than the findings of an exhaustive analysis. Such a study appears not to have been carried out.

In the end, it is contended that few studies have gone through systematically analysing what Japanese deaths would have been caused. Here, therefore, is an analysis backed up by reasoning.

Total of predicted Japanese fatalities resulting from a conventional invasion of Japan, starting in November 1945 and terminating in December 1946.

Caveat: the death toll could vary from that arrived at here through all sorts of factors – sudden surrender in the forces abroad after encirclement by the Allies, especially if their communications were disrupted; revolt and revolution within the Home Islands; surrender after the first phase of the two-part invasion strategy; and more. Nevertheless, each section here constitutes a reasonable analysis and totaling of fatalities.

Type of person dead	Cause of death	Number dead	Notes
Japanese Army within the Home Islands	Combat and refusal to surrender	2,232,500	Based on the Pacific island defence campaigns, at a 95% KIA rate. See explanatory note below. From a total of 2,350,000.
Japanese Army in the rest of Asia	Combat and refusal to surrender	3,277,500	Based on the Pacific island defence campaigns, at a 95% KIA rate. See explanatory note below. From a total of 3,450,000.[115]
Japanese Navy	Combat and refusal to surrender	1,166,963	Based on a 99% KIA rate from a total of 1,178,750. See explanatory note below.
Militia	Combat deaths	240,000	From a total of 4,000,000, assuming a 30% casualty rate. 1,200,000 casualties, with one in five being fatalities and the others wounded.
Co-opted armed civilians	Combat deaths	1,680,000	From a total of 28 million, assuming a 30% casualty rate. 8,400,000 casualties, with one in five being fatalities and the others wounded.
Sub-total – combat deaths		**8,596,963**	**Total combat force of 38,127,500.**
Civilians dying from lack of food	Operation Starvation, and Allied naval blockades	14,000,000	Seven million by mid-1946 would continue at a million a month dying from starvation by the end of the invasion in December 1946.[116]

Type of person dead	Cause of death	Number dead	Notes
Sub-total		22,596,963	Total of those already in the forces and those dying from starvation
Civilians	Collateral damage	5,282,754	10% of the population left over would have died – that is, 5,827,537 from the population of 72,147,000 – given predicted Allied Rules of Engagement.[117]
All Japanese deaths		27,879,717	Total resulting from a conventional invasion of the Home Islands lasting until the end of 1946.

Rationale

Force totals

Frank estimates 2.9 million uniformed men in the homeland area. He cites ULTRA decrypts as showing 14 Japanese Army divisions, as well as tank and infantry brigades – at least 680,000 strong in southern Kyushu. Figuring in the militia, the three local prefectures contained 3.8 million adults. If only one in ten died, a lower loss rate than Okinawa, then the total Japanese fatalities would have come to 580,000 to 630,000.[118] Hoyt suggests '2.5 million soldiers on duty in the homeland'.[119] Toland cites 53 infantry divisions, and 25 brigades – a total of 2,350,000 troops. These would be backed up by four million defence civilians; 'a special garrison force of 250,000', and a civilian militia of 28 million.[120]

Figures on the Imperial Japanese Navy's strength by mid-1945 are very difficult to obtain. Its vessels were largely inoperative, either through disrepair, or being blockaded to the extent it would have been suicidal to put to sea. Not that the Navy was averse to suicide: the final voyage of the *Yamato* had shown that. But we must presume some degree of strategic sanity in its senior command, which would want to use its assets to bring about enemy losses. Therefore, it is assumed they would fight and die rather than do the unthinkable: refuse to participate.

The Navy's air forces were in somewhat better shape both numerically and capability-wise. It was used to operating off land bases, and indeed, had carried out much, if not most, of the fighter and bomber missions in SE Asia. For example, in the 208 missions flown against the Australian landmass, only two were carried out by the Army.[121] The Navy's air forces, which could be gathered for the Home Islands, is difficult to discern but overall it appears to be 291,537. The Navy's overall strength was 1,178,750. [122]

Loss rates

The Army loss rates are based around the experiences of the island campaigns. Interestingly, scholars and politicians making estimates of Japanese losses have not factored in the loss of life that would have taken place in Japan's armed forces outside of the Home Islands. But we can't assume these forces would have stopped fighting. Rather, the converse would have happened: once they heard that the Home Islands were being invaded they would have fought all the harder, seeking out Allied forces to attack. The Japanese rationale behind that is simple: Allied forces engaged elsewhere were not invading the Home Islands.

The Navy's loss rate figures are based around the assumption that given the type of battle, any ship in action would take with her to the seabed almost all of her ship's company. Is there any doubt that both Army and Navy would have fought to the end, given previous experience? There is but very little doubt; however, with the sacred Home Islands being invaded, there would have been even less reason to surrender.

The militia and armed civilians are seen as behaving as troops usually do, unless they're World War II professional Japanese military. In general, a force will break and run with a 30 percent casualty rate; that is, participants falling, seeing others fall, seeing dead and wounded around them, and then finally throwing down their weapons and running. Of those who are casualties, there will be four wounded and one dead out of that 30 percent. That civilians would have been ordered *en masse* to sacrifice their lives is in little doubt: it will be recalled that the Navy's Admiral Onishi had offered to spend '20 million lives' in kamikaze attacks to stop any invasion.[123] [124] Mitsuo Fuchida, leader of the Pearl Harbor attack, said post-war: 'Every man, woman and child would have resisted the invasion, with sticks and stones if necessary.'[125] But we can't presume the same high fatality rate for Japanese quasi-military as we do for the professionals: these pressed civilians would not have had the same psychological hardening, training and experience. Therefore they are treated in the fatality count with this 'discounted' rate.

The eight million total for Japanese combat deaths might seem high. But it should be remembered that Okinawa saw a loss of life in the defending force of around two hundred thousand. That was for a small island in a campaign of weeks. The invasion of the Home Islands would have taken up until the end of 1946, in a campaign encompassing around 1050 miles/1700 kilometres.[126] The country is a little bigger than Italy, with a landmass of 145,834 square miles, or 377,708 square kilometres.

It is predicted that the Allies would have tried to prevent unnecessary casualties. But a collateral death rate of 10 percent of the civilian population – those left over from combat operations, and if not dying already from hunger – seems a fairly realistic loss rate.[127] The B-29 raids would have continued: although Le May had concluded that there was a list of targets no longer worth bombing. However, they were cities he was referring to, not towns. With the Japanese practice of mixing light industry into suburbs, that meant the targeting of a local blacksmith – not that such precision was possible – would mean that his house-dwelling neighbours would be hit too.

Figures for D-Day as an example are much debated, but it is thought that between 15,000 and 20,000 French civilians were killed during the Normandy Campaign alone, and that was with nearly a year left of the European war to go. They of course were not potential combatants, which every Japanese was said to be, so the Allied willingness to shoot first would have been much higher as they advanced across Japan. One can't see white tablecloths being hung out of windows there, as was the case in France and Germany as the Allies progressed. So the civilian death toll would have been very high. Given, as previously noted, a plan to use up six atomic weapons in the advance on the Kyushu peninsula, it can be seen that the Allies would have exacted huge civilian losses in an effort to ensure there was no resistance to their incoming troops.

Regarding the losses from starvation, it will be recalled that Japan's Lord Keeper of the Privy Seal, wrote:

> Everything became scarce. The food situation was gradually becoming worse and worse. Under such conditions even the soldiers had not too much to eat …. With winter ahead, I said I cannot bear the responsibility for the lives of tens of millions of people dying a dog's death from hunger and exposure.[128]

The totality of this number is, however, almost impossible to gauge. It has been totaled here at a million a month, but that could have been more (the winter might well have been very harsh) or less (the Japanese, organised in so many ways, might have succeeded in organising more growth of their own food). 'Starvation' is also a very difficult causal factor to gauge, as no one would have been very concerned with determining exactly how a person died – from cold, hunger, natural causes, illness due to a weakened immune system, or whatever. The Japanese would have also incurred massive losses from the diseases spread by the breakdown of sewage systems, drinking water supplies, government heating programs and so on. Hence we might caveat it two million each way, but this makes a useful reference point.

Conclusion

The death toll for Japanese who died in the two atomic blasts was probably about 200,000. If they had not been sacrificed, the deaths of an approximately 28 million Japanese would have been exacted in a conventional assault.

CHAPTER EIGHTEEN
BLAMING AMERICA

How an attitude developed that
the A-bombs were morally wrong

Overview: In this chapter, we discuss how an attitude has developed among many that the use of the A-bombs was not necessary and/or ethically wrong. This chapter also examines how those viewpoints developed and how accurately they are based on fact. Was, for example, the A-bomb attacks merely the 'White Man' attempting to wipe out a race they perceived as inferior? Why does much of the children's literature on the bombings minimise Japanese fault? The chapter concludes with an elaboration of how successive generations have gradually misunderstood the extent of World War II and the many factors necessitating the use of the A-weapons. It looks briefly at four alternative scenarios, before delivering a final judgment.

Ironically, much of the post-war analysis contained several authoritative viewpoints that the use of the atomic weapons had made things easier. Hisatune Sakomizu, secretary to the Japanese cabinet in 1945: 'If the A-bomb had not been dropped, we would have had great difficulty in finding a good reason to end the war.'[1] Marquis Koichi Kido, adviser to the Emperor in 1945: 'The presence of the atomic bomb made it easier for us politicians to negotiate peace. Even then the military would not listen to reason.'[2]

General Sweeney, the *Enola Gay* pilot, initially noted that there were no questions about the use of the bomb: 'Because in 1945, the events of the war were seared into the consciousness of the nation and the world, I wasn't asked any questions about whether it had been necessary to drop the atomic bombs.'[3]

This changed over time, to a stage in the 1990s where Sweeney and many others had to defend the atomic attack missions, in what became an internationally famous argument about how to display his bomber in American museums. Writing about inspecting the proposed Smithsonian Institute commemoration of 50 years since the atomic missions, Sweeney wrote:

> Today, we veterans of World War II find ourselves confronted by a persistent and ideologically driven attempt to erode the truth of the war – to distort America's motives, its role in the war, and the nature of the enemy we faced – not unlike the erosion of the Enola Gay, sitting stored away and forgotten for all those years.[4]

A globe indicating nations who had exploded nuclear weapons, shown by quantity, in Nagasaki Atomic Bomb Museum in 2015. This section shows the USA. (Author photo)

Why did the reverse attitude develop? In many ways the revisionist attitude was the product of the decades of political thinking. The 1960s especially had seen revolutionary attitudes develop with the rise of feminism – new concepts of race, especially in the United States, and much more besides. There were now varying agendas at work.

Here, for example, is the argument that the West was essentially at fault in World War II: the use of the atomic weapons was primarily a racist attack. In 1995, there was a degree of this analysis appearing in the public arena around the time of the 50th anniversary of the A-bomb raids. For example, journalist and author Mick Hume wrote an essay: 'Hiroshima: remembering "the White Man's Bomb"' which has been widely reprinted since, especially at significant anniversaries of the attacks. He essentially argues that:

> Two broader political considerations made up Truman's mind. First, the politics of international power dictated that the United States would definitely drop the bomb somewhere, regardless of the state of the war. And second, the politics of racial superiority determined that that somewhere would definitely be Japan.[5]

Hume uses several arguments for his point:

a. The United States never contemplated using the bomb on Germany: 'There was no high-level discussion about using the bomb in Europe against Nazi Germany'. This ignores the reality of the Trinity test explosion in July taking place after the German surrender in May 1945, and that Roosevelt himself at one stage asked General Groves of the Manhattan Project whether a bomb could be readied to use against the Germans.[6]

b. Gar Alperovitz (already discredited here) proved the Allies knew Japan was surrendering.

c. The United States wanted to demonstrate its power to the USSR, Asia and the world. The Japanese were the target because the United States 'considered them to be a lower race'. [7] Strangely, Hume then uses pre-combat dismissive attitudes about Japanese combat abilities as evidence of Western racism. The fact, demonstrated across the Pacific for three and a half years, that the Japanese were *not* inferior soldiers, is dismissed.

If, however, the West's plan was intent on wiping out the Japanese as inferior, critics such as Hume seem to have further avoided logic. Japan could in fact have been devastated by firestorm raids until it was no more – that did not happen, beyond a few attacks around the time of the surrender, when certain capitulation was not evident. Japan could have been denied any opportunity to surrender merely by destroying its command centres in Tokyo, thus denying any radio offers of capitulation – that did not happen. It could indeed have been subjugated into slavery and wholesale slaughter after the surrender – that did not happen.

It is a strange racist overlord indeed who would not take advantage of such opportunities, especially given the outright hatred of the Japanese prevalent at the time in the Allied forces and involved countries. Instead, Japan was pacified, politically civilised and assisted into becoming one of the biggest economic powerhouses of the 20th century. Meanwhile, in the United Kingdom, food rationing continued until July 1954 – the Japanese Occupation ended two years earlier in April 1952. Strange that a 'racist overlord' endured privations – while former enemies such as Germany and Japan were assisted in their recovery.

Nevertheless, there have been plenty of critics of the A-bomb who have continually argued that the attack was merely a racist move. For example, students from Hiroshima, under the leadership of activist Ceri Dingle, also in the 1990s, and for the next 20+ years, have engaged in an international mission to rally attention to the same cause:

> The school students' mission was not to elevate nuclear weapons as uniquely destructive, or dictate who can have them or demand apologies. No, it was to challenge the racial thinking that legitimised 'the White Man's Bomb'. They set out to tell the truth about the war – that the Japanese were viewed as vermin to be eradicated, that Japan was on its knees when this great experiment in human annihilation was conducted.[8]

Proponents of the 'racist' cause, such as Hume and Dingle, routinely employ the argument that Japan would have surrendered 'soon' – the oft-touted date is the end of 1945. Just as routinely, they never employ any research to show how many Allied military and conquered nations personnel were dying every month: around 40,000 military personnel and 250,000 people in Japanese-held lands – every 30 days.

If the war had continued until the end of 1945, the grim total over that six months would have been 240,000 Allied military dead; 1.5 million civilians, and the 300,000 POWS to be killed as soon as the Home Island invasion began. And the Japanese at nine million deaths would make it 11.4 million dead – all so the world would wait for a Japanese capitulation by the end of 1945, rather than use the A-bombs.

Speaking of students, there has been a pervasive attitude within children's books that depict the atomic raids as being wrong. It is hardly surprising that the children of the post-war generation have grown up with a perception that the A-bomb attacks killed thousands rather than saved millions. A small study of Western children's books was carried out to examine this situation. The results were startling:

- Not one of the books surveyed for this study mentioned that Hiroshima and Nagasaki residents were given Allied advice to evacuate their cities.

- Not one of the books surveyed mentioned that many of the Japanese military were so keen to pursue the war that they rose in rebellion after the Emperor's surrender order.

- Only just over half – 53 percent – of the children's books analysed mention the Japanese and Allied casualties that would have been incurred in a conventional invasion.[9]

- Pearl Harbor, as a cause of the war, is mentioned by the majority – 80 percent – of the writers; but the invasion of China by Japan was included by just over half – 60 percent.

- If the degree of blame overall for the war is averaged out, then 55 percent of the writers ascribed fault to the Japanese, while 45 percent of averaged blame saw the Allies as responsible.

A peace banner in the Nagasaki Atomic Bomb Museum in 2015. (Author photo)

Instead, writers concentrated on the individual story of despair and tragedy. Perhaps the most famous of these is the sad story of the 1000 paper cranes, commemorated at the Hiroshima memorial and in numerous other places. At the age of two, Sadako Sasaki was exposed to radiation from the Hiroshima bomb. Ten years later she developed leukemia. In hospital, she was told of the legend of the crane, a sacred bird in Japan, which lives for a hundred years. If a sick person folds 1000 paper cranes, so the story went, then that person would get well.

After hearing the legend, Sadako decided to fold 1000 cranes in the hope that she would get well again. Despite sickness, she managed to fold 644 cranes before she died. Thirty-nine of Sadako's classmates felt saddened by the loss of their close friend and decided to form a paper crane club to honour her.[10] This led to a call for a permanent monument, which later was developed with assistance from more than 3200 schools in Japan and nine donor countries. The memorial was opened on 5 May 1958 and is a major drawcard in the Hiroshima complex featuring the Ground Zero building and the underground museum.[11] It is immensely sad that Sadako died – and that anyone died in the Hiroshima blast – but it is hardly a logical argument to replace analysis with emotion. If around 300,000 people a month had died if the war had continued, how many of those would have been children? Who indeed folded paper cranes for the millions of children who had already died?

の成果を誇示する目的もあった。また、ソ連との冷たい戦争の最初の作戦という性格も持っていた。

The Road to the Atomic Bombing

The German scientists who discovered nuclear fission in 1938 realized that the phenomenon could be applied to a bomb. The United States launched the Manhattan Project in 1942 and allotted a sum of money greater than the entire national budget of Japan for the development of the atomic bomb. The bomb was intended for use against Germany, but by the end of 1944 the target had changed to Japan. Hiroshima and Nagasaki, two of 17 cities including Kyoto chosen as candidates, were subjected to atomic bombings on August 6 and 9, 1945. It is said that the atomic bombs were used to hasten the end of World War II. But another purpose was to display the success of the Manhattan Project, into which two billion dollars had been invested. The atomic bombings were also the first strategic move in the Cold War between the United States and the Soviet Union.

导致原子弹投下的经过

1938年(昭和13年)在德国发现了核分裂,启发了人们可应用原子弹爆炸。1942年(昭和17年)美国策划了曼哈顿计划,拿出了超过当时日本国家预算的巨额研制并开发了原子弹。原子弹光时以结写业业业士后把目标转向

A sign arguing one of the main purposes of the A-bombs use was to justify the money spent on it. Nagasaki Atomic Bomb Museum in 2015. (Author photo)

At the Hiroshima Peace Memorial library, the staff members estimate that there have been 110 published Japanese language children's books that relate to the attacks. These include around ten volumes of comic books, which are especially popular in Japan.[12] While little analysis has been attempted of these, inspection of only a few suggest their themes relate closely to those published in the West.[13]

Barefoot Gen, for example, tells the story of Gen, a young boy living in Hiroshima at the time of the bombing. It does not examine or show anything but a young boy and his family impacted by the bomb. Elements of the mystical are included by having ants coming into the house minutes before the bomb is dropped, the implication being that even the natural world retreated before the evil of the Allies. The bomb – dropped from a far lower height than it was in actuality – and the crew of the B-29 are briefly seen from the ground. There is no rationale given for why the bomb is dropped. Then the reader follows Gen through torturous times battling for survival.

It is easy to see how the rationale for the bomb, and the reader's emotion, is being manipulated here:

- Even Nature retreats before the Allied strike, the implication being the attack was 'evil'.

- Without a reason, children are attacked.

- The aircrew are seen, thus portraying that they were heartless people who attacked the target, and were not an emotionless machine.

- No warning is given to the population below the aircraft.

- The millions of leaflets actually dropped over the city do not feature in the story.

- No history of Japan in the war is given. In fact, we are not even shown Japan is at war.

- There is nothing around the family to show an attack necessity. We do see one soldier in uniform.

- Gen's father is present – of fighting age – but we are not told of his occupation.

- He dies heroically, telling Gen to save his mother and her unborn baby.

In essence, *Barefoot Gen* tells the reader that Japan was doing nothing wrong, and then for no reason, it was attacked. Its civilians were blameless; they were not involved in the war, and yet they were mercilessly bombed.

Other books – non-fiction – aimed at children, are also often quite obviously pushing a no-nuclear agenda. *Nuclear Arms Control*, by Justin Healey, for example, is quite overt in its message. One of the most significant stances the book takes is its proclamation that: 'Nuclear weapons pose a direct and constant threat to people everywhere. Far from keeping the peace, they breed fear and mistrust among nations.'[14] The fact that fear of nuclear retaliation kept the USSR at bay in the Cold War is not mentioned.

Other aspects are more subtle.

Above, the proclamation cited is a cartoon figure of a young person brandishing a loud-hailer while wearing a sign proclaiming 'No War' and holding a red 'Stop' sign. The bright colours and attractive graphic aligns the reader into the message. And for young naive readers, who can't be moved by the simplistic message that war must be avoided, there is no discussion of the young citizens of Paris and London, or indeed of Pearl Harbor, Singapore, and Darwin, who died before the advance of the Axis war machine.

It is not always the case though that children's history books on the A-bomb subject have an agenda or are unbalanced. The Heinemann Library's *Hiroshima: the shadow of the bomb*, for example, presents a variety of arguments for using the weapons, while at the same time analysing the possible courses of action for demonstration, conventional warfare and blockade. It cites the Okinawa statistics and asks: 'If that was the price to be paid for taking one island … what would it cost to take Japan itself.'[15] One argument the book doesn't examine, however, is the cost to the 300,000 Allied POWs if Japan was invaded.

Up to the present day, it is not unusual to find manipulative, vitriolic attacks on the decision. This following one is worth repeating in full before giving some analysis. It was from a radio program[16] on the 70th anniversary of the Hiroshima strike:

MICHAEL BRISSENDEN: Seventy years ago, the world changed forever when America dropped the first atomic bomb on the Japanese city of Hiroshima.

The Americans said they took the drastic step to put an early end to World War II and save the lives of hundreds of thousands of US soldiers.

But as North Asia correspondent Matthew Carney reports, this official narrative is now being overturned.

MATTHEW CARNEY: On the 6 August 1945, the world's first atomic bomb was exploded over Hiroshima, wiping out the city centre and killing about 140,000 by the year's end. Keiko Ogura was eight at the time and only 2.4 kilometres from the hypocenter.

KEIKO OGURA (translated): I was engulfed with a dazzling flash of light and the blast slammed me to the ground and I lost consciousness. I woke up, it was dark and everyone was crying.

MATTHEW CARNEY: Keiko says the atomic bombings of Hiroshima, and another at Nagasaki three days later, were war crimes.

Many historians say the bombings did not lead to the Japanese surrender and that the Soviet declaration of war on Japan two days later was a bigger shock. It put an end to any hope that the Soviets would negotiate a favourable surrender for Japan.

The severely weakened Japanese Imperial Army had no capacity to fight the Soviets on a second front in China and Northern Japan.

Yuki Tanaka, a Japanese historian, says the country had no choice. The Soviets would have killed Emperor Hirohito. He was seen as the heart and soul of imperial Japan.

YUKI TANAKA: The Soviet Union would demolish the emperor system and they will execute the emperor as well as all other members of the royal family.

MATTHEW CARNEY: America believed the shock and awe of the devastating power of the new bombs would force Japan into surrender, but experts say inside Japan it was viewed very differently.

The Americans had already destroyed 66 Japanese cities with a massive fire bombing campaign. In just one night, 100,000 civilians were killed in Tokyo.

Jeffrey Kingston is director of Asian Studies at Tokyo's Temple University.

JEFFREY KINGSTON: If you look at it from the perspective of the Japanese military, it doesn't really make a big difference whether people are dying from fire bombs or atomic bombs. So it's two additional city centres that are destroyed.

MATTHEW CARNEY: The atomic bombings probably did play a part in averting a bloody ground invasion and saving thousands of US lives. But historians say the bombs were also about sending a message to the Soviets.

Jeffrey Kingston again:

JEFFREY KINGSTON: We have this incredible new weapon, we have a monopoly on it, and we are going to emerge from this war the strongest superpower. And so in a sense, this was the opening salvo of the Cold War.

(Sound of children singing)

MATTHEW CARNEY: On the eve of 70th anniversary, the children of Hiroshima sing for a future free of nuclear weapons. But today, more countries than ever have the bomb.

America's atomic attacks on Japan started a nuclear arms race, which has brought the world to the brink of destruction.

This is Matthew Carney reporting for AM in Hiroshima.

An analysis of this is illuminating. The program is 'fast and loose' with the truth. It manipulates data to an end of condemning America, and it further uses emotion to cloud judgment to further that aim. It does this in the following ways:

- The program plays on emotion rather than facts:

  i. It uses the testimony of a child to arouse pity in the listener.

  ii. It uses the sound of children singing to arouse sympathy from the listener.

- The program purports to tell the listener that 'many historians [plural] say', but then it only quotes one.

- The script-writer employs the phrase 'shock and awe', which was used in the controversial 2003 invasion of Iraq, to parallel the attack of the United States on Japan in World War II, so as to elicit hostility to the concept of the A-bomb strikes.

- The program quotes selectively from someone who disagrees with the A-bomb strikes, and allows him to posit unchallenged the concept that the United States recognised the USSR as a power of equal in World War II, when it is obvious the USSR in 1945 was no such thing:

  i. It possessed not one aircraft carrier, one of the most significant weapons of the war, being vastly outnumbered in such capacity by both the RN and the USN.

  ii. It possessed no long-range bomber fleet.

iii. It possessed little in the way of modern amphibious forces.[17]

iv. Oddly, and illogically, the USSR is both held up to be a threat to the United States – the A-bombs are a demonstration of power – but the United States at the same time is shown to possess weapons superior to the A-bombs anyway: the firestorm capacity, which killed more in a single night than either A-bomb.

Facebook advert from 9 August 2018. (Author photo)

- The program ends with a pejorative phrase that is demonstrably false: 'America's atomic attacks on Japan started a nuclear arms race which has brought the world to the brink of destruction.'

  i. It is undeniable there has not been a third world war in 70 years, whereas before World War II, there was global conflict a mere 20 years previously.

ii. The implication is that without the A-bombs the world would have been a more peaceful place, with the USSR being less aggressive, not more, as it was in Hungary, Czechoslovakia, as well as the Balkans, Afghanistan, and so on.

iii. There have been only slightly more people killed by warfare (per capita, by year) in the 20th century than there was beforehand. Given population rises, warfare technology's greater efficiency, and competition over resources, that is surprising.[18]

iv. The number of deaths from warfare[19] since World War II has steadily declined:

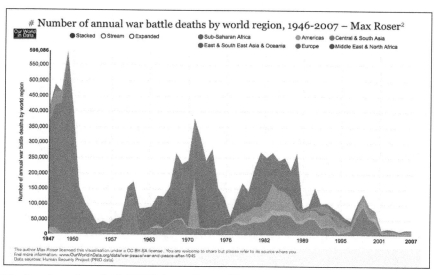

Number of annual war deaths WWII–2007. (Our World in Data)

The accusations of doing the 'wrong thing' occur most usually at the anniversary of the bombings. For example, the Mises Institute prominently feature this on their website:

Every year during the first two weeks of August the mass news media and many politicians at the national level trot out the 'patriotic' political myth that the dropping of the two atomic bombs on Japan in August of 1945 caused them to surrender, and thereby saved the lives of anywhere from 500,000 to one million American soldiers, who did not have to invade the islands. Opinion polls over the last 50 years show that American citizens overwhelmingly (between 80 and 90 percent) believe this false history which, of course, makes them feel better about killing hundreds of thousands of Japanese civilians (mostly women and children) and saving American lives to accomplish the ending of the war. [20]

Or in defiance of logic, the USSR myth that keeps being repeated:

Nuclear weapons shocked Japan into surrendering at the end of World War II – except they didn't. Japan surrendered because the Soviet Union entered the war. Japanese leaders said the bomb forced them to surrender because it was less embarrassing to say they had been defeated by a miracle weapon.[21]

Although *Atomic Salvation* is a book of military analysis, it should close on one of philosophical reflection. And that is one related to the philosophy of utilitarianism. The analysis that has been carried out shows clearly that over a million Allied troops, and millions of Japanese, would have died in the event of *four possible courses of action* other than using the A-bombs.

Logically, these are:

First – containment through naval blockade. Millions of Japanese would have starved. Thousands of Allied military personnel would have died, either from defending themselves in the case of Japanese attack, or through accidents. Throughout Asia, Japan would have continued the fight.

Second – a continuation of air bombing. Although thousands of Japanese would have died, due to their preparations and the country's topography nothing decisive would have been achieved. A steady loss of Allied lives would have entailed through Japanese attacks wherever possible, and accidents.

Third – the first and second courses could have been combined to create a third – a combination of starvation and air attacks.

But once again, it would have taken months and months, and the Japanese would have continued to fight. Who knows when their will would have been broken? Indeed, as has been mentioned, an Allied lessening of impetus may well have encouraged them to make assaults and breakouts in the style of the Battle of the Bulge. The Allies would have suffered steady losses.

Fourth – eventually, discouraged, with lower morale, and suffering the outrage of those who felt their loved ones' lives had been needlessly lost, 'conventional assault', would have been taken.

We can state with certainty that the Japanese would have died en masse, with civilians acting as soldiers against the formidable might of the Allies, whose skills, tactics, techniques, and equipment had been honed through their attacks on Europe.

As it was, the two atomic attacks killed probably killed around 200,000 people. Loss of life in war is always tragic. But better 200,000 should die than around 30 million, and as many as 35 million, the combined possible total of all Allied and Japanese deaths in a conventional invasion.

And that is why this book is entitled *Atomic Salvation*.

APPENDIX
CHILDREN'S BOOKS ON THE ATOMIC BOMBINGS

Adams, Simon. *Eyewitness World War II.*

Reason for A-bombing: not mentioned

Degree of blame for Japan /Degree of blame for Allies: 10/90

Was Pearl Harbor mentioned? Yes, but only in a timeline appendice

Was Japan's attack on China mentioned? No

Were potential Japanese casualties mentioned via conventional invasion? No

Were potential Allied casualties mentioned via conventional invasion? No

Was the idea of a "quick end" to the war mentioned? No

Was the leaflet drop urging surrender mentioned? No

Was the attempted military coup mentioned? No

Dugan, Michael. *Children in Wartime.*

Reason for A-bombing: to end the war

Degree of blame for Japan /Degree of blame for Allies: ambivalent but probably 80% Japan to blame

Was Pearl Harbor mentioned? Yes

Was Japan's attack on China mentioned? No

Were potential Japanese casualties mentioned via conventional invasion? No

Were potential Allied casualties mentioned via conventional invasion? No

Was the idea of a "quick end" to the war mentioned?

Was the leaflet drop urging surrender mentioned? No

Was the attempted military coup mentioned? No

Ganeri, Anita. *The top ten events that changed the world*

Reason for A-bombing: To bring the war to an end, or the Japanese would fight "to the bitter end, for years if necessary." (p. 18)

Degree of blame for Japan /Degree of blame for Allies: Japan 50% / Allies 50%

Was Pearl Harbor mentioned? Yes

Was Japan's attack on China mentioned? No

Were potential Japanese casualties mentioned via conventional invasion? Yes

Were potential Allied casualties mentioned via conventional invasion? No

Was the idea of a "quick end" to the war mentioned? Yes

Was the leaflet drop urging surrender mentioned? No

Was the attempted military coup mentioned? No

Grant, RG. *Hiroshima and Nagasaki* *[i]

    Reason for A-bombing: To save Allied lives / To save Japanese lives

    Degree of blame for Japan /Degree of blame for Allies: Japan 80% / Allies 20%

    Was Pearl Harbor mentioned? Yes

    Was Japan's attack on China mentioned? Yes

    Were potential Japanese casualties mentioned via conventional invasion? Yes

    Were potential Allied casualties mentioned via conventional invasion? Yes

    Was the idea of a "quick end" to the war mentioned? Yes

    Was the leaflet drop urging surrender mentioned? No

    Was the attempted military coup mentioned? No

Harris, Nathaniel. *Witness to History: Hiroshima* *

    Reason for A-bombing: "…by shortening the war it saved lives – even, in the long run, Japanese lives." (p. 24) Presents arguments for and against, including deterrence of Russia

    Degree of blame for Japan /Degree of blame for Allies: Japan 80% / Allies 20%

    Was Pearl Harbor mentioned? Yes

    Was Japan's attack on China mentioned? Yes

    Were potential Japanese casualties mentioned via conventional invasion? Yes

    Were potential Allied casualties mentioned via conventional invasion? Yes, "half a million casualties" although disagreement with as "low as 40, 000." (p. 24)

    Was the idea of a "quick end" to the war mentioned? Yes

    Was the leaflet drop urging surrender mentioned? No

    Was the attempted military coup mentioned? No

Hillman, Robert. *Australians at War: World War II*

    Reason for A-bombing: not mentioned

    Degree of blame for Japan /Degree of blame for Allies: 50/50

    Was Pearl Harbor mentioned? Yes

    Was Japan's attack on China mentioned? Yes

    Were potential Japanese casualties mentioned via conventional invasion? Implied: "the Japanese had no surrender plan. It was to be a fight to the last man, and to the last woman – the Japanese had trained and armed women to fight with sharpened bamboo spears, in the event of invasion." (p. 23)

    Were potential Allied casualties mentioned via conventional invasion? Yes, "a minimum of 50, 000 lives" (p. 25)

    Was the idea of a "quick end" to the war mentioned? No

    Was the leaflet drop urging surrender mentioned? No

    Was the attempted military coup mentioned? No

Hook, Jason. *Hiroshima* *

    Reason for A-bombing: To avoid enormous casualties on both sides

    Degree of blame for Japan /Degree of blame for Allies: Japan 80% / Allies 20%

    Was Pearl Harbor mentioned? Yes

---

i   * = deals with the sole topic of the A-bombings

Was Japan's attack on China mentioned? Yes

Were potential Japanese casualties mentioned via conventional invasion? Indirectly, citing "28 million civilians willing to fight to the death" (p. 20)

Were potential Allied casualties mentioned via conventional invasion? Yes, via comparison with Okinawa, and via General LeMay's statement

Was the idea of a "quick end" to the war mentioned? Yes

Was the leaflet drop urging surrender mentioned? No

Was the attempted military coup mentioned? No

Huey, Lois Miner. *Voices of World War II. Stories from the front lines*

　　Reason for A-bombing: "Japan refused to surrender" (p. 25)

　　Degree of blame for Japan /Degree of blame for Allies: Japan 50% / Allies 50%

　　Was Pearl Harbor mentioned? Yes

　　Was Japan's attack on China mentioned? Yes

　　Were potential Japanese casualties mentioned via conventional invasion? No

　　Were potential Allied casualties mentioned via conventional invasion? No

　　Was the idea of a "quick end" to the war mentioned? Implied

　　Was the leaflet drop urging surrender mentioned? No

　　Was the attempted military coup mentioned? No

Langley, Andrew. *Living Through World War II.*

　　Reason for A-bombing: "to finish the war as soon as possible." (p. 63)

　　Degree of blame for Japan /Degree of blame for Allies: Japan 80% / Allies 20%

　　Was Pearl Harbor mentioned? Yes

　　Was Japan's attack on China mentioned? Yes

　　Were potential Japanese casualties mentioned via conventional invasion? Yes: "vast numbers more on both sides." (p. 63)

　　Were potential Allied casualties mentioned via conventional invasion? Yes: "vast numbers more on both sides." (p. 63)

　　Was the idea of a "quick end" to the war mentioned? "The Allies wanted to finish the war as soon as possible." (p. 63)

　　Was the leaflet drop urging surrender mentioned? No

　　Was the attempted military coup mentioned? No

Lawton, Clive. *Hiroshima: the story of the first atom bomb* *

　　Reason for A-bombing: to bring a sudden end to the war

　　Degree of blame for Japan /Degree of blame for Allies: 50/50

　　Was Pearl Harbor mentioned? Yes

　　Was Japan's attack on China mentioned? Yes

　　Were potential Japanese casualties mentioned via conventional invasion? No, brief reference: "The Allies feared that the war in the Pacific would continue until 1946, with the loss of many more lives on both sides." (p. 20)

　　Were potential Allied casualties mentioned via conventional invasion? YES, brief reference: "The Allies feared that the war in the Pacific would continue until 1946, with the loss of many more lives on both sides." (p. 20)

Was the idea of a "quick end" to the war mentioned? Yes
Was the leaflet drop urging surrender mentioned? No
Was the attempted military coup mentioned? No

Malam, John. *The Bombing of Hiroshima* *
Reason for A-bombing: "to bring the war on the Pacific to a quick end, and, therefore, to
save American lives" (p. 18) and "to get the 'upper hand' over the Soviet Union (p. 19)
Degree of blame for Japan /Degree of blame for Allies: Japan 20% / Allies 80%
Was Pearl Harbor mentioned? Yes
Was Japan's attack on China mentioned? Yes
Were potential Japanese casualties mentioned via conventional invasion? No
Were potential Allied casualties mentioned via conventional invasion? No
Was the idea of a "quick end" to the war mentioned? Yes
Was the leaflet drop urging surrender mentioned? No
Was the attempted military coup mentioned? No

Morimoto, Junko. *My Hiroshima* *
Reason for A-bombing: None given in the text, which is a personal account of the author's
experience in Hiroshima as a child.
Degree of blame for Japan /Degree of blame for Allies: Japan 20% / Allies 80%. (Japan is
mentioned as being "pro-war" at the time, but the A-weapons are said to be "the crimes
of adults."
Was Pearl Harbor mentioned? No
Was Japan's attack on China mentioned? No
Were potential Japanese casualties mentioned via conventional invasion? No
Were potential Allied casualties mentioned via conventional invasion? No
Was the idea of a "quick end" to the war mentioned? No
Was the leaflet drop urging surrender mentioned? No
Was the attempted military coup mentioned? No

Murray, Aaron R (Ed.) *World War II Battles and Allies.*
Reason for A-bombing: "Hoping to stop the war in the Pacific" (p. 91)
Degree of blame for Japan /Degree of blame for Allies: Japan 80% / Allies 20%
Was Pearl Harbor mentioned? Yes
Was Japan's attack on China mentioned? No
Were potential Japanese casualties mentioned via conventional invasion? No
Were potential Allied casualties mentioned via conventional invasion? Yes, 250k
Was the idea of a "quick end" to the war mentioned? No
Was the leaflet drop urging surrender mentioned? No
Was the attempted military coup mentioned? No

Tames, Richard. *Hiroshima: the shadow of the bomb* *
Reason for A-bombing: "...to speed the end of the war and avoid a bloody invasion." (p. 17)
Degree of blame for Japan /Degree of blame for Allies: Japan 90% / Allies 10%

Was Pearl Harbor mentioned? Yes

Was Japan's attack on China mentioned? Yes

Were potential Japanese casualties mentioned via conventional invasion? Yes, Okinawa
compared (p. 11) & "could cost an invader perhaps a million casualties." (p. 18)

Were potential Allied casualties mentioned via conventional invasion? Indirectly without number

Was the idea of a "quick end" to the war mentioned? Yes

Was the leaflet drop urging surrender mentioned? No

Was the attempted military coup mentioned? No

Stein, R. Conrad. *World at War: Hiroshima* *

Reason for A-bombing: "By the summer of 1945, Japan was already a defeated nation."
(p.33) and "Perhaps the atomic bomb helped bring an end to the war." (p. 42)

Degree of blame for Japan /Degree of blame for Allies: Japan 0% / Allies 100%

Was Pearl Harbor mentioned? No

Was Japan's attack on China mentioned? No

Were potential Japanese casualties mentioned via conventional invasion? No

Were potential Allied casualties mentioned via conventional invasion? No

Was the idea of a "quick end" to the war mentioned? No

Was the leaflet drop urging surrender mentioned? No

Was the attempted military coup mentioned? No

ENDNOTES

Introduction

1   WWII database. <http://ww2db.com/person_bio.php?person_id=255> Accessed June 2013.

2   Kase, Toshikazu. *Journey to the Missouri.* New Haven: Yale University Press, 1950. (p. 205)

3   Long, Doug, website. Hiroshima: Harry Truman's Diary And Papers. <http://www.doug-long.com/hst.htm> Accessed 1 December 2013.

4   Kase, Toshikazu. *Journey to the Missouri.* New Haven: Yale University Press, 1950. (p. 184)

5   Grant, RG. *Hiroshima and Nagasaki.* East Sussex: Wayland Publishers, 1997. (p. 20)

6   Kase, Toshikazu. *Journey to the Missouri.* New Haven: Yale University Press, 1950. (p. 180)

7   Toland, John. *The Rising Sun: The Decline and Fall of the Japanese Empire.* New York: Bantam, 1982. (p. 877)

8   Fussell, Paul. *The New Republic.* 'Thank God for the Atom Bomb' August 1981. (p. 11)

9   Birth of the Constitution of Japan website. 'Potsdam Declaration' <http://www.ndl.go.jp/constitution/e/etc/c06.html> Accessed June 2013.

10   Rotter, Andrew J. *Hiroshima – the World's Bomb.* Oxford: Oxford University Press, 2008. (pp. 189–91)

11   Rotter, Andrew J. *Hiroshima – the World's Bomb.* Oxford: Oxford University Press, 2008. (p. 192)

12   The Pacific War Research Society. *Japan's Longest Day.* Tokyo: Kodansha International Limited, 1986. (p. 21)

13   Rotter, Andrew J. *Hiroshima – the World's Bomb.* Oxford: Oxford University Press, 2008. (p. 209)

14   The Pacific War Research Society. *Japan's Longest Day.* Tokyo: Kodansha International Limited, 1986. (p. 22)

15   Harper, Stephen. *Miracle of Deliverance.* London: Sidgwick and Jackson, 1985. (p. 131)

16   Rotter, Andrew J. *Hiroshima – the World's Bomb.* Oxford: Oxford University Press, 2008. (p. 209)

17   Collie, Craig. *Nagasaki: Massacre of the Innocent and Unknowing.* Melbourne: Allen & Unwin, 2011. (p. 163)

18   Rotter, Andrew J. *Hiroshima – the World's Bomb.* Oxford: Oxford University Press, 2008. (p. 210)

19   The Pacific War Research Society. *Japan's Longest Day.* Tokyo: Kodansha International Limited, 1986. (p. 25)

20   The Pacific War Research Society. *Japan's Longest Day.* Tokyo: Kodansha International Limited, 1986. (p. 38)

21   Harper, Stephen. *Miracle of Deliverance.* London: Sidgwick and Jackson, 1985. (p. 138)

22   Rotter, Andrew J. *Hiroshima – the World's Bomb.* Oxford: Oxford University Press, 2008. (p. 206)

23   The Pacific War Research Society. *Japan's Longest Day.* Tokyo: Kodansha International Limited, 1986. (p. 41)

24 The Pacific War Research Society. *Japan's Longest Day*. Tokyo: Kodansha International Limited, 1986. (p. 46) The Allied response became known as the 'Byrnes Note' after Secretary of State James Byrnes, whose advisors included experts in the Japanese polity.

25 The Pacific War Research Society. *Japan's Longest Day*. Tokyo: Kodansha International Limited, 1986. (p. 47)

26 Frank, Richard B. *Downfall: the End of the Imperial Japanese Empire*. New York: Penguin, 1999. (p. 314)

27 Frank, Richard B. *Downfall: the End of the Imperial Japanese Empire*. New York: Penguin, 1999. (p. 316) These conversations are not recorded in The Pacific War Research Society's Japan's Longest Day, the most comprehensive account of the revolt.

28 The Pacific War Research Society. *Japan's Longest Day*. Tokyo: Kodansha International Limited, 1986. (pp. 213–14)

29 The Pacific War Research Society. *Japan's Longest Day*. Tokyo: Kodansha International Limited, 1986. (p. 332)

30 The Pacific War Research Society. *Japan's Longest Day*. Tokyo: Kodansha International Limited, 1986. (p. 333)

31 The Pacific War Research Society. *Japan's Longest Day*. Tokyo: Kodansha International Limited, 1986. (p. 333)

32 The Pacific War Research Society. *Japan's Longest Day*. Tokyo: Kodansha International Limited, 1986. (p. 333)

33 Encyclopedia Brittanica. <http://www.britannica.com/EBchecked/topic/598171/Tojo-Hideki> Accessed October 2014.

Chapter 1

1   Japanese Peace Memorial Museum. Author visit, 2015.

2   ITV. Woodhead, Leslie. (Dir). *The Day They Dropped the Bomb*. 2015.

3   Tibbets, Paul W. *Return of the Enola Gay*. Ohio: Mid Coast Marketing, 1998.

4   Timeline #2 – the 509th; The Hiroshima Mission. The Atomic Heritage Foundation. Accessed May 2013.

5   Grant, RG. *Hiroshima and Nagasaki*. East Sussex: Wayland Publishers, 1997. (p. 4)

6   Toland, John. *The Rising Sun: The Decline and Fall of the Japanese Empire*. New York: Bantam, 1982. (p. 875)

7   Hook (p. 22)

8   Toland, John. *The Rising Sun: The Decline and Fall of the Japanese Empire*. New York: Bantam, 1982. (pp. 878–79)

9   ITV. Woodhead, Leslie. (Dir). *The Day They Dropped the Bomb*. 2015.

10 Tibbets, Paul W. *Return of the Enola Gay*. Ohio: Mid Coast Marketing, 1998. (p. 230)

11 Grant, RG. *Hiroshima and Nagasaki*. East Sussex: Wayland Publishers, 1997. (p. 9)

12 Grant, RG. *Hiroshima and Nagasaki*. East Sussex: Wayland Publishers, 1997. (p. 9)

13 Giovannitti, Len, and Fred Freed. *The Decision to Drop the Bomb*. New York: Coward-MCann Inc, 1965. (p. 269)

14 Campbell, Richard H. *The Silverplate Bombers: A History and Registry of the Enola Gay and Other B-29s Configured to Carry Atomic Bombs*. North Carolina: McFarland & Company, 2005.

15 Sweeney, Major General Charles W. *War's End: an Eyewitness Account of America's Last Atomic Mission*. New York: Avon Books, 1997. (p. 114)

16   Harper, Stephen. *Miracle of Deliverance*. London: Sidgwick and Jackson, 1985. (p. 133)

17   Harper, Stephen. *Miracle of Deliverance*. London: Sidgwick and Jackson, 1985. (p. 163)

18   Inspection visits by the author in 2012 and 2015.

19   Ienaga, Saburo. *The Pacific War*. New York: Pantheon Books, 1978. (p. 202)

20   Lifton, Robert Jay, and Greg Mitchell. *Hiroshima in America*. New York: Avon Books, 1995. (p. XVII)

21   Inspection visits by the author in 2012 and 2015.

22   Fitzmaurice, Francis William; Australian Army NX38456. DOB 24 Jun 1918; Enlisted 17 Jun 1941 in Strathfield, NSW. Discharged 12 Dec 1945 as a Lance Bombardier posted to 2/1 Heavy Battery.
      Mcconnell, Reginald. Australian Army NX38462. DOB 22 May 1918; Enlisted 17 Jun 1941 in Buckley Vale, NSW. Discharged 23 Nov 1946 as a Gunner posted to 2/1 Heavy Battery.
      Jobling, Eric Murray. Australian Army VX25508. DOB 26 Jul 1918. Enlisted 12 Jun 1940 in Caulfield, Vic. Discharged 14 Dec 1945 as a Private posted to 18 Australian Anti-Tank Battery Hooper, Eric Ernest. Australian Army VX23630. DOB 27 Jul 1918. Enlisted in Goorambat, Vic. Discharged 4 Dec 1945 as a Private posted to 2/2 Australian Pioneer Battalion.
      Chick, Allan Clifford. Australian Army TX3350. DOB 19 Mar 1920. Enlisted 17 Jun 1940 in Launceston, Tas. Discharged 7 May 1953 as a Private posted to the 2/40 Battalion. See <http://www.ww2roll.gov.au> Accessed June 2015.

23   Inspection visit by the author in 2012.

Chapter 2

1   Birth of the Constitution of Japan website. (The Ministry of Foreign Affairs 'Nihon Gaiko Nenpyo Narabini Shuyo Bunsho: 1840-1945' vol.2, 1966) 'Potsdam Declaration' <http://www.ndl.go.jp/constitution/e/etc/c06.html> Accessed June 2013.

2   Giovannitti, Len, and Fred Freed. *The Decision to Drop the Bomb*. New York: Coward-MCann Inc, 1965. (p. 275)

3   Weintraub, Stanley. *The Last Great Victory*. New York: Truman Talley Books, 2001. (p. 452)

4   Matsushiro Underground Imperial Headquarters brochure. 'From the Darkness of the Hidden History.' Obtained in a 2015 visit – author collection.

5   The Japan Times. 'Secret navy bunker gives a glimpse of the war's final days.' 27 June 2015. (p. 3)

6   Inspection by the author of the Nagasaki complex, and explanation from the nearby Nagasaki Museum of History and Culture. June 2015.

7   Kerr, E Bartlett. *Flames Over Tokyo*. New York: Donald I Fine, Inc, 1991. (p. 272)

8   Rotter, Andrew J. *Hiroshima – the World's Bomb*. Oxford: Oxford University Press, 2008. (p. 210)

9   Wilcox, Robert K. *Japan's Secret War: Japan's Race Against Time to Build Its Own Atomic Bomb*. New York: Marlowe and Company, 1995. (p. 177)

10   Giovannitti, Len, and Fred Freed. *The Decision to Drop the Bomb*. New York: Coward-MCann Inc, 1965. (p. 85) Grew was the USA's Acting Secretary of State from April to July 1945, and Undersecretary of State from July to August 1945.

11   Giovannitti, Len, and Fred Freed. *The Decision to Drop the Bomb*. New York: Coward-MCann Inc, 1965. (p. 299)

12   Harper, Stephen. *Miracle of Deliverance*. London: Sidgwick and Jackson, 1985. (p. 138)

13   Bradley, James. *Flyboys*. Boston: Little, Brown and Company. 2003. (pp. 148-149)

14   Giovannitti, Len, and Fred Freed. *The Decision to Drop the Bomb*. New York: Coward-MCann Inc, 1965. (p. 41)

15   The Pacific War Research Society. *Japan's Longest Day*. Tokyo: Kodansha International Limited, 1986. (p. 8)

16   Nagasaki Atomic Bomb Museum. *The Light of Morning*. (No page number available)

17   Powers, D. BBC-History. World Wars: Japan: No Surrender in World War Two. [online] Bbc.co.uk. <http://www.bbc.co.uk/history/worldwars/wwtwo/japan_no_surrender_01. shtml. 2019> Accessed May 2019.

18   Fussell, Paul. *The New Republic*. 'Thank God for the Atom Bomb.' August 1981. (p. 3)

19   Hoyt, Edwin P. *Japan's War*. London: Hutchinson, 1986. (p. 403) Japan's population was around 71 million, but the 100 million figure was often used in propaganda.

20   Nagasaki Atomic Bomb Museum. Letters from the end of the World. (No page number available)

21   Rotter, Andrew J. *Hiroshima – the World's Bomb*. Oxford: Oxford University Press, 2008. (p. 203)

22   Nagasaki Atomic Bomb Museum. *The Light of Morning*. (No page number available)

23   Giovannitti, Len, and Fred Freed. *The Decision to Drop the Bomb*. New York: Coward-MCann Inc, 1965. (p. 42)

24   The Pacific War Research Society. *Japan's Longest Day*. Tokyo: Kodansha International Limited, 1986. (p. 115)

25   Miscamble, Wilson D. *The Most Controversial Decision. Truman, the Atomic Bombs, and the Defeat of Japan*. New York: Cambridge University Press, 2011. (p. 81)

26   General Headquarters, Indian Military Intelligence Directorate 9329. (US Army) Japanese in Battle. Second Edition. August 1944. (Ike Skelton Combined Arms Research Library Digital Library) (p. 3)

27   Slim, William. *Defeat into Victory*. London: Cassell, 1956. (p. 337)

28   Hallas, James H. *Killing Ground on Okinawa*. Connecticut: Praeger, 1996. (p. 127)

29   Hallas, *Killing Ground on Okinawa*. (p. 123)

30   Astor, Gerald. *Operation Iceberg: the Invasion and Conquest of Okinawa in World War II*. New York: Donald I. Fine, 1995. (p. 416)

31   Tamayama, Kazuo and John Nunneley. *Tales by Japanese Soldiers*. London: Cassell, 1992. (p. 171)

32   Frank, Richard B. *Downfall: the End of the Imperial Japanese Empire*. New York: Penguin, 1999. (p. 29)

33   Frank, Richard B. *Downfall: the End of the Imperial Japanese Empire*. New York: Penguin, 1999. (p. 30)

34   Hook, Jason. *Hiroshima*. Suffolk: Hodder Children's Books. 2003. (p. 32)

35   Frank, Richard B. *Downfall: the End of the Imperial Japanese Empire*. New York: Penguin, 1999. (pp. 79-81)

36   Grant, RG. *Hiroshima and Nagasaki*. East Sussex: Wayland Publishers, 1997. (p. 40)

37   Maddox, Robert James. 'The Biggest Decision: Why We Had to Drop the Atomic Bomb.' American Heritage. 1995. Volume Number 46. Issue Number 3 (May/June) (pp. 71-77) <http://alsos.wlu.edu/information.aspx?id=1228> Accessed July 2013.

38   Maddox, Robert James. 'The Biggest Decision: Why We Had to Drop the Atomic Bomb.' American Heritage. 1995. Volume Number 46. Issue Number 3 (May/June) (pp. 71-77) <http://alsos.wlu.edu/information.aspx?id=1228> Accessed July 2013.

39   Kuwahara, Yasuo and Gordon T. Allred. *Kamikaze: A Japanese Pilot's Own Spectacular Story of the Infamous Suicide Squadrons.* Clearfield, Utah: American Legacy Media, 2007. (p. 248)

40   Harper, Stephen. *Miracle of Deliverance.* London: Sidgwick and Jackson, 1985. (p. 146)

41   Gilbert, Martin. *The Second World War.* Great Britain: Phoenix, 1989. (p. 723)

42   Grant, RG. *Hiroshima and Nagasaki.* East Sussex: Wayland Publishers, 1997. (p. 46), quoting Giovanitti and Freed, T*he Decision to Drop the Bomb.*

Chapter 3

1   Grant, RG. *Hiroshima and Nagasaki.* East Sussex: Wayland Publishers, 1997. (p. 20)

2   Kase, Toshikazu. *Journey to the Missouri.* New Haven: Yale University Press, 1950. (p. 103)

3   History Learning Site. 'The Fire Raids on Japan'. HistoryLearningSite.co.uk. 2011. <http://www.historylearningsite.co.uk/fire_raids_on_japan.htm> Accessed May 2014.

4   Kase, Toshikazu. *Journey to the Missouri.* New Haven: Yale University Press, 1950. (p. 217)

5   History Learning Site. 'The Fire Raids on Japan'. HistoryLearningSite.co.uk. 2011. <http://www.historylearningsite.co.uk/fire_raids_on_japan.htm> Accessed May 2014.

6   The Pacific War Research Society. Japan's Longest Day. Tokyo: Kodansha International Limited, 1986. (p. 22)

7   Hook, Jason. *Hiroshima.* Suffolk: Hodder Children's Books. 2003. (p. 31)

8   The Pacific War Research Society. *Japan's Longest Day.* Tokyo: Kodansha International Limited, 1986. (p. 22)

9   The Pacific War Research Society. *Japan's Longest Day.* Tokyo: Kodansha International Limited, 1986. (p. 25)

10   The Pacific War Research Society. *Japan's Longest Day.* Tokyo: Kodansha International Limited, 1986. (p. 22)

11   Frank, Richard B. *Downfall: the End of the Imperial Japanese Empire.* New York: Penguin, 1999. (p. 313)

12   The Pacific War Research Society. *Japan's Longest Day.* Tokyo: Kodansha International Limited, 1986. (p. 27)

13   For example, David Bergamini has argued that the Imperial family knew all along how they were perceived, and how they could manipulate proceedings to their advantage. As Ian Buruma puts it in 'The Emperor's Secrets':
… far from being a hapless, pacific victim of 'military cliques,' Emperor Hirohito and his courtiers had been plotting a war against the West since the 1920s. He 'had inherited from his great-grandfather [the Meiji Emperor] a mission, which was to rid Asia of white men'. The unsavory truth, as revealed by Bergamini, was that Hirohito had not only led his nation into war by stamping military orders but, through his coterie, had also intimidated those who opposed him by conniving in bizarre Oriental intrigues, including religious frauds, blackmails, and assassinations. (The New York Review of Books, <http://www.nybooks.com/articles/archives/2001/mar/29/the-emperors-secrets/>)
Bergamini, however, came in for a great deal of criticism, and his suggestions are not generally accepted. See Bergamini, David. *Japan's Imperial Conspiracy.* New York: Morrow, 1971.

14   The Pacific War Research Society. *Japan's Longest Day.* Tokyo: Kodansha International Limited, 1986. (p. 29)

15   The Pacific War Research Society. *Japan's Longest Day.* Tokyo: Kodansha International Limited, 1986. (p. 106)

16   The Pacific War Research Society. *Japan's Longest Day.* Tokyo: Kodansha International Limited, 1986. (p. 38)

17   The Pacific War Research Society. *Japan's Longest Day*. Tokyo: Kodansha International Limited, 1986. (p. 41)

18   The Pacific War Research Society. *Japan's Longest Day*. Tokyo: Kodansha International Limited, 1986. (p. 46)

19   Kase, Toshikazu. *Journey to the Missouri*. New Haven: Yale University Press, 1950. (p. 250)

20   Kase, Toshikazu. *Journey to the Missouri*. New Haven: Yale University Press, 1950. (p. 245)

21   The Pacific War Research Society. *Japan's Longest Day*. Tokyo: Kodansha International Limited, 1986. (pp. 213–14)

22   The Pacific War Research Society. *Japan's Longest Day*. Tokyo: Kodansha International Limited, 1986. (pp. 213–14)

23   The Pacific War Research Society. *Japan's Longest Day*. Tokyo: Kodansha International Limited, 1986. (pp. 217)

24   Giovannitti, Len, and Fred Freed. *The Decision to Drop the Bomb*. New York: Coward-MCann Inc, 1965. (p. 303)

25   Ienaga, Saburo. *The Pacific War*. New York: Pantheon Books, 1978. (p.231)

26   Ienaga, Saburo. *The Pacific War*. New York: Pantheon Books, 1978. (pp. 231–32)

27   Rotter, Andrew J. *Hiroshima – the World's Bomb*. Oxford: Oxford University Press, 2008. (p.199)

28   Frank, Richard B. *Downfall: the End of the Imperial Japanese Empire*. New York: Penguin, 1999. (p. 321)

29   The Pacific War Research Society. *Japan's Longest Day*. Tokyo: Kodansha International Limited, 1986. (p. 332)

30   Frank, Richard B. *Downfall: the End of the Imperial Japanese Empire*. New York: Penguin, 1999. (p. 321)

31   The Pacific War Research Society. *Japan's Longest Day*. Tokyo: Kodansha International Limited, 1986. (p. 333)

32   Toland notes there is no US record stating the attack took place. Toland, John. *The Rising Sun: The Decline and Fall of the Japanese Empire*. New York: Bantam, 1982. (p. 838)

33   The attack is commemorated in Oita City's Yokaren Museum. The authoritative website Kamikaze Images names the admiral as a vice-admiral rather than the higher rank. See <http://www.kamikazeimages.net/museums/yokaren-oita/index.htm>

34   Frank, Richard B. *Downfall: the End of the Imperial Japanese Empire*. New York: Penguin, 1999. (pp. 321–2)

35   Toland, John. *The Rising Sun: The Decline and Fall of the Japanese Empire*. New York: Bantam, 1982. (p. 966)

36   The Pacific War Research Society. *Japan's Longest Day*. Tokyo: Kodansha International Limited, 1986. (p. 333)

37   The Pacific War Research Society. *Japan's Longest Day*. Tokyo: Kodansha International Limited, 1986. (p. 333)

38   Frank, Richard B. *Downfall: the End of the Imperial Japanese Empire*. New York: Penguin, 1999. (p. 322)

39   Kase, Toshikazu. *Journey to the Missouri*. New Haven: Yale University Press, 1950. (p. 218)

40   Kase, Toshikazu. *Journey to the Missouri*. New Haven: Yale University Press, 1950. (pp. 263–65)

41   Toland, John. *The Rising Sun: The Decline and Fall of the Japanese Empire*. New York: Bantam, 1982. (p. 974)

42   Kase, Toshikazu. *Journey to the Missouri*. New Haven: Yale University Press, 1950. (pp. 263–65)

43   United States Strategic Bombing Survey. Interrogations of Japanese Officials. OPNAV
      P-03-100. Naval Analysis Division. Interrogation NAV NO. 76. USSBS NO. 379.
      'Japanese War Planning.' Tokyo, 17 November 1945. Interrogation of Admiral Yonai,
      Mitsumasa; Navy Minister in various cabinets as follows: Hayashi Cabinet February–June
      1937; First Konoye Cabinet, June 1937–January 1939; Hiranuma Cabinet January–July
      1939. Appointed Member Supreme Military Council, August 1939; Premier January–July
      1940; Deputy Premier and Navy Minister in Koiso Cabinet, July 1944; Navy Minister in
      Suzuki Cabinet, April 1945.
      <http://www.ibiblio.org/hyperwar/AAF/USSBS/IJO/IJO-76.html> Accessed May 2014.
44   About.Com 20th Century History. 'The War is Over … Please come Out.' <http://
      history1900s.about.com/od/worldwarii/a/soldiersurr.htm>
45   Wilmott, HP, Robin Cross and Charles Messenger. *World War II*. New York: Dorling
      Kindersley, 2004. (p. 293)

Chapter 4

1   Giovannitti, Len, and Fred Freed. *The Decision to Drop the Bomb*. New York: Coward-
      MCann Inc, 1965. (pp. 146–47)
2   Grant, RG. *Hiroshima and Nagasaki*. East Sussex: Waland Publishers, 1997. (p. 20)
3   Alperovitz, Gar. *The Decision to use the Atomic Bomb: and the Architecture of an American
      Myth*. New York: Alfred A Knopf, 1995. (p. 27)
4   Grant, RG. *Hiroshima and Nagasaki*. East Sussex: Wayland Publishers, 1997. (p. 21)
      quoting Giovanitti and Freed, *The Decision to Drop the Bomb*.
5   Harper, Stephen. *Miracle of Deliverance*. London: Sidgwick and Jackson, 1985. (p. 112)
6   Harper, Stephen. *Miracle of Deliverance*. London: Sidgwick and Jackson, 1985. (p. 112)
7   Toland, John. *The Rising Sun: The Decline and Fall of the Japanese Empire*. New York:
      Bantam, 1982. (p. 839)
8   Willmott, HP. *The Second World War in the Far East*. London: Cassell, 1999. (p. 205)
9   Willmott, HP. *The Second World War in the Far East*. London: Cassell, 1999. (p. 205)
10   Frank, Richard. 'No Bomb, No End.' *What If?* (Cowley, Robert. Ed) New
      York: GP Putnam and Sons, 2001. (p. 377) <http://coachfleenor.weebly.com/
      uploads/6/6/7/3/6673552/no_bomb_no_end.pdf> Accessed July 2013.
11   Frank, Richard. 'No Bomb, No End.' *What If?* (Cowley, Robert. Ed) New
      York: GP Putnam and Sons, 2001. (p. 378) <http://coachfleenor.weebly.com/
      uploads/6/6/7/3/6673552/no_bomb_no_end.pdf> Accessed July 2013.
12   Toland, John. *The Rising Sun: The Decline and Fall of the Japanese Empire*. New York:
      Bantam, 1982. (p. 839)
13   Harper, Stephen. *Miracle of Deliverance*. London: Sidgwick and Jackson, 1985. (p. 182)
14   Willmott, HP. *The Second World War in the Far East*. London: Cassell, 1999. (p. 205)
15   Willmott, HP. *The Second World War in the Far East*. London: Cassell, 1999. (p. 205)
16   Willmott, HP. *The Second World War in the Far East*. London: Cassell, 1999. (p. 198)
      Figured rounded up from 43.46 percent.
17   Alperovitz, Gar. *The Decision to use the Atomic Bomb: and the Architecture of an American
      Myth*. New York: Alfred A Knopf, 1995. (p. 21)
18   National Archives. Minutes of Meeting held at the White House 18 June 1945. Numbered
      C072142. Declassified Authority NND943011. (In the possession of the author.)
19   For example, Mollo's *The Armed Forces of World War II* gives a total figure exceeding that: of
      'maximum strength of five million men' in March 1942, citing 140 divisions and smaller

units. (p. 253) A figure of 33,000 men is given for the Army's air units (p. 259), and a Navy total of 1,663,223 men in July 1945, its peak strength. (p. 262)

20 Liddell Hart, BH. *History of the Second World War*. New York: GP Putnam's Sons, 1971. (p. 683)

21 Slim, Field Marshall Viscount. *Defeat into Victory*. London: Pan, 1999. (p. 508)

22 Liddell Hart, BH. *History of the Second World War*. New York: GP Putnam's Sons, 1971. (p. 690)

23 MacDonald Fraser, George. *Quartered Safe Out Here*. London: Harper Collins, 1995. (p.216) Original italics.

24 For a general overview see 'The Liberation of the South-West Pacific and Burma' in Liddell Hart, BH. *History of the Second World War*. New York: GP Putnam's Sons, 1971. Yamato was lost without her main armament of big guns – the world's largest on any ship – hitting any target.

25 Nihon Kaigun. <http://www.combinedfleet.com> Accessed March 2014. 'Japan started the war with 63 ocean-going submarines (i.e., not including midgets), and completed 111 during the war, for a total of 174. However, three-quarters of these (128 boats) were lost during the conflict ....'

26 Global Security.org. 'The Battle for Okinawa.' <http://www.globalsecurity.org/military/facility/okinawa-battle.htm> Accessed December 2013.

Chapter 5

1 Kerr, E Bartlett. *Flames Over Tokyo*. New York: Donald I Fine, Inc, 1991. (p. 41)

2 Kerr, E Bartlett. *Flames Over Tokyo*. New York: Donald I Fine, Inc, 1991. (pp. 28–33)

3 Kerr, E Bartlett. *Flames Over Tokyo*. New York: Donald I Fine, Inc, 1991. (pp. 189)

4 Kerr, E Bartlett. *Flames Over Tokyo*. New York: Donald I Fine, Inc, 1991. (pp. 186)

5 Kerr, E Bartlett. *Flames Over Tokyo*. New York: Donald I Fine, Inc, 1991. (pp. 207)

6 Hoyt, Edwin P. *Japan's War. The Great Pacific Conflict 1853–1952*. London: Hutchinson, 1987. (p. 363)

7 Lifton, Robert Jay, and Greg Mitchell. *Hiroshima in America*. New York: Avon Books, 1995. (p. 34)

8 (See p. 367)

9 Except where specified, taken from Kerr's *Flames Over Tokyo*, pages 215–231. Only the significant raids in terms of result are listed. For the Tokyo 10 March raid statistics see the chapter 'The Flowers of Edo'. Kerr has a table on page 255 that has some contradictory figures compared to the text – the latter has been used.

10 Yasukuni Shrine Museum, Tokyo. Exhibit: Bombing raids in 1945. Viewed June 2015. The exhibit wording does not give a target, saying it was a daylight attack, but it does say that subsequent raids focused on 'strategic factory installations' until February 1945. This bombing raid is not cited in other documents used here for the compilation of this table.

11 Kerr suggests 200,000 – Hoyt, Edwin P. *Japan's War. The Great Pacific Conflict 1853–1952*. London: Hutchinson, 1987. (p. 385) Kerr is citing Robert Guillain's *La Guerre au Japan* (The War of Japan) specifically Chapter 14, 'Boei, Air Defence of Homeland'. Kerr also notes that if the war had gone the other way, General Le May and others involved in this attack would have been 'duly tried and executed as war criminals'. (p. 387)

12 Hillenbrand, Laura. *Unbroken*. New York, Random House, 2010. (p. 274) The second total plane count is from Louie Zamperini, who was a B-25 bombardier and a POW at the time.

13 Kerr's narrative gives accounts of planes hit and diving away. Hoyt's *Japan's War* says two aircraft were lost – see page 385.

14 Kerr suggests 200,000 – Hoyt, Edwin P. *Japan's War. The Great Pacific Conflict 1853–1952*. London: Hutchinson, 1987. (p. 385) Kerr is citing Robert Guillain's *La Guerre au Japan* (The War of Japan) specifically Chapter 14, 'Boei, Air Defence of Homeland'. Kerr also notes that if the war had gone the other way, General Le May and others involved in this attack would have been 'duly tried and executed as war criminals'. (p. 387) Harper in Miracle of Deliverance suggests 84,000 dead – see page 111. Kurt Vonnegut in his novel *Slaughterhouse 5* uses '83,793 people', which probably helped establish this number firmly into common use. (p. 86)

15 Hoyt, Edwin P. *Japan's War. The Great Pacific Conflict 1853–1952*. London: Hutchinson, 1987. (p. 389)

16 Toland says 562 aircraft. Toland, John. *The Rising Sun: The Decline and Fall of the Japanese Empire*. New York: Bantam, 1982. (p. 837)

17 Toland says 502 aircraft. Toland, John. *The Rising Sun: The Decline and Fall of the Japanese Empire*. New York: Bantam, 1982. (p. 837)

18 Toland says 'tens of thousands', but it is unclear if he is referring to this night and the previous raid of the 23rd, or indeed all of the firestorm raids to that point. Toland, John. *The Rising Sun: The Decline and Fall of the Japanese Empire*. New York: Bantam, 1982. (p. 837)

19 Hoyt, Edwin P. *Japan's War. The Great Pacific Conflict 1853–1952*. London: Hutchinson, 1987. (p. 398)

20 Toland says 517 aircraft. Toland, John. *The Rising Sun: The Decline and Fall of the Japanese Empire*. New York: Bantam, 1982. (p. 838)

21 Toland, John. *The Rising Sun: The Decline and Fall of the Japanese Empire*. New York: Bantam, 1982. (p. 838)

22 Toland, John. *The Rising Sun: The Decline and Fall of the Japanese Empire*. New York: Bantam, 1982. (p. 838)

23 Toland, John. *The Rising Sun: The Decline and Fall of the Japanese Empire*. New York: Bantam, 1982. (p. 838)

24 Sweeney, Major General Charles W. *War's End: an Eyewitness Account of America's Last Atomic Mission*. New York: Avon Books, 1997. (p. 152)

25 Hillenbrand, Laura. *Unbroken*. New York, Random House, 2010. (p. 296)

26 Sweeney, Major General Charles W. *War's End: an Eyewitness Account of America's Last Atomic Mission*. New York: Avon Books, 1997. (p. 152) James Fahey in *Pacific War Diary* (p. 371) says a radio broadcast he heard on board USS Montpelier said 820, with one B-29 failing to return; he also cited the bomb load.

27 Sweeney, Major General Charles W. *War's End: an Eyewitness Account of America's Last Atomic Mission*. New York: Avon Books, 1997. (p. 196)

28 Toland, John. *The Rising Sun: The Decline and Fall of the Japanese Empire*. New York: Bantam, 1982. (p. 950)

29 Department of Defence. Fire Effects of Bombing Attacks. Defence Liaison Office W, of The Secretary of Defence, 1950. (Ike Skelton Combined Arms Research Library Digital Library) (pp. 20–21)

30 Kerr, E Bartlett. *Flames Over Tokyo*. New York: Donald I Fine, Inc, 1991. (pp. 221–23)

Chapter 6

1 Toland, John. *The Rising Sun: The Decline and Fall of the Japanese Empire*. New York: Bantam, 1982. (p. 771)

2   The Navy Department Library. 'Tokyo - a Study in Jap Flak Defence. Headquarters AAF Intelligence Summary 45–10 (30 May 1945): 18–25. <http://www.history.navy.mil/library/online/tokyo_flak.htm> Accessed November 2013.

3   United States Strategic Bombing Survey. Interrogations of Japanese Officials. OPNAV P-03-100. Naval Analysis Division. Interrogation NAV NO. 28, USSBS NO. 112, Tokyo Air Defence. Interrogation of Major Toga, Hiroshi, IJA; staff officer of the 10th Air Division from July 1944 to October 1945. <http://www.ibiblio.org/hyperwar/AAF/USSBS/IJO/IJO-28.html> Accessed November 2013.

4   Transcribed and formatted for HTML by Charles Hall, HyperWar Foundation. <http://www.ibiblio.org/hyperwar/AAF/USSBS/IJO/IJO-28.html>

Chapter 7

1   Hoyt, Edwin P. *Japan's War. The Great Pacific Conflict 1853–1952.* London: Hutchinson, 1987. (pp. 360–61)

2   Hoyt, Edwin P. *Japan's War. The Great Pacific Conflict 1853–1952.* London: Hutchinson, 1987. (p. 369)

3   Hoyt, Edwin P. *Japan's War. The Great Pacific Conflict 1853–1952.* London: Hutchinson, 1987. (p. 374)

4   Major source: Bôeichô Bôei Kenshûjo Senshishitsu [Military History Department, National Institute of Defence Studies, the Defence Agency] ed. Ran'in Bengaru-wan hômen kaigun shinkô sakusen [The Dutch East Indies and Bengal Bay Area: Naval Advance Operations]. *Senshi Sôsho* vol. 26. Tokyo: Asagumo Shinbunsha, 1969. (p. 342) Translated by Haruki Yoshida

5   Kase, Toshikazu. *Journey to the Missouri.* New Haven: Yale University Press, 1950. (p. 101)

6   The Pacific War Research Society. *Japan's Longest Day.* Tokyo: Kodansha International Limited, 1986. (p. 75)

7   Wilcox, Robert K. *Japan's Secret War: Japan's Race Against Time to Build Its Own Atomic Bomb.* New York: Marlowe and Company, 1995. (pp. 161-162)

8   Stars and Stripes. Robin Hoecker. 'To the death. Author says Bunker Hill, WWII Kamikaze pilots relate to warfare today.' 4 December 2008. <http://www.stripes.com/news/to-the-death-1.85893> Accessed June 2014.

9   Kamikaze Images. <http://wgordon.web.wesleyan.edu/kamikaze/writings/ogawa/index.htm>

10 Kamikaze Images. <http://wgordon.web.wesleyan.edu/kamikaze/writings/ogawa/index.htm>

11 The Pacific War Research Society. *Japan's Longest Day.* Tokyo: Kodansha International Limited, 1986. (p. 8)

12 Kerr, E Bartlett. *Flames Over Tokyo.* New York: Donald I Fine, Inc, 1991. (p. 250)

13 Tagaya, Osamu. *Mitsubishi Type 1 Rikko 'Betty' Units of World War 2.* Osprey Publishing Ltd. 2001. (p. 95)

14 Tagaya, Osamu. *Mitsubishi Type 1 Rikko 'Betty' Units of World War 2.* Osprey Publishing Ltd. 2001. (p. 95)

15 Hoyt, Edwin P. *Japan's War. The Great Pacific Conflict 1853–1952.* London: Hutchinson, 1987. (p. 363)

16 Military Factory. <http://www.militaryfactory.com/aircraft/detail.asp?aircraft_id=626> Accessed January 2014.

17 US Armed Forces Manual. U.S. Technical Air Intelligence Command, May 1945. <http://www.wwiiaircraftperformance.org/japan/Jack-11-105A.pdf> Accessed January 2014.

18 Military Factory. <http://www.militaryfactory.com/aircraft/detail.asp?aircraft_id=542>

19 Francillon, Rene J. *Japanese Aircraft of the Pacific War* (1st ed.). London: Putnam & Company Ltd, 1970.

20 Military Factory. <http://www.militaryfactory.com/aircraft/detail.asp?aircraft_id=542>

21 Military Factory. <http://www.militaryfactory.com/aircraft/detail.asp?aircraft_id=542>

22 Weintraub, Stanley. *The Last Great Victory*. New York: Truman Talley Books, 2001. (p. 375)

23 Weintraub, Stanley. *The Last Great Victory*. New York: Truman Talley Books, 2001. (p. 375)

24 Military History Encyclopedia on the Web. <http://www.historyofwar.org/articles/weapons_mitsubishi_A7M.html> Accessed June 2018.

25 Kennedy, Maxwell Taylor. *Danger's Hour*. New York: Simon and Schuster, 2008. (p. 235) The Bunker's Hill data is derived from this and DiGiulian.

26 All derived from DiGiulian, except for the Franklin and St Lo figures: the latter from NavSource Online <http://www.navsource.org/archives/03/063.htm> Totals include dead and missing.

27 Kennedy suggests another 25 'smaller British and American carriers' were damaged by kamikaze strikes.

28 Kamikaze Damage to US and British Carriers. Website. DiGiulian, Tony. <http://www.navweaps.com/index_tech/tech-042.htm> Accessed February 2015. DiGiulian says the 30th.

29 US Navy records confirm. See Rdigan, Joe. NavSource Online: Aircraft Carrier Photo Archive. <http://www.navsource.org/archives/02/13t.htm>Accessed Feb 2015.

30 Kamikaze Damage to US and British Carriers. Website. DiGiulian, Tony. <http://www.navweaps.com/index_tech/tech-042.htm> Accessed February 2015. DiGiulian says the 25th.

31 Derived from DiGiulian

32 Kamikaze Damage to US and British Carriers. Website. DiGiulian, Tony. <http://www.navweaps.com/index_tech/tech-042.htm> Accessed February 2015. DiGiulian says the 21st.

33 Hellcat fighter pilot James Vernon says he joined the ship in 'early May' 1945, which would make the repair time less than six months. He also reports the *Ticonderoga* as being hit by two kamikaze strikes. See Vernon, James W. *The Hostile Sky*. Maryland, Naval Institute Press, 2003. (p. 176) This is borne out by the ship's company website, which also has her air group embarking on board on 2 May; see USS *Ticonderoga*. Website. <http://bigt.net/history-cv14.html> Accessed October 2015.

34 Derived from DiGiulian.

35 Naval History Homepage. <http://www.naval-history.net/xGM-Chrono-04CV-Formidable.htm>

36 Inoguchi, Rikihei, and Tadashi Nakajima, with Roger Pineau. *The Divine Wind: Japan's Kamikaze Force in World War II*. Annapolis: Naval Institute Press, 1958.

37 Warner, Denis, Peggy Warner, with Commander Sadao Seno. *The Sacred Warriors: Japan's Suicide Legions*. New York: Van Nostrand Reinhold, 1982.

38 Kamikaze Images. <http://wgordon.web.wesleyan.edu/kamikaze/background/ships-sunk/index.htm> Accessed December 2013. (Later source address is: <http://www.kamikazeimages.net>)

39 Harper, Stephen. *Miracle of Deliverance*. London: Sidgwick and Jackson, 1985. (p. 116)

40 Frank, Richard. 'No Bomb, No End.' <http://slantchev.ucsd.edu/courses/pdf/Frank%20-%20No%20war,%20No%20end.pdf> Accessed July 2013.

41 Weintraub, Stanley. *The Last Great Victory*. New York: Truman Talley Books, 2001. (p. 287)

42   Federation of American Scientists. <http://www.fas.org/irp/eprint/arens/chap5.htm>

43   Federation of American Scientists. <http://www.fas.org/irp/eprint/arens/chap5.htm>

44   United States Strategic Bombing Survey. Interrogations of Japanese Officials. OPNAV
      P-03-100. Naval Analysis Division. Interrogation NAV NO. 6. USSBS NO. 40. 'The
      Attack on Pearl Harbor', 'The Kamikaze Corps in Philippines and Okinawa.' Tokyo, 18
      October 1945. Interrogation of Captain Fuchida, Mitsuo, IJN, <http://www.ibiblio.org/
      hyperwar/AAF/USSBS/IJO/IJO-6.html> Accessed May 2014.

45   Federation of American Scientists. http://www.fas.org/irp/eprint/arens/chap5.htm

46   Toland, John. *The Rising Sun: The Decline and Fall of the Japanese Empire*. New York:
      Bantam, 1982. (p. 805)

47   Harper, Stephen. *Miracle of Deliverance*. London: Sidgwick and Jackson, 1985. (p. 138)

48   Harper, Stephen. *Miracle of Deliverance*. London: Sidgwick and Jackson, 1985. (p. 139)

49   Harper, Stephen. *Miracle of Deliverance*. London: Sidgwick and Jackson, 1985. (p. 138)

50   United States Strategic Bombing Survey. Interrogations of Japanese Officials. OPNAV
      P-03-100. Naval Analysis Division. Interrogation NAV NO. 6. USSBS NO. 40. 'The
      Attack On Pearl Harbor', 'The Kamikaze Corps in Philippines and Okinawa.' Tokyo,18
      October 1945. Interrogation of Captain Fuchida, Mitsuo, IJN, http://www.ibiblio.org/
      hyperwar/AAF/USSBS/IJO/IJO-6.html Accessed May 2014.

51   United States Strategic Bombing Survey. Interrogations of Japanese Officials. OPNAV
      P-03-100. Naval Analysis Division. Interrogation NAV NO. 56. USSBS NO. 228.
      Aircraft Escort Of Convoys And Anti-Submarine. Operations. Tokyo, 1 November 1945.
      Interrogation of Lieutenant (junior grade) Okuno, Y., IJN; naval aviator in a squadron
      responsible for convoy escort and anti-submarine operations. <http://www.ibiblio.org/
      hyperwar/AAF/USSBS/IJO/IJO-56.html> Accessed May 2014.

52   United States Strategic Bombing Survey. Interrogations of Japanese Officials. OPNAV
      P-03-100. Naval Analysis Division. Interrogation USSBS NO. 62. Kamikaze Corps.
      Tokyo, 15 October 1945. Interrogation of Captain Inoguchi, Rikibei, IJN, Chief of Staff
      of First Air Fleet throughout the Philippine Campaign. http://www.ibiblio.org/hyperwar/
      AAF/USSBS/IJO/IJO-12.html Accessed May 2014.

53   United States Strategic Bombing Survey. Interrogations of Japanese Officials. OPNAV
      P-03-100. Naval Analysis Division. Interrogation NAV NO. 44. USSBS NO. 193.
      'Defence Of The Philippines, 1944.' Tokyo, 26 October 1945. Interrogation of
      Commander Yamaguchi, Moriyoshi; from August 1944 to January 1945 Operations
      Officer on the Staff of Vice Admiral Fukudome, CinC Second Air Fleet (FORMOSA), and
      after 23 October CinC First Combined Base Air Force (Luzon). <http://www.ibiblio.org/
      hyperwar/AAF/USSBS/IJO/IJO-44.html> Accessed May 2014.

Chapter 8

1   Information is drawn in general from the work, except where noted: *US Naval Technical
     Mission to Japan – January 1946. US Navy World War II Technical Intelligence – Japan S-02-
     Japanese Suicide Craft-1946.* (ebook) January 1946. Accessed July 2014.

2   Actually known as Type 1 and Type 5.1, reflecting slight design changes in both. The Type
     1 had problems with the metal construction, and with the initial gearboxes. This led to a
     change to wooden construction, and the elimination of the gearbox with direct drive.

3   The general purpose behind the other designs were to achieve much higher speeds (up to
     100 knots) with much greater armament, such as multiple rocket launchers. There was a
     heat-seeking variant, which would allow the pilot to abandon the craft to its final run and

avoid suicide. Significant problems arose with the hull design allowing such higher speeds, and this led to significant time lapses with successful implementation.

4   Variations in length were common, as the vessels were made by different yards, according to one source. See Warner, Denis, and Peggy Warner, with Commander Sadao Seno. *The Sacred Warriors: Japan's Suicide Legions*. New York: Van Nostrand Reinhold, 1982. (p. 148)

5   Warner and Seno say 15–18 knots, from Toyota, Nissan and Chrysler engines. (p. 148) A 'knot' is 1.5 miles per hour, or 1.85 kilometres per hour.

6   Harper, Stephen. *Miracle of Deliverance*. London: Sidgwick and Jackson, 1985. (p. 116)

7   Hoyt, Edwin P. *Japan's War. The Great Pacific Conflict 1853–1952*. London: Hutchinson, 1987. (p. 389)

8   Skates, John Ray. *The Invasion of Japan*. South Carolina: The University of South Carolina Press, 1994. (p. 111)

9   Japanese Suicide Weapons website. <http://www.b-29s-over-korea.com/Japanese_Kamikaze/Japanese_Kamikaze05.html> Accessed July 2014.

10   Nihon Kaigun. <http://www.combinedfleet.com/OkinawaEMB.htm> Accessed July 2014.

11   Harper, Stephen. Miracle of Deliverance. London: Sidgwick and Jackson, 1985. (p. 195)

12   As noted by the author, in two visits to the island, some 15 years apart.

13   Nihon Kaigun. <http://www.combinedfleet.com/PhilippinesEMB.htm> Accessed July 2014. Warner and Seno argue 23 personnel were killed on War Hawk, and LCI (M) 974 was also sunk by this attack, which they say involved 40 boats. They point out curiosities in the account – one Army maru-ni was manned by six personnel, according to one ship's report, which was almost impossible and clearly illogical manning.

14   Fahey, James J. *Pacific War Diary*. New York: Zebra Books, 1963. (p. 280)

15   Giovannitti, Len, and Fred Freed. *The Decision to Drop the Bomb*. New York: Coward-MCann Inc, 1965. (p. 88–89)

16   Yasukuni Shrine Museum, Tokyo. Detail of exhibit. Author visit 2015.

17   Presumably 'Palaus' is Palau. See 'World War II in the Pacific – Japanese Suicide Attacks at Sea' at <http://www.ww2pacific.com/suicide.html>. Accessed May 2015. The same reference was repeated at the time in Wikipedia, giving the website as a source.

18   Tadamasa Iwai, former officer in Japan's Tokko Suicide Regiment, wrote a book entitled *Tokko*. See extract at <http://www.lcjapan.com/lectures/iwaie.html>

19   Tadamasa Iwai, former officer in Japan's Tokko Suicide Regiment, wrote a book entitled *Tokko*. See extract at <http://www.lcjapan.com/lectures/iwaie.html>

20   Takahashi, Maiko. *Bloomberg Business*. 'In the Cockpit With Japan's Kamikaze Pilots.' <http://www.bloomberg.com/news/articles/2015-02-26/two-kamikaze-pilots-two-reprieves-one-pacifist-view> Accessed June 2015.

21   Polmar, Norman and Carpenter, Dorr B. *Submarines of the Imperial Japanese Navy 1904–1945*. London: Convoy Maritime Press Ltd, 1986. (pp. 137–38)

22   Skates, John Ray. *The Invasion of Japan*. South Carolina: The University of South Carolina Press, 1994. (p. 111 for both examples)

23   Nihon Kaigun. <http://combinedfleet.com/ships/kaiten> Accessed July 2014.

24   At least four Kairyu survived the war and are on display at:
the Japanese Maritime Self-Defence Service School, Eta Jima, Japan
Yamato Museum, Kure City, Japan
Yasukuni Shrine Museum, Tokyo
US Navy Nautilus Submarine Force Library and Museum, Groton, Connecticut, USA.
Nihon Kaigun website: <http://www.combinedfleet.com/kairyu.htm> Accessed June 2013.

25 Nihon Kaigun. <http://combinedfleet.com/ships/kaiten> Accessed July 2014.

26 Toland, John. *The Rising Sun: The Decline and Fall of the Japanese Empire*. New York: Bantam, 1982. (p. 790)

27 Warner, Denis, and Peggy Warner, with Commander Sadao Seno. *The Sacred Warriors: Japan's Suicide Legions*. New York: Van Nostrand Reinhold, 1982. (p. 273, and pp. 114–17)

28 Warner, Denis, and Peggy Warner, with Commander Sadao Seno. *The Sacred Warriors: Japan's Suicide Legions*. New York: Van Nostrand Reinhold, 1982. (p. 150)

29 Harper, Stephen. *Miracle of Deliverance*. London: Sidgwick and Jackson, 1985. (p. 138)

Chapter 9

1   Frank, Richard B. *Downfall: the End of the Imperial Japanese Empire*. New York: Penguin, 1999. (p. 124). Frank gives the total of over seven million on page 128.

2   Frank, Richard B. *Downfall: the End of the Imperial Japanese Empire*. New York: Penguin, 1999. (pp 124–25)

3   Frank, Richard B. *Downfall: the End of the Imperial Japanese Empire*. New York: Penguin, 1999. (p. 130)

4   Frank, Richard B. *Downfall: the End of the Imperial Japanese Empire*. New York: Penguin, 1999. (p. 124)

5   Newman, Robert P. *Truman and the Hiroshima Cult*. East Lansing: Michigan State University Press, 1995. (p. 6)

6   Neither for that matter had Australians after the war. The same author's Carrier Attack research conducted a survey that showed that 76 percent of those surveyed had never studied at school any attacks on Australia in WWII. This is despite the country enduring 208 air incursions, including 77 air raids on the Northern Territory; scores of vessels sunk off the eastern coast, and in the sinking of one cruiser, HMAS *Sydney*, off Western Australia, the loss of more lives (645) than in that country's entire losses in the Vietnam War.

7   Frank, Richard B. *Downfall: the End of the Imperial Japanese Empire*. New York: Penguin, 1999. (pp 20–22)

8   Frank, Richard B. *Downfall: the End of the Imperial Japanese Empire*. New York: Penguin, 1999. (pp. 85–86) The actual number of troops available was 2,903,000.

9   Kase, Toshikazu. *Journey to the Missouri*. New Haven: Yale University Press, 1950. (p. 252)

10 Frank, Richard. 'No Bomb, No End.' *What If?* (Cowley, Robert. Ed) New York: GP Putnam and Sons, 2001. (p. 375) <http://coachfleenor.weebly.com/uploads/6/6/7/3/6673552/no_bomb_no_end.pdf> Accessed July 2013. Emphasis in the original.

11 Hoyt, Edwin P. *Japan's War. The Great Pacific Conflict 1853–1952*. London: Hutchinson, 1987. (p. 393)

12 Toland, John. *The Rising Sun: The Decline and Fall of the Japanese Empire*. New York: Bantam, 1982. (p. 851)

13 Sweeney, Major General Charles W. *War's End: an Eyewitness Account of America's Last Atomic Mission*. New York: Avon Books, 1997. (p. 152)

14 Demobilisation and Disarmament of the Japanese Armed Forces. Reports of General MacArthur. Library of Congress Catalog Card Number: 66-60006. Facsimile Reprint, 1994. <https://history.army.mil/books/wwii/MacArthur%20Reports/MacArthur%20V1%20Sup/Index.htm#cont> Accessed June 2018.

15 See Frank's chapter 'Ketsu Operation on Kyushu'.

16 Zaloga, Steven J. *Japanese Tanks 1939–45*. (p. 42) <https://books.google.com.

au/books?id=nbwZvfSPLTMC&pg=PA42&lpg=PA42&dq=japanese+tanks+
home+islands+1945&source=bl&ots=81kJ29bTyG&sig=uVgsYRSFbGPHI
QCWYv-UrhXjIPQ&hl=en&sa=X&ved=0CDYQ6AEwBGoVChMIr9D8_-
rzxgIVBimmCh2AMAFJ#v=onepage&q=japanese%20tanks%20home%20islands%20
1945&f=false> Accessed May 2014.

17   Newman, Robert P. *Truman and the Hiroshima Cult.* East Lansing: Michigan State
      University Press, 1995. (pp: 25–26)

18   Fahey, James J. *Pacific War Diary.* New York: Zebra Books, 1963. (p. 396)

19   Kase, Toshikazu. *Journey to the Missouri.* New Haven: Yale University Press, 1950. (p. 141)

20   Morimoto, Junko. *My Hiroshima.* Australia: Angus and Robertson, 1987. (p. 12 of text and
      pictures – no page numbers)

21   Southard, Susan. *Nagasaki. Life After Nuclear War.* London: Souvenir Press, 2015. (p. 27)

22   Toland, John. *The Rising Sun: The Decline and Fall of the Japanese Empire.* New York:
      Bantam, 1982. (p. 794)

23   Toland, John. *The Rising Sun: The Decline and Fall of the Japanese Empire.* New York:
      Bantam, 1982. (p. 851) The extension in age and the demonstration of weapons probably
      took place around 10 July.

24   Kase, Toshikazu. *Journey to the Missouri.* New Haven: Yale University Press, 1950. (p. 175)

25   Toland, John. *The Rising Sun: The Decline and Fall of the Japanese Empire.* New York:
      Bantam, 1982. (p. 771)

26   Allen, Thomas, and Norman Polmar. *Code-Name Downfall: The Secret Plan to Invade Japan –
      and Why Truman Dropped the Bomb.* New York: Simon & Schuster, 1995. (p. 97)

27   Harper, Stephen. *Miracle of Deliverance.* London: Sidgwick and Jackson, 1985. (p. 116)

28   Sweeney, Major General Charles W. *War's End: an Eyewitness Account of America's Last
      Atomic Mission.* New York: Avon Books, 1997. (p. 152)

29   If this is accurate, it would be a strange choice of weapon. The pike is an 18 foot/5.5m
      spear that is designed to be held rather than thrown, and used against infantry in a
      defensive manner and to hold off horsed troops while musketeers reloaded. It would
      have been no use whatsoever against infantry firearms and laughable if deployed against
      advancing armour.

30   Hoyt, Edwin P. *Japan's War. The Great Pacific Conflict 1853–1952.* London: Hutchinson,
      1987. (p. 391)

31   Hoyt, Edwin P. *Japan's War. The Great Pacific Conflict 1853–1952.* London: Hutchinson,
      1987. (See pages preceding 307 with photos of such training; the satchel charge concept
      only in text)

32   BBC. Hiroshima: BBC History of World War II. 2005.

33   Fahey, James J. *Pacific War Diary.* New York: Zebra Books, 1963. (p. 291)

34   Quoted in Fussell, Paul. *The New Republic.* 'Thank God for the Atom Bomb.' August 1981.
      (p. 2-3)

35   Fussell, Paul. *The New Republic.* 'Thank God for the Atom Bomb.' August 1981. (p. 9)

36   Munoz, Charles. United States Navy WWII aircrew. Emails to the author. 2015.

37   Southard, Susan. *Nagasaki. Life After Nuclear War.* London: Souvenir Press, 2015. (p. 35)

38   Drea, Edward J. *Japan's Imperial Army.* Kansas: University Press of Kansas, 2009. (p. 247)

39   Sajer, Guy. *The Forgotten Soldier.* London: Weidenfeld and Nicolson, 1971. (p. 316)

40   From the author's *Lethality in Combat: An 'Australian Military Handbook',* published in
      1941, it urges its readers – if they are an officer – to use lethal force in this situation if
      necessary in no uncertain terms: 'If any one of any rank makes a move to surrender, shoot

him and carry on. If a bunch of men have surrendered, open fire on their guards and give them a chance to get away. If their guards are mixed up with them, open fire just the same.' In advice to all ranks given earlier, it urges that if panic is 'being communicated to others, then it is your obvious duty to shoot to kill'. Mitchell, G.D. *Soldier in Battle.* Sydney; London: Angus & Robertson, 1941. (pp. 51, 166) See for several other examples Metelmann, Henry. *Through Hell for Hitler:* a dramatic first-hand account of fighting with the Wehrmacht. Wellingborough: Stephens, 1990, and Crozier, Brigadier-General F.P. *The Men I Killed.* London: Michael Joseph, 1937.

41   Sledge, EB. *With the Old Breed, at Peleliu and Okinawa.* Novato, Calif: Presidio Press, 1981. (p. 61)

42   Wright, Derrick. *A Hell of a Way to Die: Tarawa Atoll, 20–23 November 1943.* London: Windrow & Greene, 1997. (p. 105)

43   Leckie, Robert. *Helmet For My Pillow.* Garden City, N.Y: Doubleday, 1979. (p. 225)

44   MacDonald Fraser, George. *Quartered Safe Out Here.* London: Harper Collins, 1995. (p. xx [TO ADD])

45   Bergerud, Eric M. *Fire in the Sky: the Air War in the South Pacific.* Boulder, Colo.: Westview Press, 2000. (p. 421)

46   Denfeld, D Colt. *Hold the Marianas.* Pennsylvania: White Mane Publishing Company, 1997. (p. 127)

47   Brune, Peter. *A Bastard of a Place: the Australians in Papua.* Crows Nest, NSW: Allen & Unwin, 2003. (p. 548)

48   Brune, *A Bastard of a Place*, p. 408, and reporting cannibalism, pp. 241 and 587.

49   Ham, Paul. *Kokoda.* Sydney: HarperCollins, 2004. (pp. 344–48)

50   Strauss, Ulrich. *The Anguish of Surrender: Japanese POWs of World War II.* Seattle: University of Washington Press, 2003. (p. 46)

51   Barrett, John. *We Were There.* NSW: Allen & Unwin, 1995. (p. 222)

52   Hordern, Marsden. *A Merciful Journey.* The Miegunyah Press: Victoria, 2005. (pp. 229, 279)

53   Terkel, Louis. *The Good War: An Oral History of World War Two.* New York: Pantheon Books, 1984. (p. 80)

54   Barrett, John. *We Were There.* NSW: Allen & Unwin, 1995. (p. 251)

55   Young, Peter. *Storm from the Sea.* Great Britain: Wren's Park Publishing, 2002. (pp. 205, 219)

56   Bergerud, Eric M. *Fire in the Sky: the Air War in the South Pacific.* Boulder, Colo: Westview Press, 2000. (p. 413)

57   Wright, Derrick. *A Hell of a Way to Die: Tarawa Atoll, 20–23 November 1943.* London: Windrow & Greene, 1997. (p. 123)

58   DeRose, James F. *Unrestricted Warfare: How a New Breed of Officers Led the Submarine Force to Victory in World War II.* New York: John Wiley, 2000. (p. 248)

59   DeRose, James F. *Unrestricted Warfare: How a New Breed of Officers Led the Submarine Force to Victory in World War II.* New York: John Wiley, 2000. (p. 251)

60   Henri, Raymond. *The U.S. Marines on Iwo Jima.* Tennessee: Battery Press, 1987. (p. 230)

61   Brune, Peter. *A Bastard of a Place: the Australians in Papua.* Crows Nest, NSW: Allen & Unwin, 2003. (p. 551)

62   Brune, Peter. *A Bastard of a Place: the Australians in Papua.* Crows Nest, NSW: Allen & Unwin, 2003. (p. 484)

63   Barrett, John. *We Were There.* NSW: Allen & Unwin, 1995. (p. 309)

64   Bennett, Cam. *Rough Infantry.* Victoria: Warrnambool Institute Press, 1984. (p. 196)

65   Ham, Paul. *Kokoda*. Sydney: HarperCollins, 2004. (393) and see Milner, Samuel. *US Army in WWII*. 'Chapter VII
The Advance on the Beachhead.' http://www.ibiblio.org/hyperwar/USA/USA-P-Papua/USA-P-Papua-7.html Accessed 5 August 2005.

66   Ham, Paul. *Kokoda*. Sydney: HarperCollins, 2004. (p. 430)

67   Ham, Paul. *Kokoda*. Sydney: HarperCollins, 2004. (p. 434)

68   Hobbs, David. The British Pacific Fleet in 1945.
<http://www.navy.gov.au/sites/default/files/documents/Hobbs_THE_BRITISH_PACIFIC_FLEET_IN_1945.pdf> Accessed July 2014.

69   'United States Pacific Fleet Organisation. 1 May 1945.' <http://ibiblio.org/hyperwar/USN/OOB/PacFleet/Org-450501/index.html> Accessed July 2014.

70   Combined Fleet. 'Japan started the war with 63 ocean-going submarines (i.e., not including midgets), and completed 111 during the war, for a total of 174. However, three-quarters of these (128 boats) were lost during the conflict.' <http://www.combinedfleet.com/ss.htm> Accessed July 2014.

71   Combined Fleet. 'Japan started the war with 63 ocean-going submarines (i.e., not including midgets), and completed 111 during the war, for a total of 174. However, three-quarters of these (128 boats) were lost during the conflict.' <http://www.combinedfleet.com/ss.htm> Accessed July 2014.

72   USS Indianapolis website <http://www.ussindianapolis.org/mcvay.htm> Accessed June 2014.

73   Toland, John. *The Rising Sun: The Decline and Fall of the Japanese Empire*. New York: Bantam, 1982. (p. 796)

74   Toland, John. *The Rising Sun: The Decline and Fall of the Japanese Empire*. New York: Bantam, 1982. (p. 772)

75   Toland, John. *The Rising Sun: The Decline and Fall of the Japanese Empire*. New York: Bantam, 1982. (p. 773)

76   Slim, Field Marshall Viscount. *Defeat into Victory*. London: Pan, 1999. (p. 189)

77   Australian Broadcasting Corporation. Warrior: Reflections of Men at War. Courtesy Library of the Australian Defence Force Academy, Canberra. 2004. (26'30')

78   Hastings, Max. *Armageddon: The Battle for Germany 1944–1945*. USA: Macmillan, 2004. (p. 148)

79   McKee, Alexander. *Caen: Anvil of Victory*. London: Souvenir Press, 1964. (p. 313)

80   Newman, Robert P. *Truman and the Hiroshima Cult*. East Lansing: Michigan State University Press, 1995. (p. 119)

81   National Archives (NA), Record Group (RG) 165, Entry 421, ABC Decimal File 1942–48, Box 570, 'ABC 471.6, Atom (17 August 1945) Sec. 7,' Memorandum for Chief, Strategic Policy Section, Strategy and Policy Group, OPD (Operations Division), Subject: 'Use of Atomic Bomb on Japan, April 30, 1946.' Cited in Alperovitz, Gar. *The Decision to use the Atomic Bomb: and the Architecture of an American Myth*. New York: Alfred A Knopf, 1995. (p. 321)

82   Walker, J. Samuel. *Prompt and Utter Destruction: Truman and the Use of Atomic Bombs Against Japan*. Easyread: ReadHowYouWant.com, 2009.

83   Alperovitz, Gar. *The Decision to use the Atomic Bomb: and the Architecture of an American Myth*. New York: Alfred A Knopf, 1995. (p. 322)

84   Fussell, Paul. *The New Republic*. 'Thank God for the Atom Bomb.' August 1981. (p. 2)

85   Skates, John Ray. *The Invasion of Japan*. South Carolina: The University of South Carolina Press, 1994. (p. 179)

86   Fussell, Paul. *The New Republic*. 'Thank God for the Atom Bomb.' August 1981. (p. 3)

87   Fussell, Paul. *The New Republic*. 'Thank God for the Atom Bomb.' August 1981. (p. 2)

88   Fussell, Paul. *The New Republic*. 'Thank God for the Atom Bomb.' August 1981. (p. 2)

89   Fussell, Paul. *The New Republic*. 'Thank God for the Atom Bomb.' August 1981. (p. 2)

90   Manchester, William. *Goodbye, Darkness: a Memoir of the Pacific War*. London: Berlinn Limited, 2001. (p. 288)

91   Manchester, William. *Goodbye, Darkness: a Memoir of the Pacific War*. London: Berlinn Limited, 2001. (p. 355)

92   Garrison, Gene, with Patrick Gilbert. *Unless Victory Comes: Combat with a World War II Machine Gunner in Patton's Third Army*. London: NAL Calibre, 2004. (p. 244)

93   Garrison, Gene, with Patrick Gilbert. Unless Victory Comes: Combat with a World War II Machine Gunner in Patton's Third Army. London: NAL Calibre, 2004. (p. 216) A Panzerfaust was the German equivalent of a bazooka, a tubed weapon firing one heavy armour-piercing shot used against heavy vehicles. A tank-destroyer was a lightly armoured version of a tank that was used against enemy tanks, taking advantage of its comparative speed.

94   Manchester, William. *Goodbye, Darkness: a Memoir of the Pacific War*. London: Berlinn Limited, 2001. (pp. 342–43)

95   Manchester, William. *Goodbye, Darkness: a Memoir of the Pacific War*. London: Berlinn Limited, 2001. (p. 339)

96   Manchester, William. *Goodbye, Darkness: a Memoir of the Pacific War*. London: Berlinn Limited, 2001. (p. 311)

97   Skates, John Ray. *The Invasion of Japan*. South Carolina: The University of South Carolina Press, 1994. (pp 110–115)

98   Harper, Stephen. *Miracle of Deliverance*. London: Sidgwick and Jackson, 1985. (pp. 88–89)

99   Sledge, EB. *With the Old Breed, at Peleliu and Okinawa*. Novato, Calif: Presidio Press, 1981. (pp. 65–66)

100   Sledge, EB. *With the Old Breed, at Peleliu and Okinawa*. Novato, Calif: Presidio Press, 1981. (p. 116)

101   Ambrose, Stephen E. *Band of Brothers: E Company, 506th Regiment, 101st Airborne: from Normandy to Hitler's Eagle's Nest*. New York: Simon & Schuster, 1992. (p. 80)

102   Slim, Field Marshall Viscount. *Defeat into Victory*. London: Pan, 1999. (p. 455)

103   Metelmann, Henry. *Through Hell for Hitler: a Dramatic First-hand Account of Fighting with the Wehrmacht*. Wellingborough: Stephens, 1990. (p. 149)

104   Hastings, Max. *Armageddon: The Battle for Germany 1944–1945*. USA: Macmillan, 2004. (pp. 99–100)

105   Metelmann, *Through Hell for Hitler*, 70.

106   Metelmann, *Through Hell for Hitler*, 138.

107   Sajer, *The Forgotten Soldier*, 363.

108   Small, Ken, and Mark Rogerson. *The Forgotten Dead – Why 946 American Servicemen Died Off The Coast Of Devon In 1944 – And The Man Who Discovered Their True Story*. London: Bloomsbury. 1988. The total is made up of an E-Boat attack on one of the training convoys on the night of 27 April, and the live-fire accidents. See also: <http://www.exercisetigerslapton.org/exercise-tiger/history/>

109   Hillenbrand, Laura. *Unbroken*. New York: Random House, 2010. (pp. 61, 80)

110   Toland, John. *The Rising Sun: The Decline and Fall of the Japanese Empire*. New York: Bantam, 1982. (p. 789)

111   Liddell-Hart, BH. *History of the Second World War*. New York: GP Putnam's Sons, 1971. (p. 688)

112   Liddell-Hart, BH. *History of the Second World War*. New York: GP Putnam's Sons, 1971. (p. 688)

Chapter 10

1   Speer, Albert. *Inside the Third Reich*. London: Weidenfeld and Nicolson. 1970.

2   Wu, Tien-wei. 'A Preliminary Review of Studies of Japanese Biological Warfare and Unit 731 in the United States.' <http://www.zzwave.com/cmfweb/wiihist/germwar/731rev.htm> Accessed August 2013. The article is written in polemical language; accuses the USA of conspiracy to acquire the weaponry developed and of ensuring silence thereafter, and it lacks reference detail for interviews and the like. It has been reviewed with some perceptive comments as to the authenticity of the sources. See Fouraker, Lawrence. Review of Sheldon H. Harris. Factories of Death: Japanese Biological Warfare, 1932–1945, and the American Cover-up. New York and London: Routledge, 2002. Published on H-Japan (February, 2004). <http://www.h-net.org/reviews/showrev.php?id=8907>

3   Keiichi, Tsuneishi. *Japan Focus*. 'Unit 731 and the Japanese Imperial Army's Biological Warfare Program.' Translated by John Junkerman. November 20, 2005. <http://www.japanfocus.org/-Tsuneishi-Keiichi/2194> Accessed June 2013.

4   Keiichi, Tsuneishi. *Japan Focus*. 'Unit 731 and the Japanese Imperial Army's Biological Warfare Program.' Translated by John Junkerman. 20 November 2005. <http://www.japanfocus.org/-Tsuneishi-Keiichi/2194> Accessed June 2013.

5   China through a Lens. Chen Chao and Daragh Moller, 4 December 2003. 'WWII Japanese Chemical Weapons in China Explained: An Interview.' <http://www.china.org.cn/english/2003/Dec/81536.htm> Accessed March 2014. Other news items on the same website refer to various incidents involving mustard gas.

6   Griffith, Paddy. *Battle Tactics of the Western Front*. London: Yale University Press, 1994. Griffith presents a readable study of how alternative methods of advancement for infantry were trialed in WWI.

7   Frank, Richard B. *Downfall: the End of the Imperial Japanese Empire*. New York: Penguin, 1999. (pp. 324–25)

8   Wu, Tien-wei. 'A Preliminary Review of Studies of Japanese Biological Warfare and Unit 731 in the United States.' <http://www.zzwave.com/cmfweb/wiihist/germwar/731rev.htm> Accessed August 2013.

9   Keiichi, Tsuneishi. *Japan Focus*. 'Unit 731 and the Japanese Imperial Army's Biological Warfare Program.' Translated by John Junkerman. 20 November 2005. <http://www.japanfocus.org/-Tsuneishi-Keiichi/2194> Accessed June 2013. The report of this is said to list 106 deaths, 'reported in a survey, conducted by two Ningbo researchers and published in March 1994 by Dongnan University Press'.

10   Keiichi, Tsuneishi. *Japan Focus*. 'Unit 731 and the Japanese Imperial Army's Biological Warfare Program.' Translated by John Junkerman. 20 November 2005. <http://www.japanfocus.org/-Tsuneishi-Keiichi/2194> Accessed June 2013.

11   Sixty-eight fighter interceptions were made against these balloons that were launched from Japan, so the jet stream at altitude would carry them to their target of the continental United States. 'Of the 10,000 balloons launched, they were found as far east as Michigan, and as far south as Texas and northern Mexico. In the five years after the end of the war, eight more were found, three in the 1950s, and two in the 1960s. In 1978, a gondola with

its barometre, some of the squibs and ballast was found in Oregon.' Tails through Time. 'The Japanese Balloon Offensive of 1944–1945.' <http://aviationtrivia.blogspot.com. au/2010/12/japanese-balloon-offensive-of-1944-1945.html> Accessed May 2014.

12 Toland, John. *The Rising Sun: The Decline and Fall of the Japanese Empire*. New York: Bantam, 1982. (p. 771)

13 Wilcox, Robert K. *Japan's Secret War: Japan's Race Against Time to Build Its Own Atomic Bomb*. New York: Marlowe and Company, 1995. (p. 16)

14 Wilcox, Robert K. *Japan's Secret War: Japan's Race Against Time to Build Its Own Atomic Bomb*. New York: Marlowe and Company, 1995. (p. 39)

15 Kristof, Nicholas D. 'Japan's A-Bomb Project: One of War's "What Ifs"'. 8 August 1995. <http://www.nytimes.com/1995/08/08/world/japan-s-a-bomb-project-one-of-war-s-what-ifs.html> Accessed June 2017.

16 The book has been listed on Amazon, according to some, in Japanese only.

17 The Atomic Heritage Foundation. 'The Alsos Mission'. <http://www.atomicheritage.org/mediawiki/index.php/The_Alsos_Mission> Accessed December 2013.

18 Atomic Heritage Foundation. 'Japanese Atomic Bomb Project.' 25 May 2016. <http://www.atomicheritage.org/history/japanese-atomic-bomb-project> Accessed Sep 2016.

19 Wilcox, Robert K. *Japan's Secret War: Japan's Race Against Time to Build Its Own Atomic Bomb*. New York: Marlowe and Company, 1995. (p. 170)

20 Rotter, Andrew J. *Hiroshima – the World's Bomb*. Oxford: Oxford University Press, 2008. (p. 36, and p. 81)

21 Walker, Mark. *German National Socialism and the Quest for Nuclear Power*. Cambridge: UP Cambridge 1993. (p. 174) See also page 157, where Walker tellingly describes the Allied concerns over German ambitions as a 'bad dream'.

22 Hook, Jason. *Hiroshima*. Suffolk: Hodder Children's Books. 2003. (p. 37)

23 Tames, Richard. *Hiroshima: the Shadow of the Bomb*. Oxford, England: Heinemann, 1998. (p. 15)

24 Giovannitti, Len, and Fred Freed. *The Decision to Drop the Bomb*. New York: Coward-MCann Inc, 1965. (p. 300)

25 Adelstein, Jake. 'New evidence of Japan's effort to build atom bomb at the end of WWII.' <http://www.latimes.com/world/asia/la-fg-japan-bomb-20150805-story.html> 5 August 2015. Accessed 9 February 2017.

Chapter 11

1 Sledge, EB. *With the Old Breed, at Peleliu and Okinawa*. Novato, Calif: Presidio Press, 1981. (pp. Xiii–xiii)

2 Hillenbrand, Laura. *Unbroken*. New York, Random House, 2010. (p. 80)

3 Sweeney, Major General Charles W. *War's End: an Eyewitness Account of America's Last Atomic Mission*. New York: Avon Books, 1997. (p. 195)

4 Hillenbrand, Laura. *Unbroken*. New York, Random House, 2010. (p. 80)

5 Weintraub, Stanley. *The Last Great Victory*. New York: Truman Talley Books, 2001. (p. 438)

6 Frank, Richard B. *Downfall: the End of the Imperial Japanese Empire*. New York: Penguin, 1999. (p. 124)

7 Sledge, EB. *With the Old Breed, at Peleliu and Okinawa*. Novato, Calif: Presidio Press, 1981. (p. 243)

8 Sledge, EB. *With the Old Breed, at Peleliu and Okinawa*. Novato, Calif: Presidio Press, 1981. (p. 187)

9   Fussell, Paul. Wartime. *Understanding and Behaviour in the Second World War*. New York: Oxford University Press, 1989. (p. 142)

10   Fussell, Paul. Wartime. *Understanding and Behaviour in the Second World War*. New York: Oxford University Press, 1989. (p. 142)

11   Giovannitti, Len, and Fred Freed. *The Decision to Drop the Bomb*. New York: Coward-McCann Inc, 1965. (p. 80)

12   Giovannitti, Len, and Fred Freed. *The Decision to Drop the Bomb*. New York: Coward-McCann Inc, 1965. (pp. 146–163)

13   Giovannitti, Len, and Fred Freed. *The Decision to Drop the Bomb*. New York: Coward-McCann Inc, 1965. (p. 80)

14   Frank, Richard B. *Downfall: the End of the Imperial Japanese Empire*. New York: Penguin, 1999. (p. 27)

15   Giovannitti, Len, and Fred Freed. *The Decision to Drop the Bomb*. New York: Coward-McCann Inc, 1965. (p. 111)

16   Giovannitti, Len, and Fred Freed. *The Decision to Drop the Bomb*. New York: Coward-McCann Inc, 1965. (p. 114)

17   Rotter, Andrew J. *Hiroshima – the World's Bomb*. Oxford: Oxford University Press, 2008. (p. 99)

18   Rotter, Andrew J. *Hiroshima – the World's Bomb*. Oxford: Oxford University Press, 2008. (p. 127)

19   D-Day Museum. <http://www.ddaymuseum.co.uk/d-day/d-day-and-the-battle-of-normandy-your-questions-answered#troops> Accessed June 2014.

20   Tibbets, Paul W. *Return of the Enola Gay*. Ohio: Mid Coast Marketing, 1998. (p. 243)

21   Anthony, Sebastian. 'The Apollo 11 moon landing, 45 years on: Looking back at mankind's giant leap'. 21 July 2014. <https://www.extremetech.com/extreme/186600-apollo-11-moon-landing-45-years-looking-back-at-mankinds-giant-leap> Accessed June 2017.

Chapter 12

1   Toland, John. *The Rising Sun: The Decline and Fall of the Japanese Empire*. New York: Bantam, 1982. (p. 877)

2   Fussell, Paul. *The New Republic*. 'Thank God for the Atom Bomb.' August 1981. (p. 11)

3   Birth of the Constitution of Japan website. 'Potsdam Declaration' <http://www.ndl.go.jp/constitution/e/etc/c06.html> Accessed June 2013.

4   Craughwell, Thomas J. *The War Scientists*. London: Pier 9, 2010. (p. 228)

5   Wilcox. *Japan's Secret War*. (p. 180)

6   Central Intelligence Agency. 'The Information War in the Pacific, 1945. Paths to Peace.' Josette H. Williams. <https://www.cia.gov/library/center-for-the-study-of-intelligence/csi-publications/csi-studies/studies/vol46no3/article07.html> Accessed 1 December 2013.

7   Frank, Richard B. *Downfall: the End of the Imperial Japanese Empire*. New York: Penguin, 1999. (p. 314)

8   Giovannitti, Len, and Fred Freed. *The Decision to Drop the Bomb*. New York: Coward-McCann Inc, 1965. (p. 292)

9   Kase, Toshikazu. *Journey to the Missouri*. New Haven: Yale University Press, 1950. (p. 213)

10   Giovannitti, Len, and Fred Freed. *The Decision to Drop the Bomb*. New York: Coward-McCann Inc, 1965. (p. 176)

11   Giovannitti, Len, and Fred Freed. *The Decision to Drop the Bomb*. New York: Coward-McCann Inc, 1965. (p. 111)

12   Giovannitti, Len, and Fred Freed. *The Decision to Drop the Bomb*. New York: Coward-MCann Inc, 1965. (p. 146–171)

13   Giovannitti, Len, and Fred Freed. *The Decision to Drop the Bomb*. New York: Coward-MCann Inc, 1965. (p. 142)

14   Giovannitti, Len, and Fred Freed. *The Decision to Drop the Bomb*. New York: Coward-MCann Inc, 1965. (p. 109)

15   Michael B. Stoff. *Manhattan Project: A Documentary History* (Philadelphia: Temple University Press, 1991), 122–124. Nuclear Files Org. <http://nuclearfiles.org/menu/key-issues/nuclear-weapons/history/pre-cold-war/interim-committee/interim-committee-discussion.htm> Accessed July 2014.

16   Giovannitti, Len, and Fred Freed. *The Decision to Drop the Bomb*. New York: Coward-MCann Inc, 1965. (p. 167)

17   Giovannitti, Len, and Fred Freed. *The Decision to Drop the Bomb*. New York: Coward-MCann Inc, 1965. (p. 108)

18   Harper, Stephen. *Miracle of Deliverance*. London: Sidgwick and Jackson, 1985. (p. 102)

19   Miscamble, Wilson D. *The Most Controversial Decision. Truman, the Atomic Bombs, and the Defeat of Japan*. New York: Cambridge University Press, 2011. (p. 103)

20   Frank, Richard B. *Downfall: the End of the Imperial Japanese Empire*. New York: Penguin, 1999. (p. 312)

21   Tibbets, Paul W. *Return of the Enola Gay*. Ohio: Mid Coast Marketing, 1998. (p. 242)

22   Giovannitti, Len, and Fred Freed. *The Decision to Drop the Bomb*. New York: Coward-MCann Inc, 1965. (p. 152)

23   Giovannitti, Len, and Fred Freed. *The Decision to Drop the Bomb*. New York: Coward-MCann Inc, 1965. (p. 154)

24   Giovannitti, Len, and Fred Freed. *The Decision to Drop the Bomb*. New York: Coward-MCann Inc, 1965. (p. 140)

Chapter 13

1   Kase, Toshikazu. *Journey to the Missouri*. New Haven: Yale University Press, 1950. See the chapters in particular of 'Over my dead body' and 'Riding a tiger'.

2   Frank, Richard B. *Downfall: the End of the Imperial Japanese Empire*. New York: Penguin, 1999. (p. 356)

3   Frank, Richard. 'No Bomb, No End. What If?' (Cowley, Robert. Ed) New York: GP Putnam and Sons, 2001. (p. 379) <http://coachfleenor.weebly.com/uploads/6/6/7/3/6673552/no_bomb_no_end.pdf> Accessed July 2013.

4   Maddox, Robert James. 'Gar Alperovitz – Godfather of Hiroshima Revisionism.' *Hiroshima in History – the Myths of Revisionism*. Missouri: University of Missouri Press, 2007. (p. 8–9)

5   Kingston, Jeff. *The Japan Times*. 'Why did Japan surrender in World War II?' 6 August 2016. <http://www.japantimes.co.jp/opinion/2016/08/06/commentary/japan-surrender-world-war-ii/#.WUtoCHdh2Jb> Accessed 23 June 2017.

6   Speer, Albert. *Inside the Third Reich*. London: Weidenfeld and Nicolson. 1970.

7   Kase, Toshikazu. *Journey to the Missouri*. New Haven: Yale University Press, 1950. (p. 217)

8   Ienaga, Saburo. *The Pacific War*. New York: Pantheon Books, 1978. (p. 231)

9   Walker, J. Samuel. *Prompt and Utter Destruction. Truman and the Use of Atomic Bombs Against Japan*. USA: University of North Carolina Press, 2005. (p. 88, and other references)

10   Alperovitz, Gar. *The Decision to use the Atomic Bomb: and the Architecture of an American*

Myth. New York: Alfred A Knopf, 1995. (p. 87). See the general chapter 'Phase 1: from Pearl Harbor to the Death of Roosevelt'.

11   Ienaga, Saburo. *The Pacific War*. New York: Pantheon Books, 1978. (p. 201)

12   See *Jane's Fighting Ships of World War II*. London: Studio Editions, 1990, (p. 229) and Bennighof, Mike: 'Stalin's Aircraft Carriers' <http://www.avalanchepress.com/SovietCarriers.php> Accessed June 2016.

13   Alperovitz, Gar. *The Decision to use the Atomic Bomb: and the Architecture of an American Myth*. New York: Alfred A Knopf, 1995. (p. 272–73)

14   Soviet Russia operated the four-engined Petlyakov Pe-8 during the war, although it had been withdrawn from service as obsolete in 1939. Its range and speed were roughly half that of the B-29. The Pe-8 had replaced the Tupolev TB-3, with significant performance increases, but the USSR continued to operate the TB-3 as well throughout the conflict. The Soviets operated the twin-engined medium US B-25 Mitchell, and the British Hampden through Lend-Lease. See for example: Military Factory. 'Lend-Lease Soviet Aircraft of WWII (1939–1945)'. <https://www.militaryfactory.com/aircraft/ww2-soviet-lend-lease-aircraft.asp> Accessed June 2018.

15   The National Interest. 'Russia Battled Japan Using American Landing Ships – After Japan Surrendered.' <http://nationalinterest.org/blog/the-buzz/russia-battled-japan-using-american-landing-ships%E2%80%94after-23768> 23 December 2017. Accessed January 2018.

16   Jane's Fighting Ships of World War II says that approximately 100 submarines were present in the USSR orbat; the same publication lists 286 for the USN – neither force used midget boats.

17   Skates, John Ray. *The Invasion of Japan*. South Carolina: The University of South Carolina Press, 1994. (p. 229)

18   Alperovitz, Gar. T*The Decision to use the Atomic Bomb: and the Architecture of an American Myth*. New York: Alfred A Knopf, 1995. (p. 113)

19   Alperovitz, Gar. *The Decision to use the Atomic Bomb: and the Architecture of an American Myth*. New York: Alfred A Knopf, 1995. (p. 114)

20   Alperovitz, Gar. *The Decision to use the Atomic Bomb: and the Architecture of an American Myth*. New York: Alfred A Knopf, 1995. (p. 114)

21   Ienaga, Saburo. *The Pacific War*. New York: Pantheon Books, 1978. (p. 201)

22   Alperovitz, Gar. *The Decision to use the Atomic Bomb: and the Architecture of an American Myth*. New York: Alfred A Knopf, 1995. (p. 153)

23   Alperovitz, Gar. *The Decision to use the Atomic Bomb: and the Architecture of an American Myth*. New York: Alfred A Knopf, 1995. (p. 154)

Chapter 14

1   Grant, RG. *Hiroshima and Nagasaki*. East Sussex: Wayland Publishers, 1997. (p. 15)

2   Grant, RG. *Hiroshima and Nagasaki*. East Sussex: Wayland Publishers, 1997. (p. 13)

3   Frank, Richard B. *Downfall: the End of the Imperial Japanese Empire*. New York: Penguin, 1999. (p. 26)

4   Grant, RG. *Hiroshima and Nagasaki*. East Sussex: Wayland Publishers, 1997. (p. 14)

5   Japanese WWII POW Camp Fukuoka #17 – Omuta. 'POWs of the Japanese: Death Rates by Nationalities.' <http://www.lindavdahl.com/FrontPage_Links/pows_of_the_japanese.htm> Quotes source: Horyo Saishu Ronkoku Fuzoku-sho B, 19 February 1948. Accessed June 2017.

6   Giovannitti, Len, and Fred Freed. *The Decision to Drop the Bomb*. New York: Coward-MCann Inc, 1965. (p. 262)

7   Fussell, Paul. W*artime. Understanding and Behaviour in the Second World War*. New York: Oxford University Press, 1989. (p. 285)

8   *Encyclopedia Britannica*. 'Bataan Death March.' <https://www.britannica.com/event/Bataan-Death-March> Accessed September 2016.

9   Australian War Memorial. 'Sandakan memorial.' <https://www.awm.gov.au/collection/ART92680> Accessed September 2016.

10   Hook, Jason. *Hiroshima*. Suffolk: Hodder Children's Books. 2003, (p. 10) quoting Laurens Van Der Post, who later wrote about his experiences in *Night of the New Moon*.

11   Hillenbrand, Laura. *Unbroken*. New York: Random House, 2010. (p. 320)

12   Rotter, Andrew J. *Hiroshima – the World's Bomb*. Oxford: Oxford University Press, 2008. (p. 128)

13   Rotter, Andrew J. *Hiroshima – the World's Bomb*. Oxford: Oxford University Press, 2008. (p. 192)

14   Harper, Stephen. *Miracle of Deliverance*. London: Sidgwick and Jackson, 1985. (p. 170)

15   Fussell, Paul. 'Thank God for the Atom Bomb.' Thank god for the atom bomb and other essays. New York: Summit Books, 1988. (p. 5)

16   BBC. Hiroshima: BBC History of World War II. 2005.

17   Conversation with son John Armstrong. July 2018.

18   Munoz, Charles. United States Navy WWII aircrew. Emails to the author. 2015.

19   Giovannitti, Len, and Fred Freed. *The Decision to Drop the Bomb*. New York: Coward-MCann Inc, 1965. (p. 263)

20   Manchester, William. *Goodbye, Darkness: a Memoir of the Pacific War*. London: Berlinn Limited, 2001. (p. 210)

21   The Gun Plot website. 'Survival at sea: In the whaler after the sinking of HMAS Armidale in 1942. A personal account by Rex Pullen.' <http://www.gunplot.net/main/content/hmas-armidale-survivors-story> Accessed June 2013. Used with permission of Russ Graystone, Webmaster/Owner.

22   Hook, Jason. *Hiroshima*. Suffolk: Hodder Children's Books. 2003. (p. 37)

23   In the Mind Field website. <http://www.inthemindfield.com/2012/06/12/paul-fussell-a-remembrance/> Accessed July 2014.

24   Fussell, Paul. *The New Republic*. 'Thank God for the Atom Bomb.' August 1981. (p. 9)

25   Lifton, Robert Jay, and Greg Mitchell. *Hiroshima in America*. New York: Avon Books, 1995. (p. 9)

26   Lifton, Robert Jay, and Greg Mitchell. *Hiroshima in America*. New York: Avon Books, 1995. (p. 33)

27   Fahey, James J. *Pacific War Diary*. New York: Zebra Books, 1963. (p. 374)

28   Fussell, Paul. *The New Republic*. 'Thank God for the Atom Bomb.' August 1981. (p. 10)

29   Frank, Richard B. *Downfall: the End of the Imperial Japanese Empire*. New York: Penguin, 1999. (p. 331)

30   Grant, RG. *Hiroshima and Nagasaki*. East Sussex: Wayland Publishers, 1997. (p. 46)

31   Rotter, Andrew J. *Hiroshima – the World's Bomb*. Oxford: Oxford University Press, 2008. (p. 190)

32   MacDonald Fraser, George. *Quartered Safe Out Here*. London: Harper Collins, 1995.

33   Johnson, Gordon. Royal Australian Navy sailor in WWII. Interview with the author. Darwin. 13 May 2014.

34   Winspear, Brian. Bomber wireless operator/gunner, personal interview, Tasmania, December 2013.

35 Roberts, Lysle. Spitfire pilot. Interview with the author on the Anzac Ghan train, 2012.

36 Vernon, James W. *The Hostile Sky*. Maryland, Naval Institute Press, 2003. (p. 176)

37 Giovannitti, Len, and Fred Freed. *The Decision to Drop the Bomb*. New York: Coward-MCann Inc, 1965. (p. 261)

38 The Australian. 'Last crew member of Enola Gay dies in US.' 30 July 2014. <http://www.theaustralian.com.au/news/latest-news/last-crew-member-of-enola-gay-dies-in-us/story-fn3dxix6-1227006763027> Accessed 30 July 2014.

39 Conversation with the author, Sydney, November 2016.

40 Lifton, Robert Jay, and Greg Mitchell. *Hiroshima in America*. New York: Avon Books, 1995. (p. 33)

41 Federation of Atomic Scientists. <http://www.fas.org/irp/eprint/arens/chap5.htm> Accessed June 2018.

42 Email from Geoff Brown to the author, 17 January 2017.

43 Extracted from a discussion on 'The Gunroom' mailing list, for the novels of Patrick O'Brian. 16 February 2014. Used with permission.

44 Moyle, John. Army Maritime Services soldier. Personal interview, Darwin, June 2013.

45 MacDonald Fraser, George. *Quartered Safe Out Here*. London: Harper Collins, 1995. (p. 217)

46 MacDonald Fraser, George. *Quartered Safe Out Here*. London: Harper Collins, 1995. (p. 221)

47 Rotter, Andrew J. *Hiroshima – the World's Bomb*. Oxford: Oxford University Press, 2008. (p. 235)

48 Kuwahara, Yasuo and Gordon T. Allred. *Kamikaze: A Japanese Pilot's Own Spectacular Story of the Infamous Suicide Squadrons*. Clearfield, Utah: American Legacy Media, 2007. (p. 248)

Chapter 15

1 Harper, Stephen. *Miracle of Deliverance*. London: Sidgwick and Jackson, 1985. (p. 186)

2 Harper, Stephen. *Miracle of Deliverance*. London: Sidgwick and Jackson, 1985. (p. 186)

3 Harper, Stephen. *Miracle of Deliverance*. London: Sidgwick and Jackson, 1985. (p. 182) This figure will be referred to later, but it should be noted that due to poor record-keeping in the camps, and record destruction as part of the course of the war, it seems impossible to determine accurately how many POWs the Japanese were holding in mid-1945. It should be noted too that the prisoners were not only 'Western' nations imprisoned by the Empire, but those of British Dominion countries, such as India.

4 Sweeney, Major General Charles W. *War's End: an Eyewitness Account of America's Last Atomic Mission*. New York: Avon Books, 1997. (p. 142–43)

5 Australian War Memorial. 'General information about Australian prisoners of the Japanese.' <https://www.awm.gov.au/articles/encyclopedia/pow/general_info> Accessed June 2017.

6 Winstanley, Lt. Col. Peter, OAM RFD. Website: Prisoners of war of the Japanese. 'Survival – At Sea and On Land. A Wartime Resume of an Australian Sailor.' <http://www.pows-of-japan.net/articles/61.htm> Accessed May 2015.

7 Extracted from Falle Sam: *My Lucky Life: In War, Revolution, Peace and Diplomacy*. 'Rescued from the sea by the Japanese Navy.' <http://ww2today.com/2nd-march-1942-rescued-from-the-sea-by-the-japanese-navy> Accessed February 2014.

8 Fussell, Paul. 'Thank God for the Atom Bomb.' *Thank God for the atom bomb and other essays*. New York: Summit Books, 1988. (p. 5)

9   Frank, Richard B. *Downfall: the End of the Imperial Japanese Empire*. New York: Penguin, 1999. (p. 161)

10 Bradley, James. *Flyboys*. Boston: Little, Brown and Company, 2003. (p. 295.)

11 Hillenbrand, Laura. *Unbroken*. New York: Random House, 2010. (pp. 292–93 with the dates mentioned frequently across the remaining pages. Page 198 contains the text of the order.)

12 Rivett, Rohan D. *Behind Bamboo*. Sydney and London: Angus and Robertson, 1947. (p. 375)

13 As told to the author by a relative in 2018, who noted that it was the early 1980s, before Leo would buy a Japanese-made car.

14 Rotter, Andrew J. *Hiroshima – the World's Bomb*. Oxford: Oxford University Press, 2008. (p. 153)

15 Hillenbrand, Laura. *Unbroken*. New York: Random House, 2010. (p. 315)

16 Sweeney, Major General Charles W. *War's End: an Eyewitness Account of America's Last Atomic Mission*. New York: Avon Books, 1997. (p. 142)

17 Toland, John. *The Rising Sun: The Decline and Fall of the Japanese Empire*. New York: Bantam, 1982. (p. 962)

18 Rotter, Andrew J. *Hiroshima – the World's Bomb*. Oxford: Oxford University Press, 2008. (p. 145)

19 Toland confirms 62 aircraft. Toland, John. *The Rising Sun: The Decline and Fall of the Japanese Empire*. New York: Bantam, 1982. (p. 837)

20 SBS One. (Special Broadcasting Service, Australia). 33'35'. Revealed: The Luckiest Man in World War Two. 4 August 2014. Note: 'FEPOW' stand for 'Far East Prisoners of War', a group of historians researching on that subject.

21 Hillenbrand, Laura. *Unbroken*. New York: Random House, 2010. (p. 198)

22 Fahey, James J. *Pacific War Diary*. New York: Zebra Books, 1963. (p. 294)

23 The History Place. Genocide in the 20th Century. 'The Rape of Nangking.' <http://www. historyplace.com/worldhistory/genocide/nanking.htm> Accessed June 2012.

24 Newman, Robert P. *Truman and the Hiroshima Cult*. East Lansing: Michigan State University Press, 1995. Quoted in Frank, Richard B. *Downfall: the End of the Imperial Japanese Empire*. New York: Penguin, 1999. (pp. 162–63)

25 *Wall Street Journal*. Tenney, Lester. 'Watching the Atomic Bomb Blast as a POW Near Nagasaki.' <http://www.wsj.com/articles/the-end-of-the-japanese-illusion-1438793428> Accessed August 2015.

26 *The Australian*. 'Imperial Japan recalled.' 7 August 2015. <http://www.theaustralian.com.au/opinion/letters/an-insider-thinks-the-labor-party-is-not-fit-to-be-registered-as-such/story-fn558imw-1227473043820> Accessed 7 August 2015.

Chapter 16

1   Sweeney, Major General Charles W. *War's End: an Eyewitness Account of America's Last Atomic Mission*. New York: Avon Books, 1997. (p. 270)

2   Giangreco, DM. *Hell to Pay: Operation Downfall and the Invasion of Japan, 1945–47*. USA: Naval Institute Press, 2009. Audio book, Chapter 3, 9'34'. See also World War II Foundation. <https://www.wwiifoundation.org/students/wwii-facts-figures/> which cites 'of deaths, in total, sustained by U.S. forces during World War II: 405,000'. Accessed June 2018.

3   Giangreco, DM. *Hell to Pay: Operation Downfall and the Invasion of Japan, 1945–47*. USA: Naval Institute Press, 2009. Audio book, Chapter 3, 11'10'.

4   Demographia. <http://www.demographia.com/db-uspop1900.htm> Accessed June 2014.

5   Giangreco, DM. *Hell to Pay: Operation Downfall and the Invasion of Japan, 1945–47*. USA: Naval Institute Press, 2009. (pp. 5, 815, 275) Audio book, Chapter 3, 14'10'.

6   Sweeney, Major General Charles W. *War's End: an Eyewitness Account of America's Last Atomic Mission*. New York: Avon Books, 1997. (p. 235)

7   Hyperwar. Battle and Nonbattle Deaths. <http://www.ibiblio.org/hyperwar/USA/ref/ Casualties/Casualties-2.html#personnel> Accessed August 2017. (Note: figures are originally from Statistical and Accounting Branch Office of the Adjutant General, Office of the Comptroller of the US Army.)

8   (US) Navy History and Heritage Command. 'US Navy Personnel in World War II. Service and Casualty Statistics.' <https://www.history.navy.mil/research/library/online-reading-room/title-list-alphabetically/u/us-navy-personnel-in-world-war-ii-service-and-casualty-statistics.html> Accessed April 017.

9   United States Marines Virtual Birthplace Memorial. <http://www.usmarinesbirthplace. com/US-Marine-Corps-Casualties.html> Accessed June 2017.

10   Rotter, Andrew J. *Hiroshima – the World's Bomb*. Oxford: Oxford University Press, 2008. (p. 130)

11   Collie, Craig. *Nagasaki: Massacre of the Innocent and Unknowing*. Melbourne: Allen & Unwin, 2011. (p. 168)

12   Sweeney, Major General Charles W. *War's End: an Eyewitness Account of America's Last Atomic Mission*. New York: Avon Books, 1997. (p. 235)

13   Fussell, Paul. *The New Republic*. 'Thank God for the Atom Bomb.' August 1981. (p. 3)

14   Fussell, Paul. *The New Republic*. 'Thank God for the Atom Bomb.' August 1981. (p. 3)

15   Alperovitz, Gar. *The Decision to use the Atomic Bomb: and the Architecture of an American Myth*. New York: Alfred A Knopf, 1995. (p. 341)

16   Ienaga, Saburo. *The Pacific War*. New York: Pantheon Books, 1978. (p.150)

17   Hook, Jason. *Hiroshima*. Suffolk: Hodder Children's Books. 2003. (p. 15)

18   Hook, Jason. *Hiroshima*. Suffolk: Hodder Children's Books. 2003. (p. 16)

19   Frank, Richard B. *Downfall: the End of the Imperial Japanese Empire*. New York: Penguin, 1999. (See pages 338–40 and extensive footnotes therein.)

20   Grant, RG. *Hiroshima and Nagasaki*. East Sussex: Wayland Publishers, 1997. (p. 22)

21   Frank, Richard. 'No Bomb, No End. What If?' (Cowley, Robert. Ed) New York: GP Putnam and Sons, 2001. (p. 375) <http://coachfleenor.weebly.com/uploads/6/6/7/3/6673552/ no_bomb_no_end.pdf> Accessed July 2013. Emphasis in the original.

22   Grant, RG. *Hiroshima and Nagasaki*. East Sussex: Wayland Publishers, 1997. (p. 22)

23   Harris, Nathaniel. *Witness to History: Hiroshima*. Oxford: Heinemann Library, 2004. (p.24)

24   ITV. Woodhead, Leslie. (Dir). *The Day They Dropped the Bomb*. 2015.

25   Dunnigan, James F. *How to Make War*. New York: William Morrow and Company, 1982. See for example, Chapter 24 – 'Attrition'.

26   American Heritage. 'Half A Million Purple Hearts.' December 2000. <http://www.americanheritage.com/content/half-million-purple-hearts> Accessed June 2008.

27   Harper, Stephen. *Miracle of Deliverance*. London: Sidgwick and Jackson, 1985. (p. 76)

28   BBC. 'The War Goes On For Us – Part Two – Operation Zipper'. By brssouthglosproject. <http://www.bbc.co.uk/history/ww2peopleswar/stories/04/a5275604.shtml>

29   Harper, Stephen. *Miracle of Deliverance*. London: Sidgwick and Jackson, 1985. (p. 166)

30   Harper, Stephen. *Miracle of Deliverance*. London: Sidgwick and Jackson, 1985. (p. 168)

31   Harper, Stephen. *Miracle of Deliverance*. London: Sidgwick and Jackson, 1985. (pp. 168–170)

32   Harper, Stephen. *Miracle of Deliverance*. London: Sidgwick and Jackson, 1985. (p. 175)

33   Harper, Stephen. *Miracle of Deliverance*. London: Sidgwick and Jackson, 1985. (p. 178)

34   American Heritage. Maddox, Robert James. 'The Biggest Decision: Why We Had to Drop the Atomic Bomb.' Volume number 46, issue 3, 1995. (pp: 71–77) <http://matnyc-post1945-2013.wikispaces.com/file/view/Maddox+Biggest+Decision.pdf>

35   Atomic Archive. 'The Manhattan Project: Making the Atomic Bomb.' <http://www.atomicarchive.com/History/mp/> Accessed November 2013.

36   Atomic Archive. 'The Manhattan Project: Making the Atomic Bomb. Part IV: The Manhattan Engineer District in Operation.' <http://www.atomicarchive.com/History/mp/p4s37.shtml> Accessed June 2014.

37   'The Manhattan Project: Making the Atomic Bomb.' <http://www.atomicarchive.com/History/mp/p2s1.shtml> Accessed November 2013. 'During summer and fall 1943, the first electromagnetic plant began to take shape. The huge building to house the operating equipment was readied as manufacturers began delivering everything from electrical switches to motors, valves, and tanks. While construction and outfitting proceeded, almost 5000 operating and maintenance personnel were hired and trained.' <http://www.atomicarchive.com/History/mp/p4s7.shtml>

38   'Now there were to be 50 four-story buildings (2,000,000 square feet) in a U-shape measuring half a mile by 1000 feet. Innovative foundation techniques were required to avoid setting thousands of concrete piers to support load-bearing walls. Since it was 11 miles from the headquarters at Oak Ridge, the K-25 site developed into a satellite town. Housing was supplied, as was a full array of service facilities for the population that reached 15,000.' <http://www.atomicarchive.com/History/mp/p4s9.shtml> At Hanford in late 1944, the population working on atomic associated developments reached 50,000, although the weaponising aspects would have been concealed to many. <http://www.atomicarchive.com/History/mp/p4s23.shtml>

39   Wellerstein, Alex. 'The Worst of the Manhattan Project leaks.' 20 September 2013. <http://blog.nuclearsecrecy.com/2013/09/20/worst-manhattan-project-leaks/> Accessed June 2017.

40   AtomicArchive.com. The Manhattan Project: Making the Atomic Bomb <http://www.atomicarchive.com/History/mp/p5s6.shtml> Accessed May 2014.

41   AtomicArchive.com. The Manhattan Project: Making the Atomic Bomb <http://www.atomicarchive.com/History/mp/p5s8.shtml> Accessed May 2014.

42   Astor, Gerald. *Operation Iceberg: the Invasion and Conquest of Okinawa in World War II*. New York: Donald I. Fine, 1995. (p. 414) Quoted in the author's *Lethality in Combat*.

43   'Over 425,000 Allied and German troops were killed, wounded or went missing during the Battle of Normandy. This figure includes over 209,000 Allied casualties, with nearly 37,000 dead among the ground forces and a further 16,714 deaths among the Allied air forces.' D-Day Museum and Overlord Embroidery. <http://www.ddaymuseum.co.uk/d-day/d-day-and-the-battle-of-normandy-your-questions-answered> Accessed November 2013.

44   Hallas, James H. *Killing Ground on Okinawa*. Connecticut: Praeger, 1996. (123) Quoted in the author's *Lethality in Combat*.

45   Astor, Gerald. *Operation Iceberg: the Invasion and Conquest of Okinawa in World War II*. New York: Donald I. Fine, 1995. (p. 416) Quoted in the author's Lethality in Combat.

46   Toland, John. *The Rising Sun: The Decline and Fall of the Japanese Empire*. New York:

Bantam, 1982. (p. 803)

47   Tamayama, Kazuo and John Nunneley. *Tales by Japanese Soldiers*. London: Cassell, 1992. (p. 171) Quoted in the author's *Lethality in Combat*.

48   Donovan, Robert J. *PT109, John F. Kennedy in World War II*. New York: McGraw-Hill, 1961. (p. 30) Quoted in the author's *Lethality in Combat*.

49   Sweeney, Major General Charles W. *War's End: an Eyewitness Account of America's Last Atomic Mission*. New York: Avon Books, 1997. (pp. 279–80)

50   Walker, J. Samuel. *Prompt and Utter Destruction. Truman and the Use of Atomic Bombs Against Japan*. USA: University of North Carolina Press, 2005. (p. 93)

51   Giovannitti, Len, and Fred Freed. *The Decision to Drop the Bomb*. New York: Coward-MCann Inc, 1965. (pp. 146–47)

52   Fussell, Paul. Wartime. Understanding and Behaviour in the Second World War. New York: Oxford University Press, 1989. (p. 295)

53   'Over 425,000 Allied and German troops were killed, wounded or went missing during the Battle of Normandy. This figure includes over 209,000 Allied casualties, with nearly 37,000 dead among the ground forces and a further 16,714 deaths among the Allied air forces.' D-Day Museum and Overlord Embroidery. <http://www.ddaymuseum.co.uk/d-day/d-day-and-the-battle-of-normandy-your-questions-answered> Accessed November 2013.

54   See Hillenbrand, Laura. *Unbroken*. New York: Random House, 2010. (p. 80) for the USAAF figure.

55   D-Day Revisited. 'The Cost of Battle.' <http://d-dayrevisited.co.uk/d-day/cost-of-battle.html> Accessed June 2017.

56   <http://www.fas.org/irp/eprint/arens/chap5.htm>

57   'Over 425,000 Allied and German troops were killed, wounded or went missing during the Battle of Normandy. This figure includes over 209,000 Allied casualties, with nearly 37,000 dead among the ground forces and a further 16,714 deaths among the Allied air forces.' D-Day Museum and Overlord Embroidery. <http://www.ddaymuseum.co.uk/d-day/d-day-and-the-battle-of-normandy-your-questions-answered> Accessed November 2013.

58   Quoted in Grant, RG. *Hiroshima and Nagasaki*. East Sussex: Wayland Publishers, 1997. (p. 22)

59   See Sweeney, Major General Charles W. *War's End: an Eyewitness Account of America's Last Atomic Mission*. New York: Avon Books, 1997. (p. 270)

60   Harper, Stephen. *Miracle of Deliverance*. London: Sidgwick and Jackson, 1985. (p. 182) Laurens Van der Post's figure in *The Prisoner and the Bomb* is 200,000–400,000. Newman uses this figure on page 122 in *Truman and the Hiroshima Cult*, p. 150.

61   Newman, Robert P. *Truman and the Hiroshima Cult*. East Lansing: Michigan State University Press, 1995. (p. 139) Miscamble repeats the figure, and notes 200,000 to 300,000 people died each month under the Japanese following Pearl Harbor. Miscamble, Wilson D. *The Most Controversial Decision. Truman, the Atomic Bombs, and the Defeat of Japan*. New York: Cambridge University Press, 2011. (p. 114)

62   See Skates, John Ray. *The Invasion of Japan*. South Carolina: The University of South Carolina Press, 1994. (p. 111), and Japanese Suicide Weapons website. <http://www.b-29s-over-korea.com/Japanese_Kamikaze/Japanese_Kamikaze05.html> Accessed July 2014.

63   See Nihon Kaigun. <http://www.combinedfleet.com/OkinawaEMB.htm> Accessed July 2014.

Chapter 17

1   Dunnigan, James F. and Albert A Nofi. *The Pacific War Encyclopedia*. New York: Checkmark Books, 1998. (p. 513)

2   Slim, Field Marshall Viscount. *Defeat into Victory*. London: Pan, 1999. (p. 421)

3   Slim, Field Marshall Viscount. *Defeat into Victory*. London: Pan, 1999. (p. 538)

4   Slim, Field Marshall Viscount. *Defeat into Victory*. London: Pan, 1999. (p. 528)

5   Harper, Stephen. *Miracle of Deliverance*. London: Sidgwick and Jackson, 1985. (p. 89)

6   Hook, Jason. *Hiroshima*. Suffolk: Hodder Children's Books. 2003. (p.12)

7   Combined Fleet. <http://combinedfleet.com/ships/yamato> Accessed August 2014.

8   Maritimea. 'The Battle of Leyte Gulf.' Dr Tom Lewis. Millennium House. 2012.

9   Fussell, Paul. Wartime. *Understanding and Behaviour in the Second World War*. New York: Oxford University Press, 1989. (p. 283)

10 Flashback Television. The Lost Evidence. 50'00'.

11 Schneider, Carl J. *World War II*. New York: Checkmark Books, 2003. (p. 237)

12 Giangreco, DM. *Hell to Pay: Operation Downfall and the Invasion of Japan, 1945–47*. USA: Naval Institute Press, 2009. (pp. 5, 275, 815) Audio book, Chapter 28'00'.

13 Toland, John. *The Rising Sun: The Decline and Fall of the Japanese Empire*. New York: Bantam, 1982. (p. 846)

14 Yamashita, Samuel Hideo. *Daily Life in Wartime Japan, 1940–1945*. Lawrence: University Press of Kansas, 2015. Quoted in a review of the book by David R Ambaras in the Society for Military History's *The Journal of Military History*, Volume 80, Number 4, October 2016.

15 Hastings, Max. 'The unspeakable war and the savage Japanese soldiers who would never surrender.' *The Daily Mail*. 14 September 2007. <http://www.dailymail.co.uk/columnists/article-481881/The-unspeakable-war-savage-Japanese-soldiers-surrender.html#ixzz4TKt0GdWa> Japan's population was around 70 million, but it was routinely overstated to 100 million in government material.

16 Bradley, James. *Flyboys*. Boston: Little, Brown and Company, 2003. (p. 145)

17 Bradley, James. *Flyboys*. Boston: Little, Brown and Company, 2003. (p. 144)

18 Bradley gives only the figure of the defenders. Colt Denfeld cites 28,500 Japanese dying.

19 Denfeld, D Colt. *Hold the Marianas*. Pennsylvania: White Mane Publishing Company, 1997. (p. 97)

20 Bradley, James. *Flyboys*. Boston: Little, Brown and Company. 2003. (pp. 146–47)

21 Trevor-Roper, HR. *The Last Days of Hitler*. London: Pan, 1972. (pp. 92–97)

22 Lucas, James. *Last Days of the Reich*. London: Cassell, 1986. (p. 79)

23 SBS One. (Special Broadcasting Service, Australia). Revealed: The Luckiest Man in World War Two. 4 August 2014.

24 Calley, William L. *His Own Story*. New York: The Viking Press, 1971. (pp. 10–11)

25 Calley, William L. *His Own Story*. New York: The Viking Press, 1971. (pp. 147–48)

26 Schneider, Carl J. *World War II*. New York: Checkmark Books, 2003. (p. 228)

27 Astor, Gerald. *Operation Iceberg: the Invasion and Conquest of Okinawa in World War II*. New York: Donald I. Fine, 1995. (p. 216)

28 Astor, Gerald. *Operation Iceberg: the Invasion and Conquest of Okinawa in World War II*. New York: Donald I. Fine, 1995. (pp. 431, 439)

29 Toland, John. *The Rising Sun: The Decline and Fall of the Japanese Empire*. New York: Bantam, 1982. (p. 820)

30   Flashback Television. *The Lost Evidence*. 35'00'.

31   Flashback Television. *The Lost Evidence*. 18'30'.

32   Flashback Television. *The Lost Evidence*. 38'00'.

33   Manchester, William. *Goodbye, Darkness: a Memoir of the Pacific War*. London: Joseph, 1981. (pp. 385, 388)

34   Manchester, William. *Goodbye, Darkness: a Memoir of the Pacific War*. London: Joseph, 1981. (p. 383)

35   Flashback Television. *The Lost Evidence*. 53.00'.

36   Harding, William. *A Cockney Soldier*. Devon: Merlin Books, 1989. (p. 120)

37   Bennett, Cam. *Rough Infantry*. Victoria: Warrnambool Institute Press, 1984. (p. 80)

38   Griffiths-Marsh, Roland. *The Sixpenny Soldier*. NSW: Angus and Robertson, 1990. (pp. 172–75)

39   McKee, Alexander. *Caen: Anvil of Victory*. London: Souvenir Press, 1964. (pp. 65–67)

40   Blandford, Edmund L. *Green devils - red devils: untold tales of the Airborne Forces in the Second World War*. London: Leo Co-oper, 1993. (pp. 43–45)

41   Young, Peter. *Storm from the Sea*. Great Britain: Wren's Park Publishing, 2002. (p. 82)

42   Harding, William. *A Cockney Soldier*. Devon: Merlin Books, 1989. (p. 134)

43   Arthur, Max. *Forgotten Voices of the Second World War*. London: Ebury Press, 2005. (p. 51)

44   Arthur, *Forgotten Voices*, 53. Presumably the rank is an error – lieutenant-commander is a naval term.

45   Terkel, Louis. *The Good War: an oral history of World War Two*. New York: Pantheon Books, 1984. (p. 417)

46   Hastings, Max. *Armageddon: The Battle for Germany 1944–1945*. USA: Macmillan, 2004. (p. 323)

47   Dwight D. Eisenhower Library, Joe Lawton Collins Papers, Box 2, 201 Files – Personal Letters 1943. Via Internet discussion group H-NET Military History Discussion List H-WAR@H-NET.MSU.EDU 9 October 2004. Courtesy member Joerg Muth.

48   Bergerud, Eric. *Touched with Fire: the Land Warfare in the South Pacific*. New York: Viking, 1996. (Photographs in-between pages 166 and 167.)

49   Young, Peter. *Storm from the Sea*. Great Britain: Wren's Park Publishing, 2002. (p. 216)

50   Slim, William. *Defeat into Victory*. London: Cassell, 1956. (p. 418)

51   Tamayama, Kazuo and John Nunneley. Tales by Japanese Soldiers. London: Cassell, 1992. (p. 202)

52   Schneider, Carl J. *World War II*. New York: Checkmark Books, 2003. (p. 187)

53   Hallas, James H. *Killing Ground on Okinawa*. Connecticut: Praeger, 1996. (p. 127)

54   Hallas, *Killing Ground on Okinawa*. Connecticut: Praeger, 1996. (p. 194)

55   Astor, Gerald. *Operation Iceberg: the Invasion and Conquest of Okinawa in World War II*. New York: Donald I. Fine, 1995. (pp. 439, 451)

56   Manchester, William. *Goodbye, Darkness: a Memoir of the Pacific War*. London: Joseph, 1981. (p. 381)

57   Baker, Clive and Greg Knight. *Milne Bay 1942*. NSW: Baker-Knight Publications, 1991. (p. 260)

58   Baker, Clive and Greg Knight. *Milne Bay 1942*. NSW: Baker-Knight Publications, 1991. (p. 299)

59   Baker and Knight, *Milne Bay 1942*, (p. 140)

60   Baker, Clive and Greg Knight. *Milne Bay 1942*. NSW: Baker-Knight Publications, 1991. (p. 217)

61   Baker, Clive and Greg Knight. *Milne Bay 1942*. NSW: Baker-Knight Publications, 1991. Appendix 9: pp: 435-438.

62   Manchester, William. *Goodbye, Darkness: a Memoir of the Pacific War*. London: Joseph, 1981. (p. 166)

63   Schneider, Carl J. *World War II*. New York: Checkmark Books, 2003. (p. 205)

64   Bergerud, Eric M. *Fire in the Sky: the Air War in the South Pacific*. Boulder, Colo.: Westview Press, 2000. (p. 421)

65   Denfeld, D Colt. *Hold the Marianas*. Pennsylvania: White Mane Publishing Company, 1997. (p. 127)

66   Brune, Peter. *A Bastard of a Place: the Australians in Papua*. Crows Nest, NSW: Allen & Unwin, 2003. (p. 548)

67   Bergerud, Eric M. *Fire in the Sky: the Air War in the South Pacific*. Boulder, Colo.: Westview Press, 2000. (p. 413)

68   Wright, Derrick. *A Hell of a Way to Die: Tarawa Atoll, 20–23 November 1943*. London: Windrow & Greene, 1997. (p. 123)

69   Henri, Raymond. *The U.S. Marines on Iwo Jima*. Tennessee: Battery Press, 1987. (p. 230)

70   Brune, Peter. *A Bastard of a Place: the Australians in Papua*. Crows Nest, N.S.W: Allen & Unwin, 2003. (p. 484)

71   Brune, Peter. *A Bastard of a Place: the Australians in Papua*. Crows Nest, N.S.W: Allen & Unwin, 2003. (p. 484)

72   Barrett, John. *We Were There*. NSW: Allen & Unwin, 1995. (p. 309)

73   Bennett, Cam. *Rough Infantry*. Victoria: Warrnambool Institute Press, 1984. (p. 196)

74   Ham, Paul. *Kokoda*. Sydney: HarperCollins, 2004. (393) and see US Army in WWII. Samuel Milner, 'Chapter VII The Advance on the Beachhead.' http://www.ibiblio.org/hyperwar/USA/USA-P-Papua/USA-P-Papua-7.html 5 August 2005.

75   Ham, *Kokoda*, (p. 430)

76   Ham, *Kokoda*, (p. 434)

77   Wright, *A Hell of a Way to Die*, (p. 131)

78   Wright, *A Hell of a Way to Die*, (p. 156)

79   Holmes, *Firing Line*, (p. 323)

80   Leckie, Robert. *Helmet for My Pillow*. Garden City, N.Y: Doubleday, 1979. (p. 271)

81   Denfeld, *Hold the Marianas*, (p. 97)

82   Ham, Paul. *Kokoda*, p. 517)

83   Denfeld, *Hold the Marianas*, (p. 206)

84   Schneider, Carl J. *World War II*. New York: Checkmark Books, 2003. (p. 205)

85   Bergerud, *Touched with Fire*, (p. 422)

86   Dexter, David. *The New Guinea Offensives*. Canberra: Australian War Memorial, 1961. (pp. 407–408)

87   Bergerud, Eric. Comment on the H-War Internet discussion list. 23 September 2004.

88   Bourke, Joanna. *An Intimate History of Killing: face-to-face killing in twentieth-century warfare*. London: Granta Books, 1999. (p. 184) Bourke also accuses the Allied troops of having a 'propensity … to kill anyone who attempted to surrender'. As Bergerud and others show, this is not the case.

89   Dunnigan, James F. and Albert A Nofi. *The Pacific War Encyclopedia*. New York: Checkmark Books, 1998. (p. 513)

90 Wright, Derrick. *A Hell of a Way to Die: Tarawa Atoll,* 20–23 November 1943. London: Windrow & Greene, 1997. (p.105)

91 Leckie, Robert. *Helmet for my Pillow.* Garden City, N.Y: Doubleday, 1979. (p. 225)

92 Bergerud, *Touched with Fire,* (p. 407)

93 Bergerud, *Touched with Fire,* (p. 405–06)

94 Stouffer, Samuel A. (et al) *The American Soldier.* Princeton, N.J: Princeton University Press, 1949. (p. 162)

95 Bergerud, *Touched with Fire,* (p. 371)

96 The author's service saw him routinely sleep in a sealed concrete building with sandbagged windows, in an area that was surrounded by guards on perimeter walls. Nevertheless, you slept with your rifle under your bunk, or hooked up nearby if on the top bunk, your ammunition magazines close to hand. Your pistol belt with its holstered weapon and its magazine pouches in the belt was also nearby. Being able to snatch these up in an emergency could mean life or death – the armed services routine of keeping weapons locked up in armouries, which was what happened in peacetime at home, was unheard of.

97 Young, Peter. *Storm from the Sea.* Great Britain: Wren's Park Publishing, 2002. (p. 208)

98 Baker, Clive and Greg Knight. *Milne Bay 1942.* NSW: Baker-Knight Publications, 1991. (p. 29)

99 Sledge, EB. *With the Old Breed, at Peleliu and Okinawa.* Novato, Calif: Presidio Press, 1981. (p. 18)

100 Young, Peter. *Storm from the Sea.* Great Britain: Wren's Park Publishing, 2002. (p. 91)

101 Hastings, Max. *Armageddon: The Battle for Germany 1944–1945.* USA: Macmillan, 2004. (p. 88)

102 McKee, Alexander. *Caen: Anvil of Victory.* London: Souvenir Press, 1964. (p. 79)

103 McKee, Alexander. *A Hell of a Way to Die.* London: Souvenir Press, 1964. (p. 200)

104 Schneider, Carl J. *World War II.* New York: Checkmark Books, 2003. (p. 172)

105 Ambrose, Stephen E. *Band of Brothers: E Company, 506th Regiment, 101st Airborne: from Normandy to Hitler's Eagle's Nest.* New York: Simon & Schuster, 1992. (p. 212)

106 History Learning Site: 'Curtis LeMay.' <http://www.historylearningsite.co.uk/curtis_lemay.htm> Accessed July 2013.

107 Australian Broadcasting Corporation. Warrior: Reflections of Men at War. Courtesy Library of the Australian Defence Force Academy, Canberra. 2004. (26'30')

108 Manchester, William. *Goodbye, Darkness: a Memoir of the Pacific War.* London: Joseph, 1981. (p. 184)

109 Harper, Stephen. *Miracle of Deliverance.* London: Sidgwick and Jackson, 1985. (p. 207)

110 Harper, Stephen. *Miracle of Deliverance.* London: Sidgwick and Jackson, 1985. (p. 210)

111 p. 367.

112 Excludes the population of Okinawa-ken, which was not surveyed. Statistics Japan. 'Population of Japan (Final Report of The 2000 Population Census).' <http://www.stat.go.jp/english/data/kokusei/2000/final/hyodai.htm> Accessed May 2014.

113 Weintraub, Stanley. *The Last Great Victory.* New York: Truman Talley Books, 2001. (p. 205)

114 Newman, Robert P. *Truman and the Hiroshima Cult.* East Lansing: Michigan State University Press, 1995. (p. 19)

115 See page 123. Demobilisation and Disarmament of the Japanese Armed Forces. Reports of General MacArthur. Library of Congress Catalog Card Number: 66-60006.

Facsimile Reprint, 1994. <https://history.army.mil/books/wwii/MacArthur%20Reports/MacArthur%20V1%20Sup/ch5.htm#b4> Accessed June 2018.

116 Harper, Stephen. *Miracle of Deliverance*. London: Sidgwick and Jackson, 1985. (p. 112)

117 Hatena Blog. 'Changes in the Population of Japan, 1920–2015.' <http://nbakki.hatenablog.com/entry/Trend_Japan_Population> Accessed 20 July 2017.

118 Frank, Richard. 'No Bomb, No End. What If?' (Cowley, Robert. Ed) New York: GP Putnam and Sons, 2001. (p. 375) <http://coachfleenor.weebly.com/uploads/6/6/7/3/6673552/no_bomb_no_end.pdf> Accessed July 2013. Emphasis in the original.

119 Hoyt, Edwin P. *Japan's War. The Great Pacific Conflict 1853–1952*. London: Hutchinson, 1987. (p. 393)

120 Toland, John. *The Rising Sun: The Decline and Fall of the Japanese Empire*. New York: Bantam, 1982. (p. 851)

121 See the same author's *The Empire Strikes South*. (Avonmore, 2017)

122 'The Japanese surrender delegation in Manila reported on 19 August that the strength of their naval personnel on 1 August was 1,024,255.' This was found to be erroneous later: 'Navy strength in Japan proper, stated to be 1,024,225, was later established at 1,178,750.' Regarding air personnel: 'All personnel of both the Army and Navy Air Forces stationed on the four islands of Japan … were reported at a strength of 262,000 Army and 291,537 Navy.' See Chapter V. Demobilisation and Disarmament of the Japanese Armed Forces. Reports of General MacArthur. Library of Congress Catalog Card Number: 66-60006. Facsimile Reprint, 1994. <https://history.army.mil/books/wwii/MacArthur%20Reports/MacArthur%20V1%20Sup/Index.htm#cont> Accessed June 2018.

123 The Pacific War Research Society. *Japan's Longest Day*. Tokyo: Kodansha International Limited, 1986. (p. 75)

124 This figure and Onishi's proclamation to advance towards it are widely known. For example see Frank, Richard B. *Downfall: the End of the Imperial Japanese Empire*. New York: Penguin, 1999. (p. 311)

125 Bill Whittle (PJTV). Jon Stewart, War Criminals & The True Story of the Atomic Bombs. <https://www.youtube.com/watch?v=VfyNNVuLCn8 >

126 Figuring on a campaign taking in a road distance from Kagoshima, Kagoshima Prefecture, to Sendai, Miyagi Prefecture, which lies to the east of Tokyo. That is not to say the Allies would not have been involved in combat operations in the upper eastern island of Honshu, which would be especially to exterminate any air operations emanating from there.

127 The figures are a little inaccurately expressed by saying that if you were dying of hunger you could not be one of that 10 percent, and with a million a month being removed from the population by starvation, therefore the population should be reduced by that too.

128 Grant, RG. *Hiroshima and Nagasaki*. East Sussex: Wayland Publishers, 1997. (p. 21) quoting Giovanitti and Freed, The Decision to Drop the Bomb.

Chapter 18

1 Grant, RG. *Hiroshima and Nagasaki*. East Sussex: Wayland Publishers, 1997. (p. 46) quoting Giovanitti and Freed, The Decision to Drop the Bomb.

2 Grant, RG. *Hiroshima and Nagasaki*. East Sussex: Wayland Publishers, 1997. (p. 46) quoting Giovanitti and Freed, The Decision to Drop the Bomb.

3 Sweeney, Major General Charles W. *War's End: an Eyewitness Account of America's Last Atomic Mission*. New York: Avon Books, 1997. (p. 261)

4   Sweeney, Major General Charles W. *War's End: an Eyewitness Account of America's Last Atomic Mission*. New York: Avon Books, 1997. (p. 266)

5   Hume, Mick. 'Hiroshima: remembering "the White Man's Bomb"'. Spiked. 1995. Edited version of essay written for Living Marxism. <https://www.spiked-online.com/2019/08/09/hiroshima-remembering-the-white-mans-bomb/> Accessed 9 August 2019.

6   Wellerstein, Alex. 'Would the atomic bomb have been used against Germany?' Restricted Data. 4 October 2013. <http://blog.nuclearsecrecy.com/2013/10/04/atomic-bomb-used-nazi-germany/> Accessed January 2016.

7   Hume, Mick. 'Hiroshima: remembering "the White Man's Bomb"'. Spiked. 1995. Edited version of essay written for Living Marxism. <https://www.spiked-online.com/2019/08/09/hiroshima-remembering-the-white-mans-bomb/> Accessed 9 August 2019.

8   Dingle, Ceri. 'The Youths Who Told The Truth About Hiroshima.' Spiked Online! <http://www.spiked-online.com/newsite/article/the-youths-who-told-the-truth-about-hiroshima/17267#.VouoF3jfKZM> 6 August 2015. Accessed July 2017.

9   See Appendix: Children's book analysis, which contains a spreadsheet of the results, and a list of the books with notations as to the above.

10   Hiroshima International School. 'The Story Of Sadako Sasaki.' <http://www.hiroshima-is.ac.jp/index.php?page=sadako-story> Accessed June 2015.

11   Hiroshima Peace Park signage detail. (Author visit, 2015)

12   Conversation with staff, June 2015.

13   Guided History. Greene, Bria. 'Japanese Remembrance of the Dropping of the Atom Bomb.' <http://blogs.bu.edu/guidedhistory/historians-craft/bria-greene/> Accessed April 2016.

14   Healey, Justin. Nuclear Arms Control. Australia: The Spinney Press, 2018. (p. 35)

15   Heinemann Library. Hiroshima: the shadow of the bomb. Great Britain: Heinemann, 2006. (p.11)

16   ABC Radio. AM. 'Hiroshima bombing was less important than Soviet declaration of war in ending WWII: historians.' <http://www.abc.net.au/am/content/2015/s4287103.htm> 5 August 2015.

17   Stuart, Rob. 'Was the RCN ever the Third Largest Navy?' <http://www.navalreview.ca/wp-content/uploads/public/vol5num3/vol5num3art2.pdf> Accessed July 2014.

18   More Right. 'Comparing Warfare Deaths per Capita in 18th vs. 20th Centuries.' <http://www.moreright.net/comparing-warfare-death-per-capita-in-18th-vs-20th-centuries/>

19   Our World in Data. 'The Absolute Number of War Deaths is Declining since 1945.' <http://socialdemocracy21stcentury.blogspot.com.au/2013/02/steven-pinker-on-deaths-by-violence-in.html>

20   Mises Institute. 'The Hiroshima Myth'. <https://mises.org/library/hiroshima-myth?> 2 August 2006. Accessed May 2016.

21   Carnegie Council. 'Did Nuclear Weapons Cause Japan to Surrender?' <https://www.carnegiecouncil.org/education/008/expertclips/010> 16 January 2013. Accessed June 2015.